D0070041

JOSH McDOWELL

EVIDENCE

FOR THE

RESURRECTION

What It Means for Your Relationship with God

SEAN McDOWELL

Regal

From Gospel Light
Ventura, California, U.S.A.

Published by Regal
From Gospel Light
Ventura, California, U.S.A.
Printed in the U.S.A.

All Scripture quotations, unless otherwise indicated, are taken from the *Holy Bible*,
New Living Translation, copyright © 1996. Used by permission of Tyndale House Publishers, Inc.,
Wheaton, Illinois 60189. All rights reserved.

Other versions used are
NASB—Scripture taken from the *New American Standard Bible,* © 1960, 1962, 1963, 1968,
1971, 1972, 1973, 1975, 1977, 1995 by The Lockman Foundation. Used by permission.
NIV—Scripture taken from the *Holy Bible, New International Version*®. Copyright © 1973,
1978, 1984 by International Bible Society. Used by permission of
Zondervan Publishing House. All rights reserved.
NKJV—Scripture taken from the *New King James Version*. Copyright © 1979, 1980, 1982
by Thomas Nelson, Inc. Used by permission. All rights reserved.

© 2009 Josh McDowell Ministry and Sean McDowell.
All rights reserved.
ISBN 978-0-8307-4785-6

Rights for publishing this book outside the U.S.A. or in non-English languages are
administered by Josh McDowell Ministry, a division of Campus Crusade for Christ International.
For additional information, please visit www.josh.org, email translations@josh.org, or write to
Josh McDowell Ministry, 660 International Parkway Suite 100, Richardson, TX 75081.

To my son, Scottie.
I love you and am so proud of you!

Sean McDowell

CONTENTS

CHRIST'S RESURRECTION— THE WORLD'S ONLY HOPE

Imagine that an intelligent alien comes from somewhere in space to visit our planet and spend a few years touring the globe. The purpose of his visit is to learn about us, to research our history and to make observations about the state of life on the earth. But also imagine that the alien's human guides deliberately withhold from him all contact with Christians, all information about Christianity and all data on Christian history. What would this alien observe, and what would he conclude from his observations?

He would tour America and Western Europe and see cultures in decline and fragmented societies in which people pursue their own self-interests. He would witness people saturating themselves in pleasure and entertainment while ignoring the human needs and growing poverty around them, failing to maintain good relationships and sinking deeper and deeper into immorality. He would see grand mansions in gated communities with inhabitants overlooking massive slums dominated by hopelessness, poverty and squalor. He would see a rising crime rate and growing dishonesty in all strata of society. He would see rampant drug use and homicides in every city.

Traveling to Africa, the alien would tour countries where masses of starving people, including children, die every day while their national leaders get rich on corruption and greed. He would find whole nations in which young people are being wiped out by disease epidemics, particularly AIDS. In the Middle East, he would see murderous repression of religions, oppression and torture of women, and infighting among tribal leaders in cultures saturated with incredible oil wealth.

In the Far East, he would find more government tyranny, repression and mass genocide. In India, he would find abject poverty and hopelessness imposed by a cruel caste system preventing upward movement.

In studying the past history of our planet, our alien visitor would quickly detect a repeating cycle in world history: nations being born; growing with idealistic hope; developing great laws, art and wellbeing for their citizens; and then deteriorating as wealth led to selfish fragmentation, corruption and decline, until the society finally collapses into ruin. He would see this pattern repeated over and over in all the great civilizations of the past and present—Egypt, Sumeria, Assyria, Babylon, Persia, Greece, Rome, the Byzantines, England and America. He would see continual wars, great and small, costing the lives of uncountable people and devastating societies for generations to come. He would see repeated epidemics of disease spreading across continents and wiping out huge percentages of the population. He would see hate and mass genocide repeated over and over in tyrants such as Stalin, Hitler and African tribal leaders.

No doubt our visiting alien would see no hope for this planet. He would perceive a corrupting flaw in the human heart that would cause these dismal patterns to repeat over and over until humans either destroyed themselves or the sun grew cold. He would board his craft and return to his own planet, shaking his head at the fatal hopelessness of our world.

Actually, we did not have to invite an alien here to demonstrate the hopelessness of our planet without Christianity. We did it solely for the dramatic effect. We could as easily have looked at the world through the eyes of the many unbelievers who also see the hurt, destruction and tragedies of life on earth as a dead-end cycle of meaningless existence. For example, consider this comment posted by an unbelieving girl on an Internet atheist website:

> I'm confused . . . I always believed science would be the cure-all for my problems, but I don't know if I can keep living without eternal life. I guess I'll just have to find a way myself to make it through this meaningless existence. I just wish I knew of someone who could show me the path to eternal life. If science can't pro-

vide the answers, though, then who or what can!? *sigh* Doesn't it seem like there is a higher power that gives our lives purpose? Well, science says there isn't, so there isn't.[1]

There you have the whole problem in a nutshell. If life as one sees it now on this misery-riddled planet is all there is, then existence is indeed meaningless and one must, as this girl says it, "find a way myself." She realizes there is one thing that would make everything meaningful: eternal life. She once expected science to find a way for humans to live forever, but she has come to realize that it cannot. She wishes there was some kind of higher power that would assure her of eternal life, for only blissful life without end would make this present troubled existence meaningful.

Many have found solace in this troubled world by dreaming of ideal societies where peace and goodwill reign, where life is filled with meaning, pain and death do not exist and the future extends forever. We all know their names—Atlantis, Arcadia, Utopia, El Dorado and even Camelot, where for one brief shining moment everything is exactly as it should be. But in the minds of the hopeless many, all such dreams are mere wishful thinking. No such perfect society exists. Even the story of Camelot, which may have been true, shows the futility of such dreams.

In the story of Camelot, King Arthur and his counselor Merlin begin a new kingdom based on honoring one another, helping the poor, rescuing the imprisoned, lifting up the downtrodden, administering justice and mercy, and existing in peace and harmony. But soon after the kingdom is established, the fatal flaws emerge: lust, the one weakness in the noble Lancelot; and spite and envy, the cancer in the heart of the outcast Mordred. Thus Camelot falls, eaten from the center by these fatal flaws, giving us a cameo picture of every civilization that has ever existed or ever will exist on this present earth.

Humankind's Last Great Hope

At one point in history, there was a band of believers who trusted in someone they fervently believed would truly change the world for good. A handful of devout Jewish people thought a man named Jesus was the Messiah—the deliverer who would break their oppressive bondage under the Romans and set up a permanent and truly godly kingdom on earth. Their prophet Isaiah had prophesied in the ancient Jewish writings that the Messiah would come and restore all things to a paradise, where there would be no more fighting, oppression, fear or death (see Isa. 11; 35). The entire earth would once again be a pristine garden, where everyone would live together in peace forever.

Imagine the terrible mental and emotional state of that small group of disciples as they stood watching the Messiah, their deliverer, breathing his last agonized breath, hung to die as a common criminal on a Roman cross. Here was the miracle worker who had shown that he could command nature, heal sickness, raise the dead and produce food with a word or gesture. They had given up everything to follow him. Here was the King they had believed would reestablish the kingdom of Israel. But now here he was, nailed up on a cross. Dying. And dying with him were all the hopes they had placed in him. They must have felt like the poor girl we quoted above. Life seemed meaningless. Everything was hopeless. There seemed to be no way out of their absurd existence, no pathway to an ideal, eternal life.

But far more than the fate of the disciples or even the fate of Israel hung on the cross that day. The fate of the entire human race and their hope of a bright tomorrow and of a life after death hung there with Christ. He was humanity's last hope. For the man who was dying on that cross was the one God had promised would come and lead all of humanity out of its pain and misery into an eternal life of bliss. But now, with his death, it seemed that all hope was gone. Eternal life was a mere dream. Death would reign forever. The hope of the promised Messiah to free humanity from the chains of darkness seemed dashed. The supposed Savior was dead, and any hope of deliverance was buried with him.

The World's Greatest Surprise

Mary Magdalene was a woman who was loyal to Christ to the end. He had exorcised seven demons from her, and from that moment on she followed him gratefully and wholeheartedly. She supported his ministry financially and believed he was the one whom God had chosen to bring eternal peace to the world. She had stayed beneath the cross and witnessed the unjust and cruel execution of her master, and now her life was in utter turmoil. She was one of Jesus' most devoted followers, and seeing him disgraced brought her tremendous anguish.

After the Roman soldiers determined that Jesus was dead, they took him down from the cross and gave his body to a wealthy Jewish official to be buried in a new tomb. Mary left the dismal scene determined to visit his tomb after the burial was completed. Early Sunday morning she went to the tomb, and there she experienced another setback. Not only had Jesus been unjustly killed, but also to her alarm, the tomb was open and his body was gone. Fearing that someone had stolen the body, she ran to Peter and John, two of Jesus' disciples, telling them what she had seen. In utter disbelief, the two men quickly ran to the tomb to check out her story for themselves.

When they arrived, they saw the collapsed shell of the graveclothes still intact, but the body was nowhere to be found. Frightened and confused, the two disciples returned home. But Mary lingered behind. She peered back in the tomb for one last look, and what she saw startled her: two men, robed in bright white, sat inside the tomb.

"Why are you crying?" the angels asked her.

"Because they have taken away my Lord," she replied, "and I don't know where they have put him" (John 20:13).

Turning around, she then saw something even more remarkable: Jesus was standing right before her, alive! But strangely, rather than recognizing him, she mistook him for a gardener. We may never know why she did not recognize him. Perhaps her eyes were filled with tears. Maybe it was still dark. Perhaps she didn't even look in his face. Or perhaps God simply prevented her from understanding who he was. Jesus asked her the same question the angels had asked:

"Dear woman, why are you crying?"

Still clueless as to whom she was speaking, she said softly, "Sir, if you have taken him away, tell me where you have put him, and I will go and get him" (John 20:15). Mary was clearly confused and distraught. She loved Jesus dearly and wanted to pay her final dues.

But then in a moment of remarkable tenderness Jesus called her by name: "Mary!" he said.

"Teacher!" she cried as she suddenly recognized him. She rushed to him, embracing him in ecstatic joy (see John 20:16).

Jesus stood before Mary alive, healthy and well because death could not hold the promised Messiah. God resurrected him to fulfill his mission and bring eternal life to a sick and dying world.

Why the Resurrection of Christ Is Crucial

When Christ was on the cross, it seemed that all had been lost. Death had won. But after three days in a rich man's tomb, Jesus appeared alive again. The news was so shocking the disciples refused to believe it until he presented himself to them personally and let them touch his wounds with their own hands. Then Jesus made an amazing claim to his disciples: In the future they too would have resurrected bodies like his. Bodies that would never deteriorate, age or perish. They would realize the one great hope that would bring meaning to an otherwise meaningless existence. They would have new life without death or pain in the presence of a loving God forever.

That is the great hope Christianity offers to a hopeless world—an afterlife with God, free of pain and suffering, and filled with boundless joy. This, as we will explain more fully later, is exactly how the Bible describes heaven. Heaven is a place of unimaginable blessing. It is a place of ecstasy and fulfillment. When we reach heaven we will all say, "This is what we were made for!" The Bible refers to the afterlife with anticipation and joy. Christians eagerly look forward to the day when all tears will be wiped away. This belief in heaven is not a mere pie-in-the-sky idea designed to make us feel good in a hopeless world, like Utopia, Arcadia or El Dorado; it is a belief built on rock-solid evidence. We will explore this evidence in the third section of this book.

When we consider our present pain and struggles in light of eternal life in heaven, we will be able to transcend our seemingly hopeless circumstances. As Mother Teresa boldly said, "From heaven the most miserable earthly life will look like one bad night in an inconvenient hotel!" We can be encouraged by the words Jesus uttered when his death was glaring at him from right around the corner: "Here on earth you will have many trials and sorrows. But take heart, because I have overcome the world" (John 16:33). It is helpful to remember during difficult trials that our own resurrection is right around the corner.

The Promise of the Resurrection

"But," you may ask, "what does Christ's resurrection mean to me? So he claims to have been raised from the dead. That's astounding, if true, but ultimately, so what? What does the death and resurrection of a man two thousand years ago have to do with me right now in the twenty-first century?"

The promise of the resurrection is this: What happened to Christ can happen for us. Like him, we will die, but his resurrection is a promise that death is not the end. His resurrection is the prototype for our own. He blazed the trail through death to eternal life, and he tells us that we can follow in his footsteps with his hand leading us the entire way. The resurrection gives us hope for a glorious, pain-free, death-free future. The dreams of paradise, Arcadia, Utopia, El Dorado and Camelot can be realized in all their imagined perfection. Our most outlandish dreams of peace, love and harmony can be fulfilled.

We know that this chapter leaves you with all kinds of questions about the meaning of the resurrection. Why was it necessary? Why is this world so messed up in the first place? If the resurrection is supposed to solve problems of the world, why do we still contend with pain, trouble and death? What about all my personal hopes? Will they be lost when I die and find myself in heaven? Will my relationships be broken forever? And what about heaven? Based on what you've heard about it, you may not really be too keen on going there. Is it really like the popular pictures and descriptions of it? Will I really be me in heaven, or will I be absorbed into God and lose my own conscious self? And the really big questions: How can I be sure that all this is true? How can I know with certainty that the resurrection really occurred? How can I know this isn't just another wishful dream?

We encourage you to read on. The purpose of this book is to help you find the answers to these crucial, all-important questions.

SECTION I

THE HUMAN NEED FOR THE RESURRECTION

1

HOW DID THINGS GET SO MESSED UP?

In the movie *Runaway Jury*, based on the popular novel by John Grisham, Jacob Wood tells his family goodbye one morning and goes to work at his downtown law office. He asks his secretary's advice on a good birthday present for his son. He is looking forward to a fun evening with his family to celebrate his young son's birthday. But Jacob's plans are not to be fulfilled. That morning a crazed gunman breaks into the law office and guns him down.

Jacob Wood, like the rest of us, had built a life for himself hoping to find joy, happiness, security, love and meaning in the world through family and vocation. But in one brief moment, it all fell apart. His life ended. In an instant, his wife became a widow, his son fatherless, and all his plans ended.

It happens every day. People try to build a good life, but their plans are destroyed. Often by death, as in Jacob Wood's case, but even more often by unexpected events that throw a wrench into our carefully meshed gears, bringing our best plans to a grinding halt. It has happened to all of us. It has happened to you, and it will happen again. We have all faced unexpected fears, pain, disappointment and tragedy. Almost every one of us deals with some form of suffering that will not go away: an unhealed childhood memory, a strained or broken relationship, a physical problem, a broken dream. Smiles at some point turn to frowns, and laughter gives way to crying. Happiness and health turn suddenly to pain and suffering. All of us will at some point experience the loss of a loved one. While some of us may have more pains and regrets than others, none of us can escape the inevitable wounding and scarring life on this planet is sure to bring.

Even the earth feels the excruciating pain of trouble and death. It groans under the stress of a sin-cursed world: tornadoes and hurricanes wreak havoc on life and property, babbling brooks flood their banks to become destructive forces, and the friendly flicker of a campfire is transformed into a raging forest inferno, consuming plants, animals and homes. Gentle animals that first roamed the earth in harmony now brutally ravage each other to survive and protect their territory. Mountains erupt, spewing out volcanic ash. Earthquakes topple buildings. The sun parches fields, bringing drought, ruin and more death.

As we struggle to make a good life amid all this pain, heartache and destruction, something inside us says, "All this makes no sense." We can see all the beauty of the earth, experience the joys of love and the satisfaction of accomplishment and sense that somewhere, something is just not right about the way things work on this earth. There is so much beauty and good that we wonder whether there's not some kind of meaning beneath all the pain and ruin we see and experience. Alongside the tornadoes, hurricanes and forest fires, we see the majesty of mountains, the lavish glory of sunsets, the wide vistas of living prairies and the mighty wonder of rolling seas. We witness the intricate balance of nature and experience the joys of friendship, family and social interaction, and we say to ourselves, "There is so much good in this world, so why does it have to be marred by all the pain, tragedy and death that dogs us so relentlessly?"

The Creation Ideal

The pain, tragedy and death that wreak havoc upon us were not present in God's original creation. The beauty we see in nature, the joy we experience in loving relationships, the satisfaction we feel in work done well and the pleasure we experience in so many ways are clues that hint at what the world was like when God first made it. Relationships were uncontaminated by pride, lust, greed or jealousy. Nature was altogether benign—no destructive storms, no droughts, no forest fires. Work was rewarded with accomplishment and satisfaction, and Murphy's Law did not exist to frustrate our efforts. Death, pain and sickness were nonexistent. The earth was in a state of utter perfection, where everything worked just as it should, and perfect joy and love were the order of the day.

We know that to many people the above paragraph sounds like a wild, idealistic dream—a fantasy of our own imagining that is simply too good to be true. But we think in our best moments, when we can see in the vestiges of the goodness still abounding in our world, that some benevolent being must have put all this together. And a being powerful enough to invent pleasure, love, happiness and joy surely would have the power to prevent the evils that infect creation now. How do we explain this? How could everything be perfect and pain-free, as in the world we described above, and then degenerate into the pain-filled and death-ravaged world we experience now?

To answer, let's look briefly at the nature of the world as God first created it. In the creation account outlined in the first chapter of Genesis, God built the world, nature and life on this planet in a six-stage process, beginning with matter and proceeding to light, land, fish and land animals. Finally, on the last day, he created humans in the form of the first couple, Adam and Eve, male and female.

These human prototypes were unique among all creation in that they alone were created in God's own image. This meant they possessed several features that God's other creatures lacked. They stood upright; they had hands to use as tools to shape their environment; they possessed reason, self-awareness and the ability to choose their own destiny. The primary difference, however, was in the fact that the man and the woman were infused with the Spirit of God himself. Whereas the animals had instinct as their controlling mechanism, the humans had the God of the universe inhabiting their lives, directing their steps and informing their decisions.

What this meant was that the man and woman were God's deputies on the earth. They were God's representatives, his agents, who were given the responsibility and power to rule over the earth in God's stead, caring for the animals and the environment, as well as managing perfectly their own personal behavior. They were lords of the earth, ruling over all nature—including their own human nature—by the power of God himself living within them.

So naturally, things went well on the earth. Everything functioned according to its created purpose, according to the order that God designed, because the man and the woman ruled over all with a beneficent hand directed by God himself, who lived within them.

Your first impulse may be to think the arrangement for Adam and Eve was essentially no better than that of the animals. Yes, they were under the direction of God instead of under the direction of intrinsic instinct, but in either case, they were under direction. It may seem to you that they were not free. But let us explain that this was not the case. Adam and Eve were completely free. Above we noted that one attribute that separated the humans from the animals was that they were free to choose their own destiny. And the choice was simple. All they had to do was tell God to get out of their lives, and he would do it. They would then be free of God, no longer under his guidance and direction, and thus free to direct their lives in any way they chose.

It would be a foolish choice, however, because God designed the humans explicitly to be inhabited by him and to rule all creation by his power. Because he designed them this way, all their happiness, joy, pleasure and satisfaction came from functioning as they were designed. You see, God loved the man and woman dearly, and he designed them to experience great joy and pleasure. He gave them everything possible to increase their joy and pleasure: all the sights, sounds, aromas and tastes of creation, as well as the ecstasy and feelings associated with love, were for their delight.

Because God loved them dearly and gave them the earth for their joy, Adam and Eve loved God dearly as well. He was their chief delight. And to make things all the better, the God that they loved dearly was not a distant deity but rather a warm, personal being who lived inside them in a relationship of deep intimacy every moment of every day. Things could not have been arranged better for the human couple. To choose to go their own way, separating themselves from God, and thus losing his guidance, direction and the direct, intimate awareness of his ongoing love, would have been the most foolhardy thing they could have done.

This was the state of things when God first created the heavens, the earth, the animals and the first humans. Everything was in perfect order because God himself ruled all through the willing agency of his beloved human beings. Pain, tragedy, ruin and death could never invade as long as Adam and Eve chose to remain in their loving relationship with God.

How Things Went Wrong

It may be likely that Adam and Eve never would have stepped out of that loving relationship with God if they had not been deceived and tempted into doing it. But the enemy of God, whom we know as Satan, invaded their perfect world, deceived the woman into stepping out of God's love, and she in turn tempted the man to do the same. They decided to follow their own path instead of God's loving way for them.

No doubt, they did not consider the devastating consequences of their choice. As a result of their decision, everything in their world changed, and not for the better. God, having given them the freedom to choose their way, honored their choice. He got out of their lives so as not to interfere with the independence and freedom they had chosen. But without God in their lives, they suddenly lacked the power and wisdom to exercise their charge to reign over nature. As a result, nature went out of control, out of balance. Storms, earthquakes and disasters could no longer be prevented. The ground no longer yielded abundantly to the plow, and weeds, rust, rot, malignant bacteria and parasites infested everything. Animals that had lovingly fawned on the man and woman now fled from them and even turned on them in fear and hunger. Pain and death became permanent features of the environment.

Even human nature went out of control. With God's loving Spirit residing in them, Adam and Eve had lived in harmony, not only with nature, but also with each other. Their own relationship had always been loving and caring. But after they rejected God and chose their own way, even domestic harmony ended. The man and woman were no longer able to control their own natures, and selfishness, pride and lust entered the picture, causing strife, misunderstandings and heartbreak, contaminating even the most intimate of relationships.

This event—the choice of the first human couple to reject God and turn to themselves as their own authority—is called sin. We think of sin as coming in many varieties, from the tiny, seemingly insignificant act of going 76 miles per hour under a 70-mph speed limit to the horribly appalling sin of mass murder. And indeed, sins do come in many varieties and in many degrees of seriousness. Yet there is one thing common to all sins, from the least to the greatest. All sin springs from that original impulse of Adam and Eve to follow their own way instead of God's. All *sins*, from speeding to mass murder, spring from the fact of *sin*—which is simply rejecting the way of God in favor of the way of self.

The aftermath of all sin is chaos, pain, tragedy, destruction and death, simply because separation from God leaves us without the power and wisdom to fulfill our created function of imposing God's benevolent order on creation. This reduction of the human condition from its magnificent creation as wielders of God's power and influence to powerless creatures looking to their empty selves for guidance is commonly called the Fall. The Fall marked mankind's descent from created perfection to the tragic, troubled and death-ridden world we know today.

If Satan's purpose in seducing the human couple was to bring fatal chaos to God's creation, he seemed to have succeeded. All he needed was to get this primeval couple to pull away from God, and then all their descendants would be born into their fallen condition—alienated from God by the free choice of their first parents, Adam and Eve.

Since God is the source of all life, alienation from him means death. Adam and Eve doomed not only themselves, but also all their descendants by their free choice to reject God and make themselves their own authority. As Paul tells us, "When Adam sinned, sin entered the world. Adam's sin brought death, so death spread to everyone, for everyone sinned" (Rom. 5:12). At the Fall of Adam and Eve, death entered God's perfect world and doomed all humankind.

Why Can't God Just Ignore Our Sin?

If God really loves us, as he says he does, why must he let sin stand between him and us? He's God, after all, and he's all-powerful, isn't he? He can do anything he wants, can't he? Why can't he just forget that we sin and save us anyway?

On the surface this seems a reasonable question, but when we dig deeper we find that it has problems. The answer has to do with the twin concepts of justice and holiness. Let's talk about justice first.

We have all fallen short of God's perfect standards. Since he is the moral ruler of the universe, he cannot look on violations of his perfect standards with indifference. We may be able to do this when we offend each other, but God cannot, because to tolerate anything less than perfection in his perfect universe would be an offense against perfect justice. There would be outrage if a judge failed to administer justice in his court. Imagine a judge who, upon hearing a court case involving a brutal murder and rape, decided to let the guilty party go free because he wanted to act lovingly! What would the family of the victim think about his ignoring such an outrageous crime? Naturally, they would cry out for justice. Letting the killer off would trivialize the brutal act and make light of the lost life of their loved one. What kind of world would we live in if every judge chose to "act lovingly and kindly" and forgive crimes instead of administering justice? We can assure you, you wouldn't like it.

God is the moral ruler of the world. He is the judge of the universe—he is the ultimate King. His laws are not arbitrary; they stem from his very character and nature, and they are given to us in order to make us more like him. Essentially all of God's laws are for our own good. He designed humans; he knows what makes us tick and how we can achieve the best performance and greatest happiness. His laws work like a manufacturer's instruction and maintenance manual. If we follow them, we will come much nearer to being what God intended us to be and reap the joy, satisfaction and fulfillment that come from it.

God is truth, and his laws are righteous. In his plea for God to save Sodom and Gomorrah from his planned destruction, Abraham cried out, "Surely you wouldn't do such a thing, destroying the righteous along with the wicked. Why, you would be treating the righteous and the wicked exactly the same! Surely you wouldn't do that! Should not the judge of all the earth do what is right?" (Gen. 18:25).

Of course, Abraham misunderstood the situation in Sodom a bit. God knew that there were no righteous people in Sodom besides Lot and his family, whom he intended to save. But the point is, Abraham made a correct statement: God, as ruler and judge of all the earth, is bound by his own character to do what is right, and this means administering justice accurately.

Sin arouses God's wrath. It is not that he irrationally loses his temper because his plans for a perfect world are fouled up. There is nothing impulsive, random or capricious about God; he is not spiteful or malevolent. His anger is neither irrational nor mysterious. He is completely principled and controlled. His anger is always provoked by wickedness and the destruction wickedness renders to the created beings he dearly loves.

The second reason God must respond to sin is because he is holy. In fact, the attribute of holiness is applied to God more than any other attribute in the Bible. Most people misunderstand the meaning of holiness. They tend to think of it as being overly religious to the point of being somewhat out of touch with everyday reality. Or more negatively, they think of holiness as being a little self-righteous and religiously elevated above ordinary folks. But the true meaning of holiness is nothing like that. God's holiness is simply incompatible with sin. God's eyes are too pure to look on evil, and because he is perfect, he cannot bear wrongdoing (see Hab. 1:13).

Because God is holy, he cannot look upon sin with indifference. He judges sinners because his perfect character demands it. The Bible uses a couple of phrases to indicate why God must do so: First, God is *provoked by sin*. The Bible tells us that he was angered when idols or foreign gods were put before him in his people's lives (see Deut. 32:16,21). This simply means that God's perfect nature causes him to react strongly to wrongdoing. He cannot tolerate idolatry, immorality or injustice. If he did, he could not be called good. He would not be holy.

Second, we are told that God *burns with anger* at the sins of mankind (see 2 Kings 13:3). Judges 3:8 says, "The Lord burned with anger against Israel." Just as our eyes burn when we look at the sun, there is something within God's nature that causes him to burn with anger at the sight of evil. Because God is holy, he simply cannot respond to sin in any other way.

Because God is holy and just, he will always do what is right. He cannot overlook our wrongdoings, for he is obligated to do what is right. The British theologian Michael Green observed that "for God just to forgive without any cost to anyone would be sheer indifferentism. It would obliterate any distinction between right and wrong. It would say that right does not matter, and that evil is a matter of indifference."[1]

So, as you can see, the sin of Adam and Eve and their subsequent fall left all mankind with a serious dilemma. They had turned their backs on God, and God, in his holiness and justice, had to render a just and holy judgment against them. This judgment was death. There is no life for those who alienate themselves from the source of life, and this is what all humanity has done through sin. We will deal more fully with this dilemma in the next chapter.

2

ARE WE DOOMED?

In the previous chapter, we set up man's cosmic dilemma. Human beings were originally created perfect and placed in a perfect world. Their lives were harmonious with God, with nature, with the animals and with each other. Their entire existence was joyful, pain-free and deathless. They were created to be God's deputies in ruling the earth, and to give them the power and wisdom to accomplish that task, he placed his own Holy Spirit inside them, giving them an intimate relationship of love with the God of the universe.

But the first man and woman rejected God and chose to set themselves up as their own gods. That act was the first sin. Adam and Eve found that, having sinned once, sin gripped them like an addiction. They couldn't stop sinning, and they passed on that terrible craving to satisfy the self to all their descendants. So now we all sin, and left to ourselves, we lack the ability to find our own way in life or to reunite ourselves with the God we rejected.

If you are among the many who think sin is overplayed by the church, all you have to do is look around you at the world today and you can see clearly that mankind has lost its ability to direct its own path to a life of fulfillment and joy. Let's take a moment and look at the evidence that clearly displays the result of the Fall of mankind in the lives of people today. As many of you know, I (Josh) have a particular concern for our youth. I have spent much of my ministry working with youth, and I am greatly alarmed and saddened by the drift of today's young people into the prevalent worldview of Western culture. I think the persistent tendency of our kids to be pulled away from godly values is one of the strongest evidences we have of our fallen condition and our need for rescue from the doom of sin.

The Worldview Crisis of Our Youth

The crisis among young people today is alarming. According to a recent study, 20 percent of high school kids have contemplated suicide over the past year, while 8 percent said they attempted suicide in the same time period. Twelve percent of kids are lonely, 25 percent feel unfulfilled in life, and nearly 50 percent say they are stressed out.[1] Many kids struggle with depression, feelings of loneliness, and rejection. According to many youth culture experts, "relational deprivation" is one of the primary characteristics of younger generations today.

Youth ministry expert Dr. Chap Clark spent a year in the world of today's teens. He researched youth trends, spent time hanging out with kids personally, and acted as a substitute teacher at a Los Angeles school in an attempt to understand contemporary teen culture. He chronicled his findings in his book *Hurt: Inside the World of Today's Teenagers*. In describing this generation of young people, Clark says, "Every student I talked to acknowledged that loneliness is a central experience . . . Today's adolescents are, as a lot, indescribably lonely."[2] As a result of this relational void in the lives of many teens, Clark says, "Every single young person who has grown up in America is only one major event or catastrophe away from falling over the edge into what most would call at-risk."[3] Even our best kids have been deeply influenced by our non-relational, fast-paced, secular culture. *Every* single kid growing up today is susceptible to the negative and dangerous aspects of that culture.

Many websites, blogs, video games, movies and musicians exploit such teen struggles. Graphic novels and video games depict dark worlds where violence and hatred reign. Contemporary musicians and movies put to music the fear and anxiety many teens feel. Some believe these entertainment venues create hopelessness, self-destruction and violence toward others. Whether or not that is true, it is inarguable that they capitalize on such feelings.

Just spend a little time with young people and you will see firsthand the emptiness that haunts so many of them. From an early age, they imbibe the cultural message that life is a pitiless pursuit of individual gratification and success, requiring extraordinary good looks, money and moral compromise. They tend to lack any sense of context, community and higher purpose. It is hardly surprising that so many of them are taking antidepressants, Attention Deficit Disorder medications, or other pills. Many more hide their sadness in eating disorders, alcohol or meaningless sexual hookups. In a rush to provide our young people with everything, we've forgotten to answer a basic question: *What is life for?*

We don't know of anything that shows more clearly that we live in a fallen world where God has been forgotten than the crisis of our youth. Their lives show that we live in a world that has abandoned hope in anything beyond tomorrow, a world that is alienated from God and trying desperately to find its own way, groping in the darkness, hoping to find a handhold that will provide them with some sense of security. It's a world that demonstrates the lack of purpose and direction humankind falls into when God is rejected in favor of doing "what is right for me." The sin of Adam and Eve reverberates loudly in our culture today.

The Confused Mission in Life

When I (Sean) ask my students what their parents want most for them in their lives, their typical response is "happiness." To find what they mean by happiness, I ask them to imagine a scene of happy people and tell me what those people are doing. They typically conjure up an image of people *having fun*. To them, having fun is laughing, playing video games and partying. Rarely will any teen mention helping others, developing deep friendships or cultivating a relationship with God—things that bring true happiness because of their connection to a larger purpose in life.

A recent dictionary defines happiness as "a pleasurable or satisfying experience."[4] Notice how happiness is connected with feelings, and more specifically, with *pleasurable* feelings. In today's culture, happiness is equated with feeling good, which is the ultimate goal of most young people. According to radio talk show host Dennis Prager, most young people believe in the equation $H = nF$, or the experience of happiness equals the number of fun experiences.[5] While there is nothing wrong with pleasurable satisfaction *per se*, we should be deeply concerned about young people who identify the pursuit of pleasure as their mission in life. And this is precisely what they are doing. The "good life" for many teenagers consists of feeling good—mentally, physically and emotionally—and buying expensive things that give them pleasure.

Generation Me

The generation of young people today under age 35 has never known a world that puts duty before self. To this generation the individual always comes first, with the number one virtue being to feel good about yourself. For previous generations, duty and responsibility superseded individual wants and desires. It was considered virtuous to sacrifice personal desires for the greater good. Such is no longer true for today's young people.

Young people today have grown up in a culture that takes it for granted that they should feel good about themselves, that they are special and that they ought to follow their own personal dreams. Just watch the auditions of thousands of young people on *American Idol*, who despite their lack of ability, are convinced that they are the next stars. The "My" in MySpace is also very telling.

Be yourself, believe in yourself, express yourself. Self, self, self! It's all about the self. Do you see the connection between today's self-emphasis and the sin of Adam and Eve? It is essentially the same sin—the rejection of God's love and direction in favor of following one's own desires and setting one's own path. Today's youth give us a clear picture of alienation from the God who is the only source of love, life and fulfillment.

So powerful has been this cultural change from the group to the individual that even the Army has followed suit. In 2001 their standard slogan became, "An Army of One." In other words, no longer do they attract recruits on the basis of joining a collective group to sacrifice one's own wants for the greater good of society. Now they must encourage young people to join because it will do something for them as individuals.

The explosion of tattoos and the changing nature of dancing are both deeply connected to this larger cultural shift towards individuality. Rather than being mere fashion trends, tattoos are often a powerful means of self-expression. They allow the individual to give an outer expression to an inner reality. In the minds of many young people, tattoos are a medium for communicating individuality. Likewise, for previous generations, dancing involved skill, customs and general rules of conduct to help partners move harmoniously together. Dancing was a romantic, stylized expression of synthesized oneness with another. But today dancing typically involves individual free-form expression with only minimal social rules. The most important thing is not to submit to mutual harmony, but to express one's individual self.

The mantra of this generation might be: *Do whatever it takes to feel good about yourself because that's the most important thing in the world.* This false understanding of happiness as pleasurable satisfaction is taking a heavy toll on youth today. Christian apologist J. P. Moreland asks a very pertinent question: "If happiness is having an internal feeling of fun or pleasurable satisfaction, and if it is our main goal, where will we place our focus all day long? The focus will be on us, and the result will be a culture of self-absorbed individuals who can't live for something larger than we are."[6] In the eyes of most youth, school, work, sports, church and even God exist as means to bring one's own personal happiness and satisfaction.

In his book *Soul Searching*, Christian Smith observes that most youth view God as a cosmic therapist who exists to meet *their* needs rather than understanding their purpose as loving God and other people. Smith concludes, "As far as we could discern, what most teens appear to believe is that religion is about God responding to the authoritative desires and feelings of people . . . religion is essentially a tool for people to use to get what they want."[7]

Ironically, when people focus primarily on their own pleasure, their lives become empty and depression is often the result. According to happiness expert Dr. Martin Seligman, baby boomers experienced a tenfold increase in depression over any previous generation.[8] The reason: They began the shift towards a focus on the self. Young people today have grown up completely with this emphasis and, as a result, they have experienced even higher degrees of depression.

Young people today have many advantages unknown to previous generations: the Internet, cell phones, easier and cheaper travel, improved medical care, better education, less physical labor, improved equal rights opportunities and, for the most part, the freedom to make their own choices. But the problem for many is that they have nothing outside themselves to focus on. This generation has been trained to focus on the self at the expense of a larger purpose in life.

Our Need for Hope

The state of our young people today gives us a clear picture of how the Fall affected humankind. Life without God is one of self-focus and lack of purpose. It's a life of desperate searching for meaning and satisfaction, but one that fails to find it because we are created to find true meaning, fulfillment and love only in connection with the God who made us. Without that connection, we are doomed to the life of purposeless searching we see in today's culture. We are doomed to follow our own meandering trails to endless dead-ends in search of something we can never find on our own.

The state of our young people today is a case study in how desperately we all need hope. Life lived by one's own standards and by seeking one's own satisfaction means continual alienation from God and persistent frustration with the lack of meaning and fulfillment. The answer for everyone—youth and adults alike—is to adopt a biblical worldview with a mission that will help us weather the storms of life. A biblical worldview simply means seeing life truthfully from God's perspective. It means understanding the truth of our hopeless condition without God and taking steps to realign our lives with his character and the true meaning of universal truth.

Philosopher J. P. Moreland explains:

> This is why truth is so powerful. It allows us to cooperate with reality, whether spiritual or physical, and tap into its power. As we learn to think correctly about God, specific scriptural teachings, the soul, or other important aspects of a Christian worldview, we are placed in touch with God and those realities. And we thereby gain access to the power available to us to live in the kingdom of God.[9]

Young people and adults alike need to understand clearly that God is calling them to see life from his perspective and join him in a mission that literally defines their eternal destiny. Abandoning dependence on self and aligning with the truth of God can bring powerful transformation that is more than equal to the present challenges we all face in today's drifting, godless culture.

But the big question is, How do we find our way back to God? We alienated ourselves from him, and he honored that choice by leaving us on our own, cut off from the source of life and floundering like a headless chicken without direction or hope. And we are doomed to remain in that hopeless condition unless God himself opens a way for us to come back to him. Since we are under judgment from his perfect justice, and since he is too holy to tolerate sin in his presence, how can we who are addicted to sin possibly get back in his good graces? We can't do it unless he provides a way. Without his reaching down to us and solving our fatal dilemma, we are doomed.

But, thank God, he has done just that. He has reached down to us and given us a way out of our doom. In the next two chapters we will explore how he provided the way for us to come back to him and overcome the doom of the Fall.

THE INCREDIBLE LOVE OF GOD

So far in this book, we have explored how things were meant to be, how they turned into the mess we experience now, and the doom that descended on humanity when we rejected God in favor of self. We closed the previous chapter by showing how our alienation from God would put us in a hopeless position unless God himself offered a solution. We are guilty of bringing the contamination of sin into his perfect universe, of causing pain and ruin to his creation and to our selves. God in his perfect justice and holiness cannot be called good if he allows sin to remain in his universe. Therefore, we, the agents of sin, are under the doom of his perfect judgment. We are guilty, and we deserve condemnation. That is our dilemma.

Little do we think of it, but God faced a dilemma as well. (At least, it is a dilemma to the limited human mind.) Strangely, he did not want to condemn us. Although the sin we carried was like a contagious virus that would eventually infect all creation if it were not eradicated from his planet, he did not want to inflict on us the doom we had earned by becoming sin-contaminated creatures. However, as we have affirmed in this book, his holiness—his perfect goodness and justice—gave him no choice but to deal with the contamination of sin that we had brought into his universe. That was God's dilemma. Our sin had to be condemned, but he didn't want to condemn us.

The natural question is, Why wouldn't God want to condemn us? We had slapped him in the face by rejecting his magnificent gift of a perfect life in a perfect world. We had rejected his love—the deepest and most gratifying love a human could ever experience. We had rejected his intimate relationship with us—a relationship so close that he would live within us himself, sharing with us his wisdom and power to be his regents over creation. He gave us all this, and yet we threw it back at him and stalked off to follow our own winding path to nowhere, looking for guidance from the emptiness of our own selves, which, without God, lacked the insight and wisdom to know what step to take next.

After spurning God this way, why would he care about us anymore? Why wouldn't he simply say, "Good riddance! If that's what they think of everything I've given them, they are not worth my time and energy." Why didn't he fire off a couple of lightning bolts right there in Eden and reduce the ungrateful couple to twin piles of ashes?

We find the answer in the fact that God loved the couple he had created. It was not that he needed us to fulfill any lack of love within himself. The essence of God's being is an intimate unity of three personalities bonded by the continual interaction of love. Yet in his infinite capacity to love, he dearly loved the man and woman he created, and the power of that love was undiluted by their fall.

Although we humans are not infinite, we can understand this love to some degree because we share it, though with a more limited capacity. Like God, we delight in having other living creatures around us upon which to lavish our affection. Though young married couples are deeply in love and blissfully wrapped up in each other, almost universally they want children. They want to expand their love to include others like themselves, whom they "create in their own image" through begetting and bearing. They delight in these little bundles of joy that they bring into the world to love, cherish, protect and raise to maturity.

We parents delight in our children. And the amazing thing is that God delighted similarly in the humans he made. Just as a mother delights in the smile of her infant, God delighted in the love of his human creatures. He loved Adam and Eve with an incredible passion and derived great pleasure from their relationship with him (see Prov. 11:20). This intimate, joyful relationship between God and humankind, with love flowing continually in both directions, was his intention, not merely for this first couple, but for all humanity for all time. He created us for his delight, and he created us to delight in him.

Even when our children stray from the path we set them on and go wrong, we continue to love them. We may grieve over what they have done, but our grieving itself shows that we care for them in spite of their wayward choices. Of course, we sometimes hear of parents who disown and reject their children because of their misdeeds, but even in those cases, the ache and sadness remain in the hearts of the parents, showing that in spite of their outward display of anger and rejection, love is still intact, even if bitter and suppressed.

In this ongoing love for our children, we reflect the loving nature of God. Although the Fall had made all humanity natural enemies to God, he was in love with us. As astounding as it seems, he could not stand the thought of losing us (see John 3:16). He looked into the future he had planned for the human race, and the thought that you and I would not exist in his presence throughout eternity broke his heart. In spite of the fact that humanity had rejected him, that amazing love of his could not bear the thought of our destruction. He wanted us back. So he refused to accept Adam and Eve's decision to reject him as the final word, and he came after us. He devised a solution that would save us from our own folly.

The Incredible Love of God

There is another reason the God of the Bible acts lovingly toward his creation. It is not necessarily because of any virtue or lovability in the object loved; it is because it is simply his nature to love. Scripture tells us that "God is love" (1 John 4:8). The very nature and character of God is love. God acts lovingly not because we are lovable or deserving of love, but simply because he is love. And the love of God consists not merely of warm feelings of affection or benevolent acts of kindness. His love is a real, active, tough love that wills the very best for us in all circumstances.

This idea may be difficult for some people to accept. With personal disasters, worldwide poverty, floods, forest fires, earthquakes, terrorism, torture, disease, death and the accumulation of pain throughout the centuries, many of us are left wondering: If God is really loving, why would he allow such terrible and rampant tragedy? Christianity offers no pat answers to this difficult question, but it does assure us of God's love and care for his creation. In fact, Scripture takes great pains to give us evidence of God's love, which we are about to explore in the next few chapters of this book. When we are assured of God's love, we will know that we can trust him. And when we are willing to trust him, he will help us transcend the pain and difficulties we encounter in this fallen world.

One of the first evidences of the depth of God's love was given to Adam and Eve right there in Eden as they stood before God facing judgment for their sin. After telling them of all the pain and agony they would endure as a result of turning from him, he then made the first announcement of his plan to save them from their headlong plunge into death. In Genesis 3:15 we hear God saying to the serpent that deceived Eve into sin, "And I will cause hostility between you and the woman, and between your offspring and her offspring. He will crush your head, *and you will strike his heel*" (*NIV*, emphasis added). This prophecy gave humankind the first hint that God had a plan in place to rescue the woman, her husband and their offspring from death. It told them that a descendant of the woman would eventually come into the world and crush Satan's head, destroying forever the grip of death he inflicted upon the human race. In the process, this descendant would be wounded—that is, his heel would be stricken, but the wound would not be fatal.

This enigmatic prophecy was the first pronouncement of God's intention to save mankind, but he had devised the plan much earlier than this. In 1 Peter 1:19-20 we read, "It was the precious blood of Christ, the sinless, spotless Lamb of God. God chose him as your ransom long before the world began, but he has now revealed him to you in these last days." Here we see the true depth of God's love for us. Even before we sinned, he loved us so much that he had already devised a way to save us if we fell. And that plan involved a huge sacrifice on God's part. He intended to take the penalty for our sin upon himself, face death nose to nose and defeat its power over us once and for all. He would be greatly wounded in the process, but he would be victorious over Satan.

So you can see that understanding the meaning of love begins by looking at the character of God rather than by consulting a dictionary. And in particular we should focus on the cross of Christ, where God made the ultimate demonstration of his love to us. First John 3:16 says, "We know what real love is because Jesus gave up his life for us." Nowhere is God's love better displayed than at Jesus' death, where he willingly accepted the penalty due to us for our sin of rejecting God. As 1 John 4:10 says, "This is real love—not that we loved God, but that he loved us and sent his Son as a sacrifice to take away our sins."

We sometimes forget how utterly lost we are without God: there is nothing we can do to fix our dilemma. Yet God, in sending his Son, paid the debt for our sins so we could come back into relationship with him. Sending his Son to face death was an act of pure, unmerited love, for God was under no obligation to reach out to us. He did it freely and without compulsion simply because he loves us. There was *nothing* God would not do to prove his love to us. God could not have paid a greater price than giving his Son to suffer agony and die for us.

The love of God cannot be understood merely by analysis or from a distance. Like a good dance or a beautiful sunset, God's love can only be known by participating in it. Love is realized in relationship, which means the love of God can only be grasped in the context of a personal commitment of trust. It is not enough to remain passive spectators to God's story in the world. If we truly want to experience his love, we must be willing to apply his truth to our lives today.

Love Means Giving Yourself

Let's explore for a moment the depth of God's love for us. We often express love by giving gifts to those with whom we have relationships. Sometimes those gifts have real meaning, and sometimes they can be poor substitutes for real love, as when a busy parent showers kids with toys and things but fails to be involved deeply in their lives. There is no greater gift we can give to someone than offering ourselves. As valuable as tangible gifts are, they don't compare to the offering of our presence. Ralph Waldo Emerson, the great writer, understood this truth as well as anyone. He said, "A gift is an excuse for *not* giving yourself." And this giving of self is exactly what God did for us in sending us his Son, Jesus Christ.

Christ was not merely an external gift. He was not an angel or an animal or a third party, but the eternal Son of the Father, who is one with God in his essential being. In giving his Son, God was giving himself. This is why Paul says, "I live by faith in the Son of God, who loved me and gave Himself up for me" (Gal. 2:20, *NASB*). John Stott astutely observes:

> If God had sent a man to us, as he had sent the prophets to Israel, we would have been grateful. If he had sent an angel, as he did to Mary at the annunciation, we would have counted it a great privilege. Yet in either case he would have sent us a third party, since men and angels are creatures of his making. But in sending his own Son, eternally begotten from his own Being, he was not sending a creature, a third party, but giving himself.[1]

God gave *himself* as the offering for the salvation of humanity. The enormous significance of this is inescapable. For how could God the Father have demonstrated his love for his creation if he had sent someone else to earth? This would not do. Since the essence of love is self-giving, then when the God of all universes gave himself to mankind, he demonstrated the greatest and most astounding act of love in history. Paul observed, "He who did not spare His own Son, but delivered Him over for us all, how will He not also with Him freely give us all things?" (Rom. 8:32, *NASB*). And Jesus said, "For God loved the world so much that he gave his one and only Son, so that everyone who believes in him will not perish but have eternal life" (John 3:16). Every act of love in history pales in comparison to God's "indescribable gift" of his Son (2 Cor. 9:15, *NASB*).

The worth of a love gift is assessed in two ways: what it costs the giver and the degree to which the beneficiary is thought to deserve it. Many young lovers will shower their beloved with expensive gifts, many times beyond what they can afford because of their sacrificial love. Jacob worked 14 years for Rachel because of his love for her. God paid the highest price he could possibly pay for us: he sent his only Son to die for us. He could not have paid a higher price. He gave everything he could for those who deserved nothing. As Romans 5:8 says, this is how God showed his great love for us—"by sending Christ to die for us while we were still sinners."

Love Means Giving Up Power

God clearly demonstrated his power to the world during Old Testament times by creating the universe, destroying Sodom and Gomorrah, bringing the plagues on Egypt, splitting the Red Sea and working other wondrous miracles. But 2,000 years ago, when he wanted his love to be fully revealed, he laid aside his power. Jesus set aside the power that would dazzle men into submission and came to us in humility. Philippians 2:6-8 says:

> Though he was God,
>   he did not think of equality with God
>   as something to cling to.
> Instead, he gave up his divine privileges;
>   he took the humble position of a slave
>   and was born as a human being.
> When he appeared in human form,
>   he humbled himself in obedience to God
>   and died a criminal's death on a cross.

God humbled himself so much that he was put to death by his own creatures. People that he created to love and to love him mocked him, spit on him and tortured him. They cried out for Jesus to demonstrate his power to save himself, but he refused. He refused because the cross was not the place for power; *it was the place for the demonstration of his love.* To our world, the way of Jesus seems like foolishness. Power is what really matters. The powerless are worthless. But Jesus ignored all temptations to power and demonstrated the nature of genuine love by his death. Genuine love is characterized by unlimited, selfless risk-taking without a guarantee of success, and a vulnerability that can be easily hurt. This is exactly what God did in giving his Son; he made himself vulnerable to the possibility that his beloved humans would reject him.

Perhaps the greatest demonstration of God's strength came when he was willing to give up his unlimited power and suffer. Philip Yancey captures the significance of this act:

> The spectacle of the cross, the most public event of Jesus' life, reveals the vast difference between a god who proves himself through power and one who proves himself through love. Other gods, Roman gods, for example, enforced worship: in Jesus' own

lifetime, some Jews were slaughtered for not bowing down to Caesar. But Jesus Christ never forced anyone to believe in him. He preferred to act by appeal, drawing people out of themselves and toward him.[2]

Because of Jesus' death on the cross, we can know God in a more intimate way. Michael Green notes:

> The Lion of God's strength is the Lamb of God's sacrifice. Self-sacrificing love is actually on the throne of the universe, and is the key to the understanding of the human history and destiny. . . . Calvary displays in time God's attitude to sinners from all eternity. There is nothing more fundamental in the whole universe than the self-sacrificing love of God. This is the ground for Christian hope.[3]

God is not only the powerful creator of the universe; he is the grieving Father who yearns for the return of his prodigal son. And it was at the cross that God's love was best displayed.

This should come as good news to us all, especially today when low self-image seems to afflict so many people. In spite of the craze to affirm everyone's self-image, many people are crippled by deep internal feelings of inferiority. Our pressure-filled society places so much emphasis on external appearance, power, cash flow and popularity, that anyone who does not measure up in all categories feels diminished in value. Often we feel loved only when we accomplish what is expected of us. Unconditional love seems almost beyond comprehension to most people. It's no wonder that so many today struggle with their self-worth.

Such feelings of low self-image and worthlessness are needless, because God has demonstrated our worth to him through his willingness to send his Son to die for our sins. It's as if God was saying, "I love you so much there is nothing I would not do to have a relationship with you. You are of infinite worth to me. I made you in my image and I yearn to know you as I yearn for you to know me. You are worth more to me than the lilies of the field, the snow-capped mountains and the fish of the sea.

My love for you is limitless. I believe in you. I desire to be a part of your life and for you to experience the immense value I place on you and the infinite love I have for you." That is a summation of what you are worth. You can never consider yourself unloved or worthless. You are the dearly beloved of the God and creator of the universe.

Many people think that I (Josh) was drawn to Jesus by the historical evidence for his death and resurrection, his deity and the reliability of Scriptures. But that is not the case at all. It was his love, which was shown to me firsthand in the lives of a handful of Christians. It wasn't logical facts about Christ that caused me to commit my life to him; it was Christ's loving heart, which reached out in mercy to form a relationship with me.

You see, the historical evidence convinced my mind that the Jesus who lived 2,000 years ago had to be the one true God. But it was his love that gripped my heart and compelled me to commit my life to Christ. It was God's love that drew me to him. God said, "I have loved you, my people, with an everlasting love. With unfailing love I have drawn you to myself" (Jer. 31:3).

In the next two chapters of this book, we will show how the incredible love of God led him to the ultimate solution for restoring us into a relationship with him, and we will demonstrate that it is because of Christ's death and resurrection we can know that our loving relationship with God will continue after death.

THE SOLUTION TO OUR DILEMMA

In the previous chapter we explained God's deep love for us and showed how it led him to sacrifice himself by dying on the cross. Obviously, his sacrificial death had to have a definite purpose. If a man were to jump into a freezing lake and drown, yelling to his girlfriend sitting on the bank as he went under for the third time, "I'm doing this because I love you," we would not think of the man as a great lover but a great fool. Unless his girlfriend was drowning and his plunge into the lake could save her, his self-sacrifice would have no saving purpose.

In the previous chapter, we explained how God's deep love for us led him to sacrifice himself by dying on the cross. But obviously, his death had to have meaning, in that it somehow accomplished the definite purpose of saving us, or it would have been merely an act of foolishness. So the natural questions are, How did Christ's sacrifice work to save us? How did his death and resurrection provide a solution to man's deadly dilemma? In this chapter, we will present God's saving acts as a two-step process, beginning with his death on the cross and culminating with his resurrection from the dead.

Step One:
The Sacrifice of Christ

God's incredible love for us and the satisfaction of his demand for justice can be seen in the crucifixion of Christ on a Roman cross in first-century Judea (see Rom. 5:8). As John Stott has observed, "The cross can be seen as a proof of God's love only when it is at the same time seen as a proof of his justice."[1] We have shown in the previous chapter how Christ's sacrifice demonstrates God's love. Now we will briefly explain how it also satisfies his demand for perfect justice, and this will tell us how his death worked to save us.

We have noted that because God is good and just, he must do something about sin. Because we humans are the guilty party that contaminates his perfect world with the addiction of sin, justice demands that we suffer the penalty for sin, which is death (see Rom. 6:23). God rescued us by acting as our substitute and taking the death we deserved in our place.

What Christ did for us was somewhat like the sacrifice of Sidney Carton for the nobleman Charles Darnay in Charles Dickens's historical novel *A Tale of Two Cities*. Carton managed to smuggle himself into the jail cell of the condemned Darnay and smuggle the convicted nobleman out to freedom. Then, when it came time for the jailors to march Darnay to the guillotine, it was Carton who took his death. Or, to clarify the concept further with another illustration, the sacrifice of Jesus is somewhat like that of a judge who sentenced his own daughter to pay a 200 dollar fine for speeding. The girl did not have the money, and as a result the law stipulated that she must spend three days in jail. The judge, bound by his office to administer justice but not wanting his dear daughter to be subject to the abuses of hardened inmates in the jail, stepped down from the bench, removed his robe and paid the fine for the girl. He paid the penalty, and she went free. Justice was satisfied, but love prevailed by freeing the guilty from condemnation.

These illustrations give us something of a picture of what Christ did for us. His death on the cross was the death we should have borne. The sins he died for were our own. The guilt he carried was ours. And since he paid the price, justice is now satisfied, and we can go free. As the apostle Peter tells us, "He personally carried our sins in his body on the cross so that we can be dead to sin and live for what is right. By his wounds you are healed" (1 Pet. 2:24). And later he writes, "Christ suffered for our sins once for all time. He never sinned, but he died for sinners to bring you safely home to God. He suffered physical death, but he was raised to life in the Spirit" (1 Pet. 3:18). Paul affirms the concept when he writes, "For God made Christ, who never sinned, to be the offering for our sin, so that we could be made right with God through Christ" (2 Cor. 5:21).

Christ took our guilt and paid the legal penalty. Therefore, we are free of guilt and freed from the condemnation our sin brought upon us.

As a result, God can now free us from the penalty of sin and treat us as if we were absolutely innocent. As Paul tells us, "So just as sin ruled over all people and brought them to death, now God's wonderful grace rules instead, giving us right standing with God and resulting in eternal life through Jesus Christ our Lord" (Rom. 5:21).

Thus we can see how the incarnation and death of Christ demonstrates both God's love and his justice: "Unfailing love and truth have met together. Righteousness and peace have kissed!" (Ps. 85:10). God is loving and just. The death of Christ both paid the legal penalty for sin and removed the barrier that sin had placed between God and our selves.

Why Did It Have to Be Jesus?

The ultimate purpose of Christ's death was to reconcile rebel humans to the loving God who created them. In any reconciliation the mediator must fairly represent both sides. For this reason, Jesus Christ is the perfect mediator between God and mankind. Why? Because Christ *was God in human flesh*. He was both God and man. He was fully God from all eternity, and he became fully man when he was born to Mary in Bethlehem.

Why did God have to become human? We noted earlier that the penalty for sin is death. God, being eternal in nature, cannot die. In order to die the physical death we incurred with our sin, Christ had to become human. There is also another reason he had to be human: Humans were the ones who had rebelled against God and had broken his laws and decrees, thereby separating themselves from his presence. Since humans had offended God, a human had to pay the price for their reconciliation with God. The problem, as Scripture makes clear, is that our sins have contaminated us so much that we cannot please God on our own. No human can qualify to pay for the sins of all humanity because every human has his or her own sins to pay for. It's as if the judge in our illustration above was bankrupt and lacked the funds to pay his daughter's fine. A third party was needed to provide the lacking resources. As Paul says, "All have turned away; all have become useless. No one does good, not a single one" (Rom. 3:12). And because none of us does the good Paul mentions, none of us has the goodness needed to pay for the sins of others.

Our substitute sacrifice had to be God, for only God has the sinless perfection necessary to qualify. Christ had to be both divine and human if his death was to adequately pay the price for our sins. The only way it could work was for God to become human himself, in the person of Christ, as our substitute for execution.

To summarize, Christ's sacrifice, his leaving heaven and descending to a messed-up earth to suffer and die, shows us the full expression of God's love and justice at the cross. God desired to restore his relationship with us. But because he is the just and moral ruler of the universe, he could not merely overlook our wrongdoings and allow us to live as sinners, contaminating ourselves and his perfect creation. A penalty must be paid—a penalty that can account for human sin, yet satisfy an infinitely just God. The sin we acquired had to be removed before we could re-enter into relationship with him. Rather than inflicting that penalty on us, he committed the ultimate act of love: He sent his very own Son to become God in human flesh and die for us. If God in Christ had not paid the price for our sins and satisfied his perfect justice, we could not have been justified. Because of his death we now stand before him as if we were sinless. And because he can now see us as sinless, our relationship with him can be restored.

Step Two:
The Resurrection—the Heart of the Christian Faith

The sacrificial death of Christ, as crucial as it is in reconciling us to God, is incomplete by itself. His death was absolutely necessary to deal with the problem of sin and remove our guilt, but one more step was required in order to restore us to life and enable us to experience the fullness of God's love. That step is Christ's resurrection from the dead. Without the resurrection, the process of restoring us to God would be incomplete. The penalty would be paid and justice would be satisfied, but the doors out of the prison of death would not yet be opened to us. Let us explain.

In previous chapters, we have compared sin to an addiction. Once Adam and Eve sinned, the compulsion to gratify the self and satisfy all cravings became embedded into their being. Throughout his letters, the apostle Paul refers to this embedded tendency as our "sinful nature." In

Romans 7:18, he writes, "I know that nothing good lives in me, that is, in my sinful nature. I want to do what is right, but I can't." Adam and Eve passed on this embedded sinful nature to their descendants, which means that every human born is afflicted with it.

While Christ's death removed our guilt and paid the penalty for our sin, it was what we might call a "legal" solution that satisfied God's justice. Christ's death allowed God to look at us as guiltless and to remove the penalty of condemnation from us. But it did not deal with the practical problem of that embedded sinful nature, which we all still possess—even those of us who have accepted Christ's sacrifice as our own and have had the guilt and penalty removed from our lives. We still have that sinful nature inherited from Adam embedded within us. And until it's dealt with permanently, no matter how hard we try to follow God's ways and do his will, we will continue to fight against that sinful nature and often slip into sinning in spite of our resolve to do otherwise.

Unfortunately, this sinful nature can't be improved, and it can't be removed. There is only one way to get rid of that sinful nature: It must be killed. The problem is that it is so embedded within us that the only way to kill the sinful nature is to kill the sinner who bears it. That is why, in spite of the forgiveness we get from God through the death of Christ, we still have to die physically. Death is the only way to rid us of that embedded sinful nature.

This brings us to the vital importance of the resurrection of Christ. His resurrection from the dead completes the process of reconciling us to God. Whereas his death removed guilt and paid the penalty for sin, if that was all he did, we would still be stuck with the imperfection of our sinful nature, which would carry us into death. And death would end our physical existence forever. But the resurrection of Christ tells us that our death need not be the end of us. His resurrection can be ours as well.

Here's how it works: When God redeems us, he accepts the sacrifice of Christ to remove our guilt for sin and claims us as one of his own, even though we still carry the contaminating nature of sin. He lets us temporarily "borrow" the perfection of Christ and looks on us as if we were truly sinless, without any error or imperfection. He lets us borrow that perfection because he knows that Christ's resurrection has provided for us a permanent way to rid ourselves of the sinful contamination and regain the true perfection he intended for us at creation. Then, when we die physically, our contaminated nature dies as well. He then gives us new bodies—magnificent, glorious, perfect bodies like those of Adam and Eve—completely free of the contamination of sin. Now perfect as we were meant to be, we will be placed on a newly renovated earth to start life over as intimate companions with God, enjoying his loving fellowship and inhabited by his Holy Spirit.

This is what the resurrection of Christ shows us. Physical death is inevitable. It is necessary to separate us from the contamination of sin. But Christ's resurrection demonstrates that we can be raised again. Jesus is the trailblazer, the one who defeated death on the cross ("It is finished," John 19:3), and because of him we can live in new bodies meant to last forever.

In *The Incredible Rumor*, a short novel that I (Josh) wrote with Thomas Williams, we used an illustration in which we compared Christ to a powerful swimmer:

> Think of death as a deep, cold river. Imagine that Satan crippled us to where we couldn't swim and then forced us into that river. We would all be doomed. But along came a giant of a man too powerful for Satan to cripple. He could swim beautifully. He offered to carry us across the river, so we climbed onto his back, attached ourselves to him, and he plunged in. The burden was great, and he sank into the depths. Satan expected him to drown, but to his surprise the swimmer came up on the far shore, bringing us up with him. That's what Jesus' death and resurrection are all about.[2]

"But," you may wonder, "how can the death and resurrection of one person pay the price and defeat death for the entire human race?" According to the apostle Paul, death entered the human race through the sins of one man, Adam. If sin entered the world through one man, then it can be defeated through the virtuous act of one man. And this is exactly what happened. Because of Jesus' death and resurrection we can all be given new life. Jesus has not only dealt with sin, he has defeated the devil. He has effectively disabled death, destroying its power over us.

Because of the resurrection of Christ, death has lost its sting. Paul shouts with an air of defiance: "O death, where is your victory? O death, where is your sting?" Of course there is no reply. So Paul shouts again, this time with an air of conquest: "But thank God! He gives us victory over sin and death through our Lord Jesus Christ" (1 Cor. 15:55,57). Since death has lost its ability to bring ultimate harm, it loses its ability to terrify.

Jesus said triumphantly, "I am the resurrection and the life. Anyone who believes in me will live, even after dying. Everyone who lives in me and believes in me will never ever die" (John 11:25-26). As John Stott has so aptly stated, "Jesus is the resurrection of believers who die, and the life of believers who live."[3]

If Jesus was truly raised from the dead in history, as the evidence we will delve into later powerfully indicates, then we can have confidence that we will someday be raised from our own death as well. The empty tomb of Jesus is a promise that our relationships will continue and that we will share in Christ's defeat of death.

The Vital Importance of the Resurrection

The historical fact of the resurrection is the very foundation for the Christian faith. It is not an optional article of faith—it is *the* faith! The resurrection of Jesus Christ and Christianity stand or fall together. One cannot be true without the other. Belief in the truth of Christianity is not merely faith in faith—ours or someone else's—but rather faith in the risen Christ of history. Without the historical resurrection of Jesus, the Christian faith is a mere placebo. Worship, fellowship, Bible study, the Christian life and the church itself are worthless exercises in futility if Jesus has not been literally and physically raised from the dead. Without the resurrection, we might as well forget God, church and following moral rules and "feast and drink, for tomorrow we die!" (1 Cor. 15:32).

On the other hand, if Christ has been raised from the dead, then he is alive at this very moment, and we can know him personally (see 1 Cor. 15:4). Our sins are forgiven (see v. 3), and he has broken the power of death (see v. 54). Furthermore, he promises that we too will be resurrected someday (see v. 22). We can trust him because he is sovereign over the world (see v. 27). He will give us ultimate victory (see v. 57), and he has a plan for our lives (see v. 58).

The resurrection has been the focus of the church since its inception. The New Testament book of Acts, which tells the story of the beginning of the Christian church, illustrates this well:

- In the first chapter the 11 apostles were trying to find a replacement for Judas. One criterion for the selection of an apostle was that he "must become a witness with us of His [Jesus'] resurrection" (Acts 1:22, *NASB*).

- In Acts 2:23-24 Peter gives his first sermon on the day of Pentecost. The keynote of his address was, "This Man, delivered over by the predetermined plan and foreknowledge of God, you nailed to a cross by the hands of godless men and put Him to death. But God raised Him up again, putting an end to the agony of death, since it was impossible for Him to be held in its power" (*NASB*).

- In Peter's second sermon he says, "But you disowned the Holy and Righteous One and asked for a murderer to be granted to you, but put to death the Prince of life, *the one* whom God raised from the dead, *a fact* to which we are witnesses" (Acts 3:15, *NASB*).

Paul refers to the resurrection of Jesus 53 times in his letters. Most of these texts assert the primacy of the resurrection, the assurance it gives us of our own future bodily resurrection or both. He emphasizes the centrality of the resurrection in his letter to the Thessalonians: "For they themselves report about us what kind of a reception we had with you, and how you turned to God from idols to serve a living and true God, and to wait for His Son from heaven, whom he raised from the dead, *that is* Jesus, who rescues us from the wrath to come" (1 Thess. 1:9-10, *NASB*, emphasis added).

British scholar N. T. Wright explains how central the resurrection has been in the life of the church:

There is no form of early Christianity known to us—though there are some that have been invented by ingenious scholars—that does not affirm at its heart that after Jesus' shameful death God raised him to life again. Already by the time of Paul, our earliest written records, the resurrection of Jesus is not just a single detached article of faith. It is woven into the very structure of Christian life and thought.[4]

Even Gerd Ludemann, an atheist scholar who has severely criticized the Gospels for their supernatural content, recognizes the importance of the resurrection to Christianity. He explains, "The resurrection of Jesus is the central point of the Christian religion. . . . Evidently everything quite simply depends on the event of the resurrection of Jesus."[5] We may disagree with this atheist about the fact of the resurrection, but he hit the nail on the head regarding its importance.

To say that Jesus, his early apostles and the Christian church have placed significant emphasis on Jesus' resurrection is to put it mildly. Everything Jesus taught and lived for depended upon his death and resurrection. All the promises and prophecies in the Bible depend on the resurrection. The whole history of God's plan to restore his relationship with man and woman depends on the resurrection. It is not overstating the facts at all to say that the resurrection of Jesus is the single most important event in the history of the world. Your life and mine depend on the resurrection.

Although the resurrection of Jesus is much *more* than a historical fact, it is nothing *less* than one. As we will show later in this book, there is powerful, verified evidence that it really happened.

SECTION II

THE PERSONAL MEANING OF THE RESURRECTION

FREEDOM FROM THE FEAR OF DEATH

It is common for humans to fear death. Job described it as "the king of terrors" (Job 18:14). Not only is it extremely difficult to imagine ceasing to exist, it is even terrifying. We are the center of our own universe. Our conscious existence is our own reference point. While we know in our minds that someday death will come, it is difficult for us to come to terms with this frightening reality.

As a society we often hide from the reality of death. Like the ancient Egyptians who sought to disarm death by preserving the dead, we spend small fortunes trying to extend our youthfulness, hoping to keep the grim reaper at bay as long as possible. Even when we die we rely on all sorts of little devices to hold the reality of death at arm's length. We have morticians paint up our corpses, dress them nicely and place them in "comfortable" coffins to soften the grim impact of what really happened. Many people simply refuse to think about death or even talk about it. Even when we do talk about death, we use euphemisms to soften or disguise the harsh reality. We prefer terms such as "passed away," "went to sleep" or "went to be with the Lord."

Why, exactly, do we fear death? Let us suggest six reasons: [1]

1. *Death is mysterious and unknown.* It is normal to fear the unknown. Getting married, moving to a new city or making a new investment can all bring a certain amount of apprehension because we don't know exactly what to expect. But death poses a greater mystery than anything else; it is the greatest of all unknowns. Once having entered that realm, no one

ever returns to tell us about it. It is something we can never truly understand until we experience it ourselves.

2. *We have to face death alone.* If we could all join together and face the unknown mysteries of death in a group, perhaps it would be easier to bear the thought of it. But we cannot. We must travel alone into that dark night.

3. *We are separated from our loved ones.* We wonder if our relationships can possibly continue after this life. Will we ever meet our loved ones again?

4. *Our personal hopes and dreams will not be realized.* When we die, our goals die with us. We cannot continue to build our dreams. Death ends the best of our plans.

5. *Death raises the possibility that we will be annihilated.* We fear that death could mean the end of everything. After our death, will we continue to exist?

6. *Death is unavoidable.* Even with today's scientific advances that extend the length of our lives, all of us will die. Even Methuselah, the Old Testament patriarch who lived almost 1,000 years, eventually succumbed to death. The Bible tells of a few people who were brought back from the dead, but all of them except Christ died again. No one can escape the inevitability of death.

Not only is death inevitable and fearsome, sometimes it hits suddenly in ways we could never have anticipated. Such uncertainty can be debilitating, even for believers in Jesus. In spite of their belief, they can still wrestle with the emotional pain of death. We grieve deeply the loss of our loved ones, even though we do not grieve as people without future hope. While the Bible never promises complete deliverance from the emotionally difficult aspects of death, we are told that victory over the utterly paralyzing fear of it is within our grasp. Anticipating heaven doesn't get rid of our apprehensions about the unknown aspects of death, but it can help to minimize the fear that death brings by putting it in a larger context and seeing it from a new perspective. Truly understanding the biblical doctrine of resurrection has the added benefit of freeing us from debilitating fear of our final journey into the unknown realm.

Finding the Right Perspective

I (Sean) often ask my students to imagine two high school seniors who both get denied acceptance to the college they want to attend. One student is terribly upset for a week or more, while the other is upset for only a day. Assuming that college acceptance was equally important to both of them, why was one student more upset than the other? The answer is that he allowed himself to be. He held a philosophy of life that allowed his daily circumstances to control his level of happiness. Like most people, he believed that events made him happy or unhappy. His emotions rose or fell in relation to the good or bad things that happened to him. He did not realize that his negative emotions came almost solely from his perspective on life—his worldview. Few people realize how little circumstances have to do with one's happiness. Far more important is how we respond to our circumstances. And our response is always based on our perspective. Having a heavenly perspective on life can bring powerful strength that enables us to live above our immediate circumstances.

Few people seem to realize that the resurrection of Jesus is the cornerstone to a worldview that provides the proper perspective to all of life. This includes our perspective on death. The resurrection makes it clear that no matter how devastating our struggles, disappointments and troubles are, they are only temporary. No matter what happens to you, no matter the depth of the tragedy or pain you face, no matter how death stalks you and your loved ones, the resurrection promises you a future of immeasurable good.

The deaths of friends and loved ones are natural causes for grief, and the prospect of our own death is also naturally scary. But if these events throw our lives into despair, it is simply because we allow our present circumstances to control our emotional and mental equilibrium and, as a result, shape the course of our lives. A critical aspect of having a heavenly perspective on life is the proper aligning of our thoughts by replacing inaccurate, discouraging thoughts with truthful, encouraging ones. The key is to be "transformed by the renewing of your mind" (Rom. 12:2) with Paul's heavenly perspective: "For I consider that the sufferings of this present time are not worthy to be compared with the glory that is to be revealed in us" (Rom. 8:18, *NASB*).

Pain is an inevitable element of death even for the strongest Christians. Jesus himself wept at the death of Lazarus (see John 11:35). Nonetheless, Paul instructs believers to focus their thoughts on eternal truths instead of their momentary troubles. Such a focus can diminish our present pain and provide strength to bear the suffering. Of course, this does not mean that we will ever progress to the place where death is not bothersome, for death is still the great enemy. But we do not have to fear death in a crippling way. Read 2 Corinthians 4:8-17 and note some of the contrasts that Paul makes between the present and future:

Present	Future
Our present bodies are decaying (vv. 10-11).	We will have future eternal bodies (vv. 10,12).
Our troubles are temporary (v. 17).	Heaven is forever (v. 17).
We experience present pain (vv. 8,11).	Eternal glory will be beyond comparison (vv. 15,17).

A Strategy for Confronting Death

In his book *The Risen Jesus and Future Hope*, Dr. Gary Habermas offers three practical steps for how the resurrection of Jesus can help us boldly confront the fear of death.[2] These are not mere academic exercises, but real-life solutions that personally helped him endure the early death of his wife to cancer. They include: internalizing the truth of eternal life, shifting our thought pattern to a heavenly perspective, and substituting truthful thoughts about death when we are anxious. Let's look at these three steps individually.

Step One: Internalizing the Truth of Eternal Life

I (Sean) recently spoke at a church in southern California on the subject "The Resurrection of Jesus: Fact or Fiction?" During the question-and-answer period following my lecture, a young man named Brian asked how he could believe more strongly in life after death. First I told him that he should look more fully into the historical evidence for the resurrection of Jesus, for the resurrection demonstrates his victory over death. The resurrection breaks the barrier of death between earth and heaven, allowing heaven to enter the present. I suggested to Brian that he determine whether the evidence for the resurrection was compelling. How did the case for the resurrection of Jesus compare with events in the lives of other ancient historical figures? He should sift through the evidence and weigh the facts carefully. I suggested to him that such a pursuit would likely strengthen his belief in life after death.

But sometimes it is not enough simply to know a historical fact, for historical facts alone can feel distant. I also encouraged Brian to find ways to internalize the truth of the resurrection, making it personal—a central part of his life. This may be done through prayer, meditation or spending time with people who firmly believe in the resurrection. The resurrection is so central to our faith that we cannot put it off to the side. We must make a decision about its truth and engrain it deeply into our beliefs and actions.

Step Two: Shifting Our Thinking to a Heavenly Perspective

In 1952, Florence Chadwick took the challenge of swimming from Catalina Island to the shore of mainland California. Having been the first woman to swim the English Channel both ways, she was confident she could conquer this challenge as well. The day of the swim was foggy and cool, so she could hardly see her accompanying boats. Even though she was utterly exhausted, her mother encouraged her to keep going, telling her how close she was to the shore. Finally, in complete exhaustion, she demanded to be taken into the boat. When she got into the boat she realized that she was not even a half-mile away from the shore. The next day at a news conference she said, "All I could see was the fog. . . . I think if I could have seen the shore, I would have made it."[3] Having the right perspective on the future can transform how one experiences the present. For Christians, our future destination is the new heaven and new earth. Maintaining a focus on our ultimate destination gives us strength as we struggle through the fog.

Paul regularly taught the importance of shifting one's thoughts from present difficulties to future glory. "Set your mind on the things above," he implored, "not on the things that are on earth" (Col. 3:2, *NASB*). The original idea contained in the Greek word translated as "set your mind on" relates to a philosophical journey or quest. It is the same word used in Luke to describe how "the Son of Man has come to *seek* and to save that which was lost" (Luke 19:10, *NASB*, emphasis added). According to Randy Alcorn, "It is a diligent, active, single-minded investigation."[4]

This is not something we do naturally; it involves a conscious effort to view the world through a heavenly lens. Rather than focusing on the daily grind of living, Paul calls his hearers to redirect their thoughts to an eternal vantage point. This shift in perspective enables us to completely transform our present experiences. Peter urges believers to apply this perspective to suffering and persecution (see 1 Pet. 5:9-10) and Jesus urges his followers to apply it to anxiety (see Matt. 6:19-34), material possessions (see Matt. 16:26) and even death (see Matt. 10:28).

Do you see what this means? It means you can live above your circumstances. You can retain meaning and joy in life even when things do not go well. Your mental and emotional equilibrium are not rooted in what happens to you, but rather in the eternal and dependable certainty that the God who loves you will bring you through the difficulty and resurrect you to a new pain- and death-free life.

Step Three: Replacing Our Fearful Thoughts

Anxiety and stress about death can cripple us from living freely in the present. Paul dealt with this in Philippians 4:6-9. He instructed his hearers to dwell on "whatever is true, whatever is honorable, whatever is right, whatever is pure, whatever is lovely, whatever is of good repute, if there is any excellence and if anything worthy of praise." Paul challenged his readers to replace their fearful, anxious thoughts with positive, truthful ones. He further encouraged them to practice this process until it became a habit.

Identifying our faulty thinking and correcting it with truth can be a freeing and edifying experience. It can help us to have the mind of Christ as opposed to a mind conformed to the fear-producing patterns of this world, and to experience the power of the resurrection in the present. This is not mere brainwashing, but a process by which we can embody in our lives the historical truth of the resurrection of Jesus. Talking to yourself with clarifying statements such as, *Death is not the end, but a step in the process of restoring my relationship to God and others,* is an example of how left-brain language can help to calm right-brain anxiety. Focusing on the facts that "I am not alone in this process" and "God has already defeated death" can take the place of internal thoughts of fear, anxiety and despair. Such a process can prepare us to experience the peace of God even amidst the most grueling of trials.

Another method is to argue against our anxieties and fears with truth. For example, it is immensely helpful to remind ourselves that this world is not all there is, that our cherished relationships will continue after death and that we will conquer death like Jesus. When fear strikes, focus on what we know to be true. Dr. Habermas explains: "How do we substitute edifying thoughts for our fear of death? One method is to identify our misbeliefs, argue against them, and replace them with truthful counterthoughts. While truth frees us, lies always enslave."[5]

When John the Baptist was wrestling with his faith in prison, Jesus responded by reminding him of key truths *he already knew*. Two of John's disciples came to Jesus enquiring as to whether he was truly the Messiah. Jesus answered them by saying, "Go back to John and tell him what you have seen and heard—the blind see, the lame walk, the lepers are cured, the deaf hear, the dead are raised to life, and the Good News is being preached to the poor" (Luke 7:22). Jesus responds to John with proof that he was the chosen one, including his ability to raise the dead. John could trust Jesus during his present struggles because he knew Jesus had power over life and death.

A cognitive approach can be very helpful in combating the fear of death. Reminding ourselves of what we know to be true about Jesus can give us confidence that his promises that we have not yet experienced—such as his promise to resurrect us from the dead—are also dependable. We infer the validity of the promise from the certainty of what we know to be true.

The Resurrection Demonstrates the Defeat of Death

Death was not the end of Jesus, and his resurrection shows that it need not mark the end for us. Easter is good news because it proclaims every year the truth that Jesus is alive—he has conquered death!

The power of the resurrection is in a class of its own. In resurrecting Jesus from the dead, God has done what we cannot do: He has conquered the powers of death. Although we may fear the process of dying, death itself need not be feared. The resurrection of the crucified Christ provides the hope that God, not death, will ultimately control our destiny.

According to several writers of the New Testament, Jesus' resurrection provides the assurance that believers will also rise from the dead. Consider the words of Paul: "But we are citizens of heaven, where the Lord Jesus Christ lives. And we are eagerly waiting for him to return as our Savior. He will take our weak mortal bodies and change them into glorious bodies like his own, using the same power with which he will bring everything under his control" (Phil. 3:20-21). This same sentiment was also professed by Luke (see Acts 4:2) and John (see 1 John 3:2). The resurrection of Jesus provides the believer with a heavenly perspective in the present and the promise of eternal life in the future (see 1 Pet. 1:3-4).

Easing the Fear of Death

As we close this chapter, let's look again at the six reasons we fear death listed earlier and show briefly how the resurrection allays those fears.

1. Death Is Mysterious and Unknown

Yes, it is mysterious and unknown, but after the resurrection of Jesus, we know something about it that we could not have known before. It is not permanent. Christ went through it, and he blazed a trail that we can follow. Some of the mystery has been removed because we now have footprints to follow that we know will lead us into new life.

2. We Have to Face Death Alone

Although from our perspective it may seem that we have to go through death alone, we now know this is an illusion. Christ is there to lead us through it. The most familiar of all psalms made the claim that we would not be alone in death: "Even though I walk through the valley of the shadow of death, I fear no evil, for You are with me; Your rod and Your staff, they comfort me" (Ps. 23:4, *NASB*). The death and resurrection of Jesus shows that this promise is not empty. Christ has actually stepped into the darkness of death and awaits us there to lead us safely through.

3. We Are Separated from Our Loved Ones

The resurrection calms this fear as well. Because God has conquered death through Jesus Christ, our loving relationships will continue after death. This belief is not a result of mere blind faith; it is rooted in fact. Just as Jesus' relationship with Mary continued after his death (as shown in her encounter with him at the tomb), our loving relationships will continue as well. Jesus said to the repentant criminal on the cross right next to him: "I assure you, today you will be with me in paradise" (Luke 23:43). When Jesus returns there will be a "reunion" in the air for his followers. And after that we will be together with the Lord and our loved ones forever (see 1 Thess. 4:17). Death may separate us temporarily from our loved ones, but the resurrection of Christ will bring us back together. Jesus is "Lord both of the living and of the dead" (Rom. 14:9), and not even death can "separate us from the love of God that is revealed in Christ Jesus our Lord" (Rom. 8:39).

Our relationships will not only continue after death; they will be utterly transformed. Revelation 21:4 describes what God will do in the new heaven and new earth: "He will wipe every tear from their eyes, and there will be no more death or sorrow or crying or pain. All these things are gone forever." Gone will be jealousy, competition, anger and resentment. We will be free like Jesus to love each other truly and to experience the love of others.

4. Our Personal Hopes and Dreams Will Not Be Realized

The resurrection also does away with this fear. In fact, it would be more accurate to say that in heaven all our hopes and dreams will be fulfilled.

C. S. Lewis suggested that the true desire behind all desires is to be with God and love him, that every desire we experience will have its legitimate fulfillment in our new life. This is affirmed in the biblical parable of the talents in which three servants are entrusted with their master's assets when he leaves for a journey (see Matt. 25:14-30). Two of the men develop and expand those assets for their master, and on his return they are rewarded with rulership over cities. The application is clear. Our hopes and dreams grow out of the abilities God has given us. We work toward developing them in this life. When we die and are resurrected to a new life in heaven, we who have developed those assets well will be given even greater responsibilities on which to continue to use and develop what God has entrusted to us.

This concept is confirmed in the phrase we read in 2 Timothy 2:12 and Revelation 20:6 where we are told that we will "reign with him." Heaven is not a place of idleness and boredom. It is filled with responsibilities that will require our talents, abilities and creativity.

5. Death Raises the Possibility that We Will Be Annihilated

Most of what we have written so far in this book clearly shows that life after death exists in abundance for those who die trusting in Christ. To be confident that this is true and not merely a wishful dream, we must carefully examine the evidence that we exist after death. And that evidence, as we will see in the final section of this book, is overwhelmingly in favor of Jesus' resurrection 2,000 years ago in Jerusalem. Paul said:

> But in fact, Christ has been raised from the dead. He is the first of a great harvest of all who have died. So you see, just as death came into the world through a man, now the resurrection from the dead has begun through another man. Just as everyone dies because we all belong to Adam, everyone who belongs to Christ will be given new life (1 Cor. 15:20-22).

6. Death Is Unavoidable

It's true that death is inevitable and no one can escape it. But as we have shown in this chapter, the inevitability of death is not necessarily a reason to fear it. Yes, it will come, but we have shown that we will go through it and come out safely in the arms of Jesus on the other side. So of death we can happily say what the apostle John said in Revelation 22:20, the penultimate verse in the entire Bible: "Come, Lord Jesus."

6

OUR HOPES AND DESIRES WILL BE FULFILLED

One of the most powerful truths the resurrection of Jesus reveals to us is that heaven is a real place that awaits us after death. The history of this fallen world will culminate with the creation of a new heaven and new earth, where resurrected people will live in a resurrected universe with the resurrected Jesus. Death is not the end; it is really the beginning. It is the doorway into eternal life.

Have you taken the time to really reflect on this truth? When we die we will eternally be with our Creator! Do you get goosebumps just thinking about it? Are you eagerly anticipating the day when this life ends and you enter into God's presence forever without any of the painful effects of sin? Frankly, many people do not feel this positive anticipation of heaven. If you are one of these, it may be that, like many, you carry in your mind a mistaken image of what heaven is like.

Science-fiction writer Isaac Asimov expressed the attitude many have about heaven when he wrote, "I don't believe in the afterlife, so I don't have to spend my whole life fearing hell, or fearing heaven even more. For whatever the tortures of hell, I think the boredom of heaven would be even worse."[1] The bitter old agnostic Mark Twain expressed similar sentiments in his tirade against Christianity, the posthumously published *Letters from the Earth*. He noted that men and women on earth spent all their time pursuing pleasures they were convinced would be utterly absent in heaven. And then, on the other hand, they claimed to look forward to a heaven where they would spend all eternity doing things they had neither interest in nor aptitude for while on earth. Few on earth enjoyed church attendance or singing, he noted. Few could play a musical instrument, and few enjoyed association with members of other races. Yet they claimed to want to go to a heaven filled with perpetual worship, perpetual music, and perpetual mixing with and loving all races and cultures. As Twain summarized man's strange attitude toward heaven, "It has not a single feature in it that he actually values. It consists—utterly and entirely—of diversions which he cares nothing about, here on earth, yet is quite sure he will like in heaven."[2]

Sadly, a similar view of the afterlife is common even among Christians. Our vision of heaven is often limited to an extended, boring, uninspiring church service. Or many, influenced by cartoons and jokes, see it as a place where we will mosey about among clouds in long, white gowns while strumming on harps. We agree that these pictures of heaven are not appealing. Somehow our image of heaven has become grotesquely distorted, and the prospect of life after death has not captured our imaginations or transformed our lives.

I (Sean) recently asked my students what they would do if they had only three days left to live before they died and went to heaven. How would they spend those few remaining days? Answers included skydiving, traveling, surfing and (of course) sex. I followed up with a simple question, "So, you think there may be pleasures and experiences in this life that if you don't do them before you die, you will miss out on them altogether because they won't exist in heaven?" All but two students answered yes. The prospect of heaven dismayed and disappointed them. It simply had not captured their imaginations, and they dreaded the idea of going there. Could the same be true for us?

Such a lack of eternal perspective sets our young people up for discouragement and sin. Many of them think that if they don't experience certain pleasures now, their chance will be gone and they never will experience them. So, since God will forgive them, why not indulge? That is why many Christian young people plunge into the pursuit of sex, money, drugs and popularity. They think that they will find pleasure and satisfaction in these activities that will be denied them in heaven. They adopt this attitude because they, along with a huge number of adults, carry in their minds a mistaken picture of what heaven is really like.

What Is Heaven Really Like?

In his provocative book *Heaven*, Randy Alcorn demonstrates that an unbiblical view of heaven has deeply infiltrated the church. In fact, he says that some of Satan's favorite lies are about heaven, for Satan knows that if we truly understood the reality of heaven, it would radically transform our present lives.[3] The truth about heaven would give us an eternal perspective from which to view the present world, and that would give us far more resolve and boldness to live truly godly lives here and now.

We have been taught too often to "spiritualize" the new heaven and the new earth with a nonphysical interpretation. Now, we must be careful in our use of that word "spiritualize" and its variant "spiritual." These terms are used in so many different ways that they can easily be misunderstood. Often when people call something "spiritual," they mean it is nonphysical. This has caused such a widespread misconception that it has led to the idea that God's physical creation is somehow inferior to truly spiritual things, which, in their minds, includes heaven. Many also believe that in heaven we will be spiritual, which to them means that we will be without solid, substantial, truly physical bodies. This view leads to an unscriptural division between the physical and spiritual, causing many to think that only the spiritual is good and the physical is temporary, disposable and, even in some ways, evil.

There are serious problems with such a view. People who believe this way tend to forget that at the end of each day of the physical creation of the world, God pronounced his work to be good. Everything he made out of atoms and molecules, cells and dirt, he called "good." The new heaven and new earth can't be merely spiritual (understood as nonphysical) because our physical bodies will be resurrected. God has gone to great lengths to redeem our bodies, and those solid, feeling, flesh-and-bone bodies will need a solid, physical environment filled with oxygen and edible food on which to survive. A nonphysical resurrection is like a colorless rainbow. It's a contradiction! When the apostle Paul describes our own resurrection, he says that:

> For when the trumpet sounds, those who have died will be raised to live forever. And we who are living will also be transformed.

For our dying bodies must be transformed into bodies that will never die; our mortal bodies must be transformed into immortal bodies. Then, when our dying bodies have been transformed into bodies that will never die, this Scripture will be fulfilled: "Death is swallowed up in victory" (1 Cor. 15:52-54).

Paul doesn't tell us here that we will be bodiless spirits. Indeed, he tells us the opposite. We will have bodies—real bodies like those we have right now, but they will be immortal. They will no longer be subject to the ravages of disease, age and death, and they will never die. They will be solid, physical bodies, but they will be eternal and incorruptible. They will be like the newly created bodies of Adam and Eve, absolutely perfect in every detail, stunningly beautiful, immensely strong, utterly healthy and impervious to aging and death.

We have misunderstood the biblical truth about the new heaven and new earth. Have you ever wondered why, if we are to "go to heaven" when we die, the Bible also speaks of a new earth? If we are destined for heaven, what is the purpose of a new earth? The book of Revelation presents the new earth as a physical place where God and his people live together. In Revelation 21 John tells of seeing a recreated earth, and then as he watches, he sees the holy city of God descend to the earth. Then John says:

I heard a loud shout from the throne, saying, "Look, God's home is now among his people! He will live with them, and they will be his people. God himself will be with them. He will wipe every tear from their eyes, and there will be no more death or sorrow or crying or pain. All these things are gone forever" (Rev. 21:3-4).

Do you get the complete picture? We will be resurrected with physical bodies to live on a new earth, where God will come down to live with us, surrounded by physical beauty with real gardens, cities, kingdoms, rivers and banquets.

We rightly call this new existence "heaven" because that is what this new earth will be. But it will be light years from the insipid, nonphysical, ethereal, falsely spiritualized heaven of popular imagination that misled Isaac Asimov, Mark Twain, our young people and so many of our fellow Christians.

What will this new earth be like? The world we live in now offers us a glimpse of the joys and pleasures that we will experience there. Randy Alcorn explains, "All our lives we've been dreaming of the New Earth. Whenever we see beauty in water, wind, flower, deer, man, woman, or child, we catch a glimpse of Heaven. Just like the Garden of Eden, the New Earth will be a place of sensory delight, breathtaking beauty, satisfying relationships, and personal joy."[4] We will not live in a sterile environment or float about among endless clouds with nothing to do. We will live on an all-new earth—just like this one, except free from storms, earthquakes, drought, floods or any other disasters. Things will grow easily, and weeds, thorns and stickers will not exist. Animals will not harm us, but rather will look to us benevolently as their leaders and benefactors. To get a clearer picture of heaven let's consider a few of the biblical descriptions.

Heaven as Home

Heaven is described as *home*. After a long trip on the road, does anything seem more appealing than going home? Sleeping in our own beds, a home-cooked meal and fellowship with family and friends are some of the greatest joys in life. When Jesus spoke of his pending death, he spoke of building us a *home* with his Father in heaven (see John 14:2). To understand heaven is to grasp the real meaning of home. Undoubtedly many people have had difficult home lives. But our true home in heaven will have all the good aspects of home, increased many times, without any of the bad. It will be a place where we feel that we belong, and have always belonged.

Heaven as Community

There will be *community* in heaven. Without the presence of sin we will be free to be more relational than we are now. Heaven is not like the Buddhist Nirvana, where people lose their individual personalities when they are swallowed up into an impersonal state of being like drops of water into the sea. Rather, we will maintain our individuality, including our identities, memories, gifts and passions to be used for God's glory and the good of the larger community.

The new Jerusalem in heaven is often described as a city, and one of dazzling beauty (see Heb. 12:22; Rev. 21:2). Cities are full of inhabitants, streets, buildings, cultural events, entertainment, athletics and other community gatherings. If the new Jerusalem didn't have these city-defining characteristics, then why would Scripture so often refer to it as a city? Heaven will have the positive aspects of the city minus the crime, poverty, pollution, slums and corruption that mar cities in our present world. To picture such a beautiful community is to take a large step toward envisioning the world God is planning to bring about as a result of the death and resurrection of Jesus.

Heaven as Rest

Heaven is described as a place of *rest*. One reason we will rest is because we will serve God in heaven. Yes, there will be work in heaven! If you find it confusing to say that we will rest because we work, let us explain. The best kind of rest is not inactivity forced on us as a result of exhaustion; the best kind of rest is activity that refreshes us because we find it exhilarating and enjoyable. When we get away from work to go to the mountains or seashore, we come back refreshed, not because we did nothing, but because we did things we enjoyed doing. We hiked, we climbed mountains, we surfed, we swam, we fished, we skied. These activities didn't exhaust us; they rejuvenated and energized us. It's much the same when you are working on something you really like and want to do. Time passes, the day ends and you can hardly believe it's time to stop. You are not exhausted and bone-weary because your creativity energized you and you enjoyed every moment of your work.

We get exhausted in our work because we often have to do things that we do not enjoy doing. Or there's trouble of one kind or another—breakdowns, problems to be solved, conflicts to resolve, repeated and difficult obstacles to overcome. The work is exhausting and not enjoyable, but we do it because we must.

Our work in heaven will be restful because it will fit us perfectly. It will be exactly what we are fitted for and love to do. It will have none of the pressures we experience in work today. There will be no outlandish deadlines, stressful coworkers or bitter competition. Things will not go wrong; Murphy's Law will have been repealed. We will feel truly fulfilled because we will work in a manner fitting to the way God designed each of us. We will be free to work for the benefit of God, others and ourselves.

Have you ever felt truly fulfilled as a person? Have you ever felt the power of truly serving other people? That was a small taste of what work will be like in heaven. And as a result of our work in heaven we will experience the most peaceful and fulfilling rest imaginable.

Heaven Will Fulfill All Desires

Unfulfilled desire is a source of great unhappiness. Perhaps the saddest novels we read are those of unrequited love in which a man or woman deeply loves and desires to marry his or her beloved, but that desire is thwarted by circumstance, rejection or death. Knowing that unfulfilled desire brings great misery, Eastern pantheistic religions see desire itself as evil. The essence of these religions is to get rid of all desire so that one no longer really wants anything. They hope to achieve a state in which they have absolutely no desire for anything at all, and only then can they step out of this evil existence and become one with their non-personal god and cease to exist as conscious individuals.

What a sad existence pantheism offers! How tragic to see the world and our own being as so evil and miserable that our life's goal is to escape existence altogether. Christianity offers the very opposite. To Christians, all creation is good. Everything was made by a loving God who desires a relationship with humankind and created us to live with him in ecstatic joy forever. Our desires were given to us so that we can experience the joy he intended for us. Before the Fall, our ultimate desire was for God himself, and relationship with him was the source of our greatest joy. Evil is with us because a malicious invader tempted our first parents into stepping out of God's will. And from that moment on, our desires turned inward, and we used them essentially to please ourselves.

Yet in spite of the invasion of evil, which brings confusion, ruin and pain to all existence, the good infused into creation remains. And God has taken amazing steps to eradicate the evil and restore the good.

We naturally desire the good because good is meant for us. Desire for good, if properly understood and seen from a cosmic perspective, leads us to desire the God who gave us the good and who wants us to experience only good forever. Thus to the Christian, desire is not evil. Desire for good is right and proper. Desire for good should lead us to desire God, as Adam and Eve did originally. God is the one source of all joy and all good.

Our problem with desire is that while living in this fallen world, it's easy to confuse ourselves about what is really good. We can desire good things, but because of our fallenness, our rampant desires can cause us to misuse the good God offers. We can become impatient to have the good and grasp at it before we should. We can use the good we desire in wrong ways. We tend to want too much of a certain good (greed), or want good that belongs to someone else (envy), or want it to make ourselves look good (pride), or want it solely for the selfish pleasure it gives us without regard to corresponding responsibility or care for others (lust).

Yet every desire we have has a legitimate satisfaction. God gave us no illegitimate desires. We make them illegitimate when we use them in the wrong ways noted above. All desires are made to be fulfilled, ultimately in heaven or in God himself.

Okay, let's address that question that lingers in the back of your mind, but that you may be hesitant to ask. Will there be sex in heaven? Sex is certainly the most pleasurable of physical experiences, and even more pleasurable because it is connected with deep love and procreation. Mark Twain noted that men would give almost anything for an opportunity to have sex, and then turn right around and say they look forward to heaven where they believe sex does not exist. But is it true that sex will not exist in heaven? While the Bible does not specifically answer this question, we know that there will be deep pleasures in heaven beyond anything we can grasp today. C. S. Lewis explains how sex is a signpost for an even greater fulfillment of the desire behind sex, which will be fully satisfied in heaven:

> I think our present outlook might be like that of a small boy
> who, on being told that the sexual act was the highest bodily

pleasure, should immediately ask whether you ate chocolates at the same time. On receiving the answer "No," he might regard absence of chocolates as the chief characteristic of sexuality. In vain would you tell him that the reason why lovers in their carnal raptures don't bother about chocolates is that they have something better to think of. The boy knows chocolate: he does not know the positive thing that excludes it. We are in the same position. We know the sexual life; we do not know, except in glimpses, the other thing which, in Heaven, will leave no room for it.[5]

Here is the big thing to remember. We may not be able to picture everything about our resurrected existence in heaven, but this we can be absolutely sure of: God created us for delight. He created the earth for our delight and pleasure. Whereas all pleasures are now tainted by the Fall in the garden, he intends none of them to be lost. All that was created will be restored. Because he loves us so deeply, he wants us to experience all the delights he originally intended when he created us for his love.

In the next chapter we'll look at exactly how God intends to restore all creation to its original ideal.

THE RESTORATION OF ALL THINGS

Stories make life interesting and understandable. We tell stories both as groups and as individuals to create meaning for our lives and to make sense of our experiences. Stories, even if fictional, are not mere exercises in entertainment. Good stories distill reality, make it comprehensible and allow us to see into the heart of our activities and discover their larger meaning. The enormous success of *The Lord of the Rings* movies points to the human yearning for our personal stories to be part of a larger story. We want a mission in life shared with fellow companions that is worth every sacrifice and hardship we have to endure.

Stories shape our worldview and our identity. Prior to inflicting the plague of locusts against Pharaoh, God impressed upon Moses the importance of storytelling to the identity of a culture: "I've also done it so you can tell your children and grandchildren about how I made a mockery of the Egyptians and about the signs I displayed among them—and so you will know that I am the LORD" (Exod. 10:2).

It is often difficult to understand a story until you reach its end. The ending brings together all of the hints, clues, secrets, misunderstandings, mysteries and events that didn't seem to make sense when they happened.

God has written the story of humankind. He has taken into account the free will he gave to the characters in the story, and when Adam and Eve seemingly ruined the story on the opening page, God merely adjusted the plot and added events to bring about the good ending he originally intended. To us—the characters who find ourselves somewhere within the yet-to-be-resolved plot—the story may not always seem to make sense. We can't always see how the chapter we're in at the moment relates to the way the book is supposed to end.

For example, we understand that in a great chapter that preceded our own, Christ's resurrection defeated Satan and overcame the curse of sin. Yet we still suffer the effects of sin in our own lives and from the sins of others. This can cause us to wonder, "If God has defeated sin, then why do I still suffer so much? Why do I have to endure this agony if sin is defeated and God is truly in control? Why do such tragedies still happen? Why do I have to hurt so much?" Sometimes we feel like David as he fled for his life from King Saul.

> I cry aloud with my voice to the Lord;
>> I make supplication with my voice to the Lord.
> I pour out my complaint before Him;
>> I declare my trouble before Him.
> When my spirit was overwhelmed within me,
>> You knew my path
> In the way where I walk
>> They have hidden a trap for me.
> Look to the right and see;
>> For there is no one who regards me;
> There is no escape for me;
>> No one cares for my soul (Ps. 142:1-4, *NASB*).

Like David, we have all experienced pain and disappointment and, like him, we wonder why God allows us to hurt so deeply—especially now, after Christ's resurrection has defeated sin and Satan, the causes of all our problems.

The answer to this question is not always clear to us because we are still in the middle of the story and it's hard for us to make sense of it. But there are answers, and we will address some of them in this chapter. However, before we can understand why we must still bear pain in spite of Christ's victory, we must understand the full scope of God's mission for the world.

God's Mission for the World

One answer to our present suffering is that God's victory over Satan is not yet complete. Paul tells us that God's ultimate intention is to restore all things to their original design and establish the kingdom of God in all its perfection on a newly created earth. That is his ultimate mission for the world. As Paul writes:

> The creation looks forward to the day when it will join God's children in glorious freedom from death and decay.... We, too, wait with eager hope for the day when God will give us our full rights as his adopted children, including the new bodies he has promised us (Rom. 8:21-23).

It's obvious that God's mission is not complete because we have not yet joined him in "glorious freedom from death and decay." Fulfillment of that promise remains in the future. God made a covenant with Abraham that the Messiah (which is the Jewish name for Christ) would come to perform the mission that Paul speaks of here. He promised to transform this earth as well as our bodies back to their originally intended perfect state. Your next question, then, might reasonably be, since Jesus has already performed the deed necessary to make all this happen, why hasn't it happened? Why are we left here in a sin-infested world, still dealing with pain, tragedy, deterioration and death?

Here is one answer: In his letter to the Romans, Paul tells us why God is delaying the final victory: "I want you to understand this mystery, dear brothers and sisters, so that you will not feel proud about yourselves. Some of the people of Israel have hard hearts, but this will last only until the full number of Gentiles comes to Christ" (Rom. 11:25).

Did you see the answer in this verse? God is allowing enough time for a great number of people to have the opportunity to submit to Christ. Since the Jews largely rejected Christ, he will make up the tally from non-Jews, or Gentile converts (see the parable of the great feast in Luke 14:16-24). He expects these converts to help bring about the final victory. He is raising an army of Christians to participate with him in the process of overcoming sin and bringing the world right again. It all goes back to the task we were given when we were created. God gave us the exalted responsibility of being lords of the earth. He told Adam and Eve to "be fruitful and increase in number; fill the earth and subdue it.

Rule over the fish of the sea and the birds of the air and over every living creature that moves on the ground" (Gen. 1:28, *NIV*). God created us to be his agents on the earth, to be its rulers and shapers. We fell down on the job, shirked our responsibility and messed up the world we were to rule and care for by contaminating it with sin. But Christ, with his death and resurrection, made it possible to renew both our lives and the earth itself.

You may wonder why, with all his power, God bothers with us bumbling humans to accomplish his purposes? Why doesn't he just say the word and let it be done? Here is the answer: He will not violate what he created us to be by horning in on our territory and doing our job for us. We are created to be his agents in caring for the world, and that responsibility still belongs to us. In spite of the Fall, we still have the responsibility we were given at creation to be his regents on the earth and to do our part in achieving the restoration his resurrection made possible. Therefore, he allows the world to remain in its present fallen condition in order for us to participate with him in bringing about the restoration of all things.

The Spirit and the Body

How is God going to work through us to bring about his mission of restoration? Paul tells us: "For there is one body and one Spirit, just as you have been called to one glorious hope for the future" (Eph. 4:4). This passage tells us that the God of restoration has given us his own power to accomplish his mission. He has given us again what he gave Adam and Eve in the beginning—his Holy Spirit. Shortly after God created Adam's body, he "breathed the breath of life into the man's nostrils" (Gen. 2:7), signifying that God put into his human creation his very own Spirit. The power of God's Spirit within the man and woman gave them the power to be God's regents on the earth, doing his will and keeping the earth as he had created it. When mankind fell, the man and woman lost that intimate connection with God, and thus they lost the power to perform as effective rulers of God's earth.

On the day of Pentecost, however, God restored his Spirit to his creation. He made himself available to live within each of our beings, giving us the power to achieve God's will on the earth. But even with the power of God's Holy Spirit in our lives, we contend with a problem that Adam and Eve did not have. The sinful nature we inherited from their fall is embedded into our being until we die and are resurrected. Even with God's Spirit in us, that sin nature will not allow us to function perfectly and effectively as Adam did. We are walking battlefields in which the sinful nature and God's Holy Spirit do battle for control of our lives. We need more help in following God's Spirit than did Adam and Eve.

God has devised a way to give us that help without invading our territory and usurping our responsibility as his regents. He has given us the church, which Paul calls Christ's body. The church is composed of men and women who choose to belong to God, to return to him, to accept his Spirit and engage with him in his mission to reestablish his eternal kingdom, first in the hearts of men and women and eventually in a recreated heaven and earth. In his church we draw strength from each other that helps us follow God's Spirit and win the internal battle against our sinful natures. We teach one another, help one another, encourage and support one another and enable one another to maintain courage in the face of adversity. The church, God's community of Christ's followers, is to bond together as his visible expression in order to spread both his gospel message and his love. "So it is with Christ's body. We are many parts of one body, and we all belong to each other" (Rom. 12:5).

If ever a message should resonate with this generation, it is this one. Our young people long for a community of people who belong to one another and lovingly support each other. They long to be part of a story that is larger than their individual lives. A girl wrote a poem for me (Sean) after hearing me speak on self-image. Titled "The Mask," she says that the smiling face most people see her wear—the eyes that sparkle, the voice that sounds happy—they're only a mask. Because she says she's lost, confused and scared, and though she has friends, she doesn't feel she belongs. Her final verse says that the day she feels she truly belongs will be the day she stops pretending—and stops wearing the mask.

I saw in this plaintive poem the yearning to have a loving, sharing community before which she could be authentic and feel a sense of genuine belonging and acceptance. For young people (and adults) to survive in their faith, they must not only be equipped with a biblical worldview, they must also sense that they are part of a loving community of believers who support each other and have a common mission in life. The God of restoration gave us exactly that: his unified body (a community of believers) to be there for each other and engage in his mission to reach a lost world and bring them to know the power through the resurrection, to restore life as God intended it to be. That is the exciting mission we must lead our young people to embrace.

The resurrection of Christ was the first step in God's plan to restore all things. His resurrection shows his power to resurrect us and restore us to new life. In addition, his victory over death demonstrates his power to overcome the effects of death that are now ravaging the planet and restore it to its Edenic perfection. That is why the resurrection of Christ is absolutely crucial to mankind.

We must help our young people not only to understand the restorative meaning of Christ's resurrection, but also to realize that it is an objectively true historical fact. There is, of course, compelling evidence in favor of the resurrection of Jesus, which we will examine in the final section of this book. As our young people come to grips with the reality of God's mission of restoration and the fact that the resurrected Christ does have the power to end all suffering and death, we are convinced that they will want to become a part of proclaiming that message.

Facing Difficulties with Joy

We could chide the disciples of Christ for thinking he didn't know what he was doing when he went willingly to his execution. Christ tried to tell them that he would be raised again, but the idea didn't sink in. No doubt it seemed too far-fetched. They were in the middle of the story, and although he told them the ending, they could not grasp it.

It's not hard for us to see the ending now. We can understand that God was in control of the entire situation surrounding Christ's death because we know the rest of the story—that he raised his Son from the grave. Now we know that the torturous death of God's Son was the means of salvation for the human race. But in spite of knowing this, we often have the same difficulty Christ's original disciples had. It's not always easy to trust in what we are told will be true. Experience interferes with faith, and emotions fog knowledge. It's not always as easy as we think to exhibit trust when you're in the middle of the story, dealing with pain, trials or tragedy—even when you know how the plot will be resolved. It's hard to have a spirit of gratitude, courage and optimism unless, of course, you actually live by the worldview that your loving God is sovereign and that he will, in fact, cause everything to work together for your good.

In Romans 8 the apostle Paul gives us several helpful insights that enable us to retain our faith and live joyfully in spite of our less-than-perfect circumstances. He first says, "And we believers also groan, even though we have the Holy Spirit within us as a foretaste of future glory, for we long for our bodies to be released from sin and suffering. We, too, wait with eager hope for the day when God will give us our full rights as his adopted children, including the new bodies he has promised us" (v. 23). Here Paul makes it clear that optimism doesn't come from denying our present pain. Our optimistic hope comes from what he tells us next: "The Holy Spirit helps us in our weakness. . . . And we know that God causes everything to work together for the good of those who love God and are called according to his purpose for them" (vv. 26,28).

Paul is not saying that everything that happens on this death-cursed world is somehow good. Death is not good. Hurt is not good. Sorrow, sadness and suffering are not good. By trusting in God, however, not only as our Savior but also as our sovereign Lord, who does all things well, we can be confident that he will cause all things to work together for our good and his glory. Even the evil things that happen to us will lead to good results. Our confidence and conviction in a God who loves us beyond words and causes all things, even tragedies, to work together for good can produce within us a spirit of gratitude, courage, optimism and joy in the face of life—and death.

Faith in a sovereign God moves us beyond a human perspective on life to an eternal perspective. The apostle Paul was himself a living example of this eternal mindset. Listen to his heart of gratitude in this God-inspired letter to the church of Corinth. Note how the hope of the resurrection provided him with a sense of courage and optimism, even in the midst of difficult times:

We are pressed on every side by troubles, but we are not crushed. We are perplexed, but not driven to despair. We are hunted down, but never abandoned by God. We get knocked down, but we are not destroyed. That is why we never give up. Though our bodies are dying, our spirits are being renewed every day (2 Cor. 4:8-9,16).

What a remarkable approach to life's problems! Paul didn't run from difficulties or live in denial of the pain they caused. He acknowledged his suffering and viewed the trials of life from an eternal perspective, knowing that the God of all comfort was there to ease his pain (see 1 Cor. 2:3-4). He trusted in a sovereign God who would cause everything to work together for good—the God of restoration who had promised to set all things right in the future. Paul's faith in a God who had everything under control enabled him to see the difficulties of this life as producing "an immeasurably greater glory that will last forever!" (2 Cor. 4:17).

Because of the resurrection, we are destined to live forever in new bodies on a new earth, an existence that will be so enjoyable that "the sufferings of this present time are not worthy to be compared with the glory that is to be revealed to us." We are "waiting eagerly for our adoption as sons, the redemption of our body" (Rom. 8:18,23, *NASB*).

In the Christian's future, "He will wipe away every tear from their eyes; and there will no longer be any death; there will no longer be any mourning, or crying, or pain," and "there will no longer be any curse, and the throne of God and of the Lamb will be in it" (Rev. 21:4; 22:3, *NASB*). We have waiting for us "an inheritance which is imperishable and undefiled and will not fade away, reserved in heaven for you" (1 Pet. 1:4, *NASB*). Every one of us who believes in Jesus is destined to have our struggles, sufferings and death transformed into blessings, joy and eternal life. That's the promise that we look forward to in our future—the promise of the resurrection: If we faithfully endure our trials and show God's love and care to the world, we will be resurrected like Jesus to live in beautiful, perfect bodies on a pristine earth just like he first created for Adam and Eve.

Through the resurrection Christ says to us, "Trust me. I am alive and in control of every situation. I will take your struggles and change them into blessings. I will take your suffering and turn it into joy. I will even take your physical death and transform it into eternal life. How can I do that? I am the sovereign, almighty Lord of the universe, who can do all things and who causes everything to work together for the good of those who love God and are called according to his purpose for them. So trust in me, no matter what." And it's the resurrection that backs up his promise and gives us confidence that it is absolutely true.

The great preacher D. L. Moody, once told the story of a sharp young 15-year-old girl named Jennifer who understood this truth. Through a sudden and shocking incident, she was left totally paralyzed on one side and almost blind. One day as she lay helpless in bed, she overheard the family doctor speaking to her parents in the corner of the room: "Poor child, she has certainly seen her best days." Fortunately, Jennifer was a believer in the resurrection of Jesus Christ. She had trusted Jesus when things were going well in her life, and she knew she could trust him now. She quickly replied, "No, doctor, my best days are yet to come, when I shall see the King in his beauty."[1]

Jennifer's hope, like ours, lies in the resurrection. She realized an absolutely profound truth: Someday her body would be transformed, and she would no longer suffer. All of her sorrow and her pain would be turned into ecstasy and joy! She firmly grasped the truth of 2 Corinthians 4:17: "For our present troubles are small and won't last very long. Yet they produce for us a glory that vastly outweighs them and will last forever!"

Jennifer's life was mired down in the middle of the plot, but she remained hopeful and joyful because she knew how the story ended and had absolute confidence in the author. She lived joyfully in the present reality because she looked forward to what she knew would happen to her when she was resurrected into a new, restored, perfect and beautiful body, just as Christ was.

The story of this present fallen world ends with our stepping into the glorious future God is preparing for us. Jesus himself promised it: "I am going there to prepare a place for you. And if I go and prepare a place for you, I will come back and take you to be with me that you also may be where I am" (John 14:2-3, *NIV*).

Our task is to live now in the reality of the completed story and not to take the pain-filled present as the true reality. In the resurrection, God has conquered sin and death. All the pain and anguish we experience as a result of the Fall is still active, but it is ultimately defeated. We are invited to participate in the defeat of it by expanding God's kingdom on the earth now, doing his will, living according to his principles, showing others the way, leading them to know him and demonstrating his nature, so that more and more may come to know him and join the mighty army of God. That army, which we know as the church, will march to final victory over our ultimate enemy and live in ecstasy with God in the restored glory of Eden forever.

That is the ultimate promise of the resurrection.

Fulfilling Our Mission of Restoration

In the last few decades, America has become a post-Christian nation. In the past, the culture-shaping institutions in America—education, entertainment, government, the media—were deeply influenced by the Judeo-Christian ethic. Even most nonbelievers were aware of the basic story line of the Bible and had respect for the role Christians played in culture. Such is no longer the case. The world around us has changed radically. The values shaping the worldviews of young people and the culture as a whole are no longer predominantly Judeo-Christian. In reality, the dominant cultural values are now anti-Christian. Few young people understand the biblical storyline and what it means for their lives. Rather, their worldview is largely shaped by the inclusive, anything goes, apathetic approach to spirituality that marks our postmodern times.

This is why we must think of ourselves as missionaries to unbelievers, especially to younger generations, and participate with God in restoring them to his kingdom. When missionaries enter a new culture, they study that culture, listen to the people and try to understand their values. They spend time getting to know individuals and building relational bridges. They ask questions such as, "What do they believe?" "How do they think?" "What is their understanding of Christianity, if they have any understanding at all?" Missionaries do not adopt the worldview of the foreign culture, but they do seek to understand the people in order to find an opening for the gospel.

In John 17, Jesus prayed, "I do not ask You to take them out of the world, but to keep them from the evil one . . . as You send Me into the world, I also have sent them into the world" (vv. 15,18, *NASB*). His prayer was not that we would create an inward-focused Christian subculture, but that we would be the salt and light to our world. Salt makes food more enticing, and light is a guiding force that attracts people. Jesus is calling us—his church—to be his hands and feet of love to others and tell them of his victory over evil and the new life to come. What an incredible mission!

There are many negative perceptions of the church, especially among younger generations. In his eye-opening book *They Like Jesus but Not the Church*, pastor Dan Kimball lists six common perceptions younger generations have of the Christian church.

1. The church is an organized religion with a political agenda.
2. The church is judgmental and negative.
3. The church is dominated by males and oppresses females.
4. The church is homophobic.
5. The church arrogantly claims all religions are wrong.
6. The church is full of fundamentalists who take the whole Bible literally.[2]

David Kinnaman, president of the Barna Research Group, came to similar conclusions in his recent book *unChristian: What a Generation Really Thinks About Christianity*. Outsiders (non-Christians) were asked to describe whether they perceived Christian churches to be loving environments where people feel unconditionally loved and accepted regardless of how they look or what they do. Sadly, only one in five outsiders viewed the church in this way. And as far as their perceptions of Christians, Kinnaman said, "Only a small percentage of outsiders strongly believe that the labels 'respect, love, hope, and trust' describe Christianity."[3]

In a culture dominated by a media largely unfriendly to the Christian cause, these misperceptions are best overcome through relationships. If we as Christians don't build genuine relationships with nonbelievers, they will continue to be misled by the popular erroneous stereotypes of what Christians are like.

The world is a mission field, and God has called us to be his personal ambassadors to it. Our mission is to tell people, as Mary did, that Jesus has risen and offers hope that we too can be resurrected into a new life. But our mission is not merely to preach this truth; it is to live out Christ's example of sacrificial love to each other and to the outside world. We agree with Dan Kimball when he wrote, "Unless we are creating cultures in our church in which people see themselves as missional in their day-to-day worlds, unless we challenge Christians to break out of the Christian bubble, only the loudest, often negative voices will be heard. We can move from being perceived as judgmental and negative to being seen as positive agents."[4]

We cannot shout this message from a distance. Rather, we must go into the world where people are. We are to follow the example of Jesus, who was known as a friend of tax collectors and sinners, and build relationships with people who feel estranged from the church. Jesus did not merely announce the kingdom of God; he demonstrated its reality by feeding the poor, healing the sick and ministering to the outcasts. Kinnaman put it this way:

> I believe part of the reason Christians are known as unChristian is because the church has lost its ability and willingness to love and accept people who are not part of the "insider" club. This failure is draining the vigor from our faith. We say we love outsiders, but in many cases we show love only if it is on our own terms, if they are interested in coming to our church, or if they respect our way of life.[5]

For the early church, belief in the resurrection meant more than merely looking forward to the life to come—the end of the story. Rather, their conviction in the resurrection caused them to participate in advancing the plot, to be agents in God's restoration by claiming the present world for his kingdom. Even though they were small in number, they trusted in a powerful God. They claimed the world for God through both action and belief. If we are going to be faithful to Jesus, how can we do any less?

OUR NEW LIFE BEGINS NOW

When the comedian Chris Farley died, a *Rolling Stone* article revealed a few facts about his tortured life. Although Chris was a gifted comedian, his inner life was terribly conflicted. He was always terrified of crowds, which was one cause of his wild behavior. It was a kind of smokescreen to cover his fear. He was terrified that his movies would fail. He was terrified that if he lost weight he would cease to be funny. He was terrified that he would never find a woman who would love him for himself and with whom he could have kids, which he wanted more than anything. And, sadly, as the article stated, "He was terrified that [his sins] would seal his fate in the afterlife."[1] Like many people today, Chris was overwhelmed with guilt.

Today we tend to avoid the topic of guilt. Rather than take personal responsibility for what we do wrong, we find ways to blame our society, our genes or some other third party. "My upbringing made me do it" or "It's the way I was made," we often say when ducking responsibility for our addictions, choices and shortcomings.

How we deal with guilt stems from our worldview. If we do not believe humans are created in the image of God with freedom to choose right and wrong, we will deny guilt. If we are not created, then we are merely accidental machines responding to stimuli and bound to follow whatever response our mechanistic brains direct us to follow. If there is no God, then there is no right or wrong, and moral choice is meaningless because morality is meaningless. Therefore, guilt cannot exist.

When a sense of guilt persists in spite of these beliefs, many will seek a therapist who dismisses the affliction as mere "guilt feelings" and tells them they are normal and that everything is okay. To escape their persistent sense of guilt, some people immerse themselves in pleasure, trying to forget any thoughts of responsibility to God or others. Other people take the opposite track and redouble their moral efforts, trying to get rid of guilt by performing and behaving better. Many comfort themselves by comparing themselves with others. No matter what you do, it's always possible to find someone who has done something worse, enabling us to say, "Well, at least I'm not as bad as *him*!"

When it comes to guilt, it's plain that there is an "elephant in the room." Isn't it at least possible that we have feelings of guilt because we are in fact *guilty*? If humans have sinned (and clearly they have), and if they are responsible for their sins (which they are), then the explanation for our guilt feelings is simple. We feel guilty because we *are* guilty. There is no other solution to feelings of guilt than to recognize our sin, own up to our responsibility, and admit that we are wrong.

Scripture makes it clear that all people have broken God's moral laws. "For all have sinned and fall short of the glory of God" (Rom. 3:23, *NASB*). Every man and woman who has ever lived has done wrong things. We have all had wrong thoughts and attitudes, and we have all made poor choices. The prophet Jeremiah said, "The human heart is most deceitful of all things and desperately wicked. Who really knows how bad it is?" (Jer. 17:9). Jesus said, "For from within, out of a person's heart, come evil thoughts, sexual immorality, theft, murder, adultery, greed, wickedness, deceit, lustful desires, envy, slander, pride, and foolishness. All these vile things come from within; they are what defile you and make you unacceptable to God" (Mark 7:21-23).

The core problem, then, is the human heart. If we claim we are without sin, we are fooling ourselves and calling God a liar. We have rebelled against God and broken his laws; we have fallen short of his standards; we have denied his love; we have rejected him from our lives. *We truly are guilty*. And until we find a solution for our guilt, we will continue to be bogged down in a life burdened with negative feelings that are hard to cope with.

In Old Testament times the Israelites had to offer animal sacrifices to pay for their guilt so God would accept them. While the blood of animals could cleanse people from ritual defilement (see Heb. 9:13), it could never fully remove sin (see Heb. 10:4). And since it was unable to remove sin,

"The sacrifices under that system were repeated again and again, year after year, but they were never able to provide perfect cleansing for those who came to worship" (Heb. 10:1).

God knew this, of course, but he had a purpose in having the people pay for their sins with blood sacrifices. As the writer of Hebrews tells us, these sacrifices were "only a shadow, a dim preview, of the good things to come, not the good things themselves" (10:1). In other words, the old system was only a temporary arrangement. Ultimate fulfillment came through the sacrifice of the Son of God, who offered himself personally and voluntarily for the sins of all mankind. Jesus dealt with sin and its guilt "once for all when he offered himself as the sacrifice for the people's sins" (Heb. 7:26-27).

Jesus was the perfect sacrifice for our sins (see Heb. 9:14). Why? Because he was sinless and blameless—he had no imperfections whatsoever. He had nothing to be guilty of, which made him capable of paying the price for our guilt.

Guilt and the Law

The basic reason we feel guilt is that we sense that we don't measure up. Each of us has within our hearts a sense of moral law, telling us what right behavior is (see Rom. 2:15). In addition, most of us are taught morality directly through sermons or Sunday school lessons, or indirectly through the laws and expectations of society in general. When our behavior doesn't match up to the right behavior in our hearts or that we've absorbed through teaching or example, we have this nuisance voice we call a conscience that lets us know that we are not measuring up to the standard of behavior that we know to be right. That sense of not measuring up to a standard is what produces our guilt.

Many people, even well-meaning Christians, deal with this guilt by trying harder to "be good," or to do a better job of obeying God's laws. They study the Bible, try their best to understand all the rules and laws and then strive with all their ability to live by them. The result is always frustration. No matter how hard we try, we humans cannot obey all the laws perfectly. The harder we try, the more obvious this fact becomes. And the more we are aware of the law and our failure to obey it, the more our guilt increases. Trying to be good by keeping God's laws is a vicious circle with no way out.

So, if we cannot keep the laws of God, why did he give them to us? One answer is that they were given for our own good, to show us how the human organism is supposed to operate. The law shows us how to live in a way that will bring us the greatest happiness, joy, health and love, and enable us to reflect the character of God. But when we find that we cannot live by these laws, they begin to look limiting and tyrannical to us. They restrict us and make us unhappy. They seem to keep us bound into a box and restrain us from experiencing all the freedom that our non-Christian friends seem to enjoy. When we look at God's laws in this way, they rob us of our freedom.

So we ask again, why did God give us laws that were impossible to obey? Another answer is that they reveal our sinful nature—our inability to follow God—and as a result, show that we are under condemnation for failing to be what God created us to be. As Jesus said, "But you are to be perfect, even as your Father in heaven is perfect" (Matt. 5:48). His point was not that we can actually be perfect, but rather the exact opposite, that by human efforts alone we can never reach perfection. The laws of God show this fact to us starkly. We compare our behavior to the behavior his laws prescribe, and we see that we do not measure up. Our failure to obey his law shows us that we are less than what God created us to be. We were made to be like him—perfect—but we are not. Thus we feel guilt. And that guilt is not merely a feeling; it is absolutely real. We feel guilty because we are guilty. Sin has alienated us from the perfect God of the universe, who made us to be like him. Sin has ruined our lives.

Our New Relationship with God

The good news of Christ's resurrection is that guilt need no longer torture us and that our relationship with God can now be restored. Because of his death and resurrection, *we no longer live under the power of the law*. Christ has redeemed us from the need to be perfect by bearing the penalty for our inability to keep the law. Therefore, "there is no condemnation for those who belong to Christ Jesus" (Rom. 8:1). He took the penalty so we could be forgiven. If we depend on the death and resurrection of Christ, we no longer bear the guilt for our sins. We need no longer feel guilty because we are no longer guilty. He took our guilt as his own and paid the penalty for it.

The resurrection of Christ demonstrated that no sin is too terrible to be forgiven. Even though he took onto his bleeding back every sin that every one of us ever committed, God still resurrected him from the dead. Even the worst of our sins were taken to the grave and left there forever. Even though we have all done terribly foul things in our lives, the empty tomb of Jesus means that we are not condemned; we are forgiven.

I (Sean) had a student come to me torn over his addiction to Internet pornography, as so many young people are today. He was deeply embarrassed at his inability to control himself. Visibly shaking, he looked me in the eyes and said, "I can control every area of my life but this one. I am so ashamed." I encouraged him to embrace God's grace and to realize that he didn't have to keep the law on his own—in fact, he couldn't.

Of course, being freed from the guilt imposed on us by the law does not mean that we no longer have to follow God's commands. It means that we have been made legally perfect by Christ's sacrifice, not by our adherence to the law. Accepting what Christ has done for us should drive us to desire obedience rather than rebellion. When we truly come to terms with the significance of what Christ did for us on the cross, we will be filled with gratitude. And a grateful heart seeks to please, not to hurt or hide.

It is only when we truly humble ourselves and realize our powerlessness that God can truly strengthen us. Paul said, "For when I am weak, then I am strong" (2 Cor. 12:10). Christ conquered the power of sin and the power of the devil. We are free from the law, and we can personally experience God's forgiveness firsthand and live new lives free from guilt and empowered by the resurrection of Christ.

How do we experience the power of the resurrection? Scripture teaches that the death and resurrection of Christ released God's Holy Spirit to come back into the life of believers (see John 7:39). It is this indwelling Spirit who gives believers the strength to conquer addictive and self-destructive habits so that they can truly live new lives free of guilt and the condemnation of sin. Paul says:

> The Spirit of God, who raised Jesus from the dead, lives in you. And just as God raised Christ Jesus from the dead, he will give life to your mortal bodies by this same Spirit living within you. Therefore, dear brothers and sisters, you have no obligation to do what your sinful nature urges you to do. For if you live by its dictates, you will die. But if through the power of the Spirit you put to death the deeds of your sinful nature, you will live (Rom. 8:11-13).

This is the essence of our new life in Christ. We live in a fallen world where we are often battered and wounded by sin, but we can live above it all, confident in the promise demonstrated by the resurrection that the power of sin over us has been defeated. We live now in a restored relationship with God, and with his Holy Spirit in us, we participate in the ultimate victory: We live our own lives free of guilt and filled with joy. And we can live our new life of freedom right now.

Does the presence of the Holy Spirit in our lives mean we no longer sin? No, we still must contend with the drag of that sin nature we inherited from Adam. That sin nature will sometimes cause us to ignore the voice of the Spirit and listen instead to the voice of the self, asserting its desires and luring us away from God's will (see Rom. 7:14-25). When we do slip into sinful acts, though, it does not mean the Holy Spirit leaves and it's all over for us. God, in his loving grace, understands our weakness, and as long as we desire to follow him, hate our sins and turn to God in penitence, he honors our intent, forgives our sin and remains with us.

Though we sin, we never forfeit our opportunity to live the full Christian life. When we turn our hearts back to God, he will reach out and embrace us in his loving arms, restoring us afresh in our relationship with him. This is what Jesus did after Peter had denied him three times. And this is what Jesus will do for us as well. We are his children, and he loves us greatly. This is why Paul says: "Now you are no longer a slave but God's own child. And since you are his child, God has made you his heir" (Gal. 4:7). That is the new life God offers—the new life we can have in him in spite of our sin and former rebellion against him.

The Community of the Resurrection

The church is primarily the community of the resurrection, a community in which we can live the new life of the Spirit. While the resurrection promises us a new and perfect life in the future, God loves us too much to leave us alone to contend with the pain, guilt and loneliness of our present life. That is why he gives us a community of people who love each other in the manner in which he loves us—a community of mutual help, support and encouragement. When the community of Christ lives in the power of the resurrection, we become God's transforming agents to each other and to a broken and hurting world.

Sadly, the church has not always lived according to the example Jesus set for it. At times the church has been an agent of repression, hypocrisy and alienation. We grieve over the pain that has been done in the name of Christ. If you have been hurt by people who claim to be followers of Christ, then we are truly sorry. But we also believe firmly that the church has been the greatest community of goodness this world has ever seen. God has created the church to be his hands and feet to bring healing to our broken world. When it truly lives according to God's plan, the church can be an incredible agent of transformation for both individuals and societies. Let's briefly look at how the church performs these functions.

It Is a Community of Hope

While Jesus was on earth, "God was in Christ, reconciling the world to himself" (2 Cor. 5:19). Now Christ is in us, and Paul says that God "has committed to us the message of reconciliation. We are therefore Christ's ambassadors, as though God were making his appeal through us" (2 Cor. 5:19-20, *NIV*). He wants to involve us in his ministry of drawing people to him, especially in times of adversity and trouble. Paul goes on to say, "We live in such a way that no one will stumble because of us, and no one will find fault with our ministry" (2 Cor. 6:3). God not only helps us fulfill our purpose by making us more and more like Christ but also draws people to himself through us. Because "if we love each other, God lives in us, and his love is brought to full expression in us" (1 John 4:12).

We often seem to fulfill that mission most effectively when we are enduring times of crisis, suffering or persecution. Most of us can exhibit love, joy, peace and patience when the wind is at our backs and we're sailing high. But how many people display gratitude, courage and optimism in the midst of a storm? When tragedy strikes, when we're hurting or mistreated and still have joy, people sit up and take notice. This is what drew Dr. Francis Collins, one of the country's leading geneticists and the former head of the Human Genome Project, to consider Christianity. In 1976, during his medical residency, Collins was shocked by the serenity of some of his mortally ill patients. He decided to investigate the evidence for the existence of God. The book that convinced him was *Mere Christianity* by C. S. Lewis, especially Lewis's argument for God on the evidence of the moral law. While the evidence convinced his mind, the hope of the suffering believers attracted his heart. The brilliant scientist became a believer in Christ.[2]

God fills you so completely with his joy and blessing during your difficulties that you actually become grateful for the trials you're experiencing. And when people see how courageous and optimistic you are during your troubled times, they will be drawn to Christ as Dr. Collins was. The late Roman Catholic priest Henri Nouwen said that some of the most joyful moments of his life were those of great emotional and physical pain, when he was "forced" to cry out to God and rely upon him as his source of hope and joy.[3]

As the body of Christ, we are called to live this hopeful reality and make it known to the outside world.

One of our heroes is a young man named Steve Sawyer. A hemophiliac from birth, Steve was infected with HIV in the early 1980s during a blood transfusion. Facing a death sentence, Steve dropped out of college and began traveling around the world telling young people that they could know God personally and face eternity with confidence and hope. We will never forget hearing Steve say that he truly thanked God for his disease because without it he would not have had such a powerful platform from which to present Jesus. Steve said, "If I had to get these diseases that are killing me for that one person to understand that they can have a relationship with Christ, then it is worth it. In light of eternity, that is all that matters."[4] Steve truly understood the hope our crucified Savior offers our broken and hurting world.

It Is a Community of Forgiveness

The Amish community of Nickel Mines, Pennsylvania, will never forget the tragedy of October 2, 2006. Charles Roberts, a non-Amish local father of three, entered the single-room Amish schoolhouse, ordered the boys to leave, and opened fire on the girls. He shot 10 girls, killing 5 before committing suicide.

In the aftermath of the tragedy the world was transfixed, not solely on the crime itself, but also on the mystery of the forgiveness that came so quickly from the Amish believers. Amish expert Donald Kraybill explained that their forgiveness "wasn't an aberration. To a person, the Amish would argue that forgiveness is the central teaching of Jesus."[5] The Amish realize that their own forgiveness was bought with a price—the cross of Christ. As a result, they graciously offer forgiveness to others.

N. T. Wright captures the reason why forgiveness is such a central feature of the Christian community: "We are in fact called to be people of forgiveness in the present because that is the life we shall be living in the future."[6] Creation will be physically restored without the damaging effects of sin. Likewise, our bodies, minds and moral natures will be renewed as well. In heaven we will be fully able to forgive ourselves and other people for the evil we have done in the fallen world. Wright explains, "The command to forgive one another, then, is the command to bring into the present what we are promised for the future, namely the fact that in God's new world all shall be well, and all manner of things shall be well."[7] It's another way we begin living the new life of our future resurrection in the present.

As believers in Jesus Christ, our responsibility is to extend God's grace to people, to be living examples of Christ's love and forgiveness. People need to see how compassionately and tenderly he treated those in sin. People need to see the lengths that Jesus went to so that we could be reconciled to God. Our task is to help people move from focusing on their mistakes to embracing God's love and forgiveness.

How seriously does God take forgiveness? Jesus said, "If you forgive those who sin against you, your heavenly Father will forgive you. But if you refuse to forgive others, your Father will not forgive your sins" (Matt. 6:14-15). It is impossible for us to withhold forgiveness from others and walk in relationship to God.

It Is a Community of Love

We live in an age marked largely by isolation, emptiness and hurt. There are two primary causes of the aloneness many feel today: technology and fatherlessness. Our age has seen unprecedented technological advances, which have benefited our world greatly. But sadly, these same inventions have caused much loneliness, disconnecting people from God and each other. People spend far more time on their computers, listening to music, playing video games and surfing the Internet than they do in face-to-face intimacy. In *Generation Me*, Dr. Jean Twenge notes that because of technology, "we're malnourished from eating a junk-food diet of instant messages, e-mail, and phone calls, rather than the healthy food of live, in-person interaction."[8]

In previous generations people watched a lot of television. This may not be good, but at least it was typically done *together*. Now many young people watch, listen and interact with media *alone,* without the supervision and accountability of other members of the family. Journalist Marya Mannes has aptly observed, "The more people are reached by mass communication, the less they communicate with each other."[9]

The deepest source of loneliness, however, is not due to technological advances, but fatherlessness. The greatest problem in the world today is not the threat of terrorism, unbridling violence or global poverty. The greatest problem facing the world today is the lack of loving fathers involved in the lives of their kids. Children with absent or neglectful fathers grow up lacking the deep, overarching love every person craves.

There are roughly 170 biblical allusions to the fatherhood of God, who is a loving father, passionately interested in the lives of his children. A relationship with God can fill the emptiness left by the neglect of an earthly father. But the only way for them to experience God's fatherly love is through people in the church who can pass it on to them in relationship. An effective way to express that love to young people is to make our homes an open and inviting place for kids to hang out. This is a powerful way for kids from broken homes to see biblical relationships modeled in action and to receive loving direction as well.

The love of God must not only be modeled in the home and inside church walls; it also needs to be taken out into our world. Biblical faith is always translated into loving and serving those around us. John says, "My little children, let us not love in word or in tongue, but in deed and in truth" (1 John 3:18, *NKJV*). Jesus demonstrated such love through his life. He touched the untouchables, loved the unlovable and approached the unapproachable. He wept over evil, responded with anger at injustice and always had time for those who were neglected. He saw beyond external appearances and loved people in a manner fitting to their true needs. Jesus called us to love our enemies, bless those who persecute us and ultimately overcome the world through the kind of love he showed to us on the cross. Such self-sacrificing love should be the foundation for all our relationships—in the church as well as outside.

A Montana church that was vandalized collected "love baskets" of gift cards and other items to send to the three teenage suspects charged with breaking into their building, breaking windows, spraying a fire extinguisher and stealing money and electronic equipment. Jason Reimer, a pastor of the church, said, "The judge will give them consequences, but as a congregation we want to reach out and extend love and mercy to them. A lot of us, whether we're churchgoers or not, have been in their shoes before and have made some bad choices. But God forgives us."[10] They wanted to be sure that the young vandals got a thorough taste of God's love.

N. T. Wright captures the idea of how self-sacrificial love should be a defining mark of the Christian church: "The call of the gospel is for the church to *implement* the victory of God in the world *through suffering love*. The cross is not just an example to be followed; it is an achievement to be worked out, put into practice."[11] The cross shows how we in the church are to love one another.

Living in Heaven Now

Paul refers to the resurrection of Jesus 53 times in his letters. Most of these texts assert the primacy of the resurrection, the assurance it gives us of our own future bodily resurrection or both. But six of these references are to the present experience of the resurrection in the life of the believer (see Rom. 6:4; Eph. 2:6; Phil. 3:10; Col. 2:12; 3:1). In other words, the resurrection is not merely an event in the past or a promise of the future; it is a present reality to be experienced in our life and relationships. While Paul writes to establish and defend the veracity of the resurrection, his main purpose is not merely to establish the fact, but to draw people into experiencing the power of the resurrection firsthand.

This is what we have attempted to show you in this chapter. The new, abundant life of assurance and victory over sin is more than just a promise waiting for us in the future. You can begin living that resurrection life right now. We can't get rid of trouble, pain and sin now—though that is indeed in our future. But we can begin living life above the debilitating influence of these afflictions by the power of God's Holy Spirit in our lives. We can live a life of joy and fellowship in relationships with those in the church who share our hope. We can live that kind of life in the presence of those who need to know Jesus, influencing them to become part of God's victory over evil and the restoration of his creation ideal. You can start living that new life right now, simply by turning your back on your sin-riddled past and placing it in the hands of God.

SECTION III

ROCK-SOLID EVIDENCE FOR THE RESURRECTION

IS IT TRUE? IS IT BELIEVABLE?

Recently I (Sean) was the guest speaker at a youth Bible camp in northern California. Throughout the week I challenged the students to use their minds to consider the claim that Jesus is the sole means of salvation (see Acts 4:12).

At the end of the week, some of the written feedback from the campers shocked me. One young woman summed up my teaching with these words: "We like his stories, but that's just *his* truth. I don't want to judge him, but I have a different truth." Her response probably should not have surprised me, since the majority of our youth (81 percent) have adopted the view that "all truth is relative to the individual and his or her circumstances."[1] The common attitude toward religion and morality is, "What is true for you may not be true for me." Many young people who claim to be Christians do not understand that the good news of Jesus is *the* truth that gives them the *only* hope for salvation and the *sole* opportunity for a relationship with the living God who created the universe.

Christian Smith demonstrates that for youth today, "the very idea of religious truth is attenuated, shifted from older realist and universalist notions of convictions of objective Truth to more personalized and relative versions of 'truth for me' and 'truth for you.'"[2] Smith says we often hear youth proclaim, "Who am I to judge?" or "If it works for them, fine." Many youth see truth pragmatically as whatever works in their lives rather than upholding the classical view of truth as "that which corresponds to reality." If Hugh Hefner's hedonistic motto, "If it feels good, do it," characterized the 1960s, the rallying cry of relativism characterizes today's youth and a growing number of adults as well: "If it works for you, it's right."

Divided Truth

Why do people think they can pick and choose religious beliefs as if they were merely choosing movies or iTunes downloads? Nancy Pearcey explains that contemporary secular culture has drawn a dividing line between the sacred and secular, ascribing religion, morality and "private" understanding to the sacred, subjective realm, and science and "public" knowledge to the secular, objective realm. "In short," she writes, "the private sphere is awash in moral relativism. . . . Religion is not considered an objective truth to which we *submit*, but only a matter of personal taste which we choose . . ."[3] Religious and moral claims are considered matters of personal preference rather than knowledgeable claims about the real world.

As a result of this cultural divide, people have been trained to compartmentalize their belief in God from their daily lives—to keep their beliefs about God in the private, subjective realm and not to consider them as objective truth. They turn to real, objective knowledge when dealing with the "secular" side of life, where a failure to observe real facts can have immediate and tangible consequences. This compartmentalization is revealed most clearly in the way youth prioritize spirituality.

A new study by the Harvard University Institute of Politics revealed that 72 percent of students consider religion "somewhat" or "very" important in their lives.[4] This at first may seem like a sign of spiritual vigor, but when researchers asked the students what they got excited about, what pressing issues they were dealing with and what experiences or routines seemed most important in their lives, their answers revealed the opposite. Rather than talking about their religious identities, beliefs or practices, most teens talked about their friends, their MySpace accounts, music, romantic interests and other personal issues. Youth culture expert Walt Mueller concludes:

> Many who hold to a more orthodox and biblical Christian faith have embraced it as something they do from time to time, rather than someone they are all of the time. Instead of integrating their faith into all of life, they live an uninte-

grated faith that only touches select parts of who they are. Consequently, their stated beliefs may be kept separate from how they view and respond to authority, how they conduct themselves in dating relationships, who they are as a student or athlete, and so on.[5]

After interviewing hundreds of students throughout the entire country, Christian Smith concluded, "What our interviews almost never uncovered among teens was a view that religion summons people to embrace an obedience to truth regardless of the personal consequences or rewards."[6] Consider what one teenager said about people who expressed opposing views of God:

> **T (Teen):** I couldn't say anything. It's their opinion. I have my own opinion.
> **I (Interviewer):** Are you right?
> **T:** Ah, I don't know. I have no idea, but . . .
> **I:** Is there a right or wrong answer when it comes to God?
> **T:** There is no right answer.
> **I:** Why not?·
> **T:** There isn't any wrong answer. 'Cause it's God, you can't prove; it's just what you believe.[7]

This girl's attitude toward truth is not unusual. It simply reflects the attitude held by many young people and a growing number of adults today. N. T. Wright has observed a deep irony in our cultural perspective on truth: "Truth is under attack on all sides, even as we insist more and more on truthfulness in terms of record keeping and checking up on one another."[8] As a result, one of the greatest obstacles we face in our ministry is a general distorted view of truth. Paul warns us that people will perish for not loving truth (see 2 Thess. 2:8-10). Unless we rebuild the foundations of truth among our youth, they will be "tossed here and there by waves and carried about by every wind of doctrine, by the trickery of men . . ." (Eph. 4:14, *NASB*).

Do People Really Care About Truth Today?

Postmodern subjectivism has affected the thinking of the current generations to the point that we are in danger of losing the idea of truth itself. Many today express doubts about whether truth is real, or, if it is real, whether it can actually be known. In spite of this postmodern disparagement of truth, Aristotle said that everyone desires to know truth. Deeply rooted somewhere in our hearts is the perhaps dormant awareness that truth is a necessary bedrock for life. We often overlook the fact that whatever people may say about truth, they inevitably organize their lives around what they believe is ultimately true. They have a latent and functional sense of truth, but their sense of what truth is suffers from the misconceptions they unwittingly have adopted from our culture.

Dan Kimball, pastor at Vintage Faith Church in Santa Cruz, California, reinforced this idea in his book *The Emerging Church*:

> I am finding that emerging generations really aren't opposed to truth and biblical morals. When people sense that you aren't just dogmatically opinionated due to blind faith and that you aren't just attacking other people's beliefs out of fear, they are remarkably open to intelligent and loving discussion about choice and truth.[9]

While people today are clearly turned off by those who arrogantly think they have all the answers, we have found that *young people respond positively to someone who can lovingly lead them to truth*.

This is where apologetics enters the picture. Apologetics, a defense of the faith, suffers from neglect and dismissal today largely because of the general dismissal of truth we described above. The purpose of Christian apologetics is *not* merely to win an argument, but to show that the beliefs we hold about God, Christ and his death and resurrection are objective facts that one should believe simply because they are literally true. They really happened in a specifically identified historical space and time.

More than ever, we need to follow the advice of Peter and give people honest reasons for believing in the truth that concurs with reality. Yet we need to do it with gentleness and respect. People today need an apologetic for the resurrection of Jesus as much as at any time in history (see 1 Pet. 3:15).

Clearing Up the Confusion About Truth

How then do we help people see that Jesus' resurrection is objective reality and simply cannot be true for one person and false for another? I (Sean) once performed the following experiment with my students. I placed a jar of marbles in front of them and asked, "How many marbles are in the jar?" They responded with different guesses, 221, 168, and so on. Then after giving them the correct number of 188, I asked, "Which of you is closest to being right?" They all agreed that 168 was the closest guess. And they all agreed that the number of marbles was a matter of objective fact, not one determined by personal preference.

Then I passed out *Starburst* candies to each student and asked, "Which flavor is right?" As you might expect, they all felt this to be a nonsense question because each person had a preference that was right for himself or herself. "That is correct," I concluded. "The right flavor has to do with a person's preferences. It is a matter of subjective opinion or personal preference, not objective fact."

Then I asked, "Are religious claims like the number of marbles in a jar, or are they a matter of personal opinion, like one's candy preference?" Most students concluded that religious claims belonged in the category of candy preference. I then opened the door for us to discuss the objective claims of Christianity. I pointed out that Christianity is based on an objective historical fact—the resurrection of Jesus. I reminded them that while many people may reject the historical resurrection of Jesus, it is not the type of claim that can be "true for you, but not true for me." The tomb was either empty on the third day, or it was occupied—there is no middle ground. Before anyone can grasp the transforming power of the resurrection of Jesus, he or she must realize that it is a matter of objective fact, not of personal preference.

The Importance of Reason in Determining Religious Belief

Another challenge we face in postmodern culture is skepticism about reason as a means of finding truth. It is not that people are unable to reason. In fact, everyone reasons every day. You reason with your boss about why you should get a raise. Kids reason with their parents for a later curfew. A wife reasons with her husband as to why they need new furniture. Every day we make important decisions—buying a new car, finding a mate, investing in the stock market. If we ignore the evidence in every aspect of life and base these decisions on a blind faith, the results could be costly. Yet today people are often reluctant to believe that reason can lead to a genuine knowledge about God.

If we use reason and insist on evidence when we approach the daily decisions of our lives, why should we discard these tools when it comes to our religious convictions? We absolutely should not! In fact, given the stakes, we should be even more careful in making our religious decisions. We should never accept religious beliefs on "blind faith," but on credible evidence.

While our reasoning ability is deeply influenced by our emotions and background, we are made in the image of God with the capacity to truly understand his revelation to the world (see Rom. 1–2). Reason is one means that God has chosen to make himself known to people. The biblical witness is based upon the premise that people—despite their sinfulness—can have truthful beliefs about God. The apostle John says, "I have not written to you because you do not know the truth, but because you do know it, and because no lie is of the truth" (1 John 2:21, *NASB*). In Acts 2:36 Paul says, "Therefore let all the house of Israel know for certain that God has made Him both Lord and Christ—this Jesus whom you crucified" (*NASB*). Paul was a great practitioner of reason. Every time he used the word "therefore," which was often, he had just set a premise and was proceeding to a reasoned conclusion. Reasoning was a key method he used to bring people to truthful beliefs. Acts 17:2 says, "And according to Paul's custom, he went to them, and for three Sabbaths reasoned with them from the Scriptures" (*NASB*). Jesus also believed in the importance of reason. He frequently debated with the religious leaders of his day, presenting evidence that he was the chosen one of God (see John 5; Matt. 22).

Professor James W. Sire developed an exercise that is a great tool to help people understand the importance of reason.[10] To begin, the class leader brainstorms with his class for ideas about why people believe as they do. The class typically responds with multiple reasons—parents, tradition, Scripture, friends, media, comfort, hope, fear, consistency, and so on. After they have come up with an extensive list, the leader places their answers into four categories—psychological, sociological, religious and philosophical. Their answers may be similar to those in the following chart.[11]

Sociological	Psychological	Religious	Philosophical
Parents	Comfort	Scripture	Consistency
Friends	Peace of Mind	Pastor	Coherence
Society	Meaning	Priest	Completeness
Culture	Purpose	Guru	(best explanation)
	Hope	Channeler	
	Identity	Church	

Then the leader asks which of these reasons for belief are valid and spends some time probing each answer carefully. Soon it becomes clear that sociological, psychological and religious reasons are problematic—parents, friends, pastors and entire cultures can be mistaken. Comforting beliefs can be false and sometimes even harmful in the long run.

The importance of this exercise is that it shows that people utilize truth as the criterion of judgment. They realize Scripture and religious authorities are only worth believing if their teachings are truthful. The objective is to get people to come to grips with how important reason is for discovering truth, and then to ask, "How do we determine whether something is true?"

With this exercise in mind, we will now consider the evidence for the historical Jesus. This is where the philosophical, scientific, historical and even personal experience can play a part. Did he really live? Did he die as the Gospels record? Was he supernaturally resurrected 2,000 years ago as the Bible and Christians claim? And, most importantly, is Jesus worth trusting with my present life and eternal destiny?

How does one go about finding true answers to these questions? A critical historian would check out the validity of the records of witnesses, confirm Jesus' death by crucifixion, go over the burial procedures and confirm the reports of the empty tomb and Jesus being seen alive on the third day. Then it would be sensible to consider every possible alternate explanation of the event. At this stage one would pursue other corroborative evidence and then draw an appropriate conclusion. Sound interesting? Hang on, because in the next section of the book, this is precisely what we will do.

Why Does It Matter Whether the Resurrection Is True?

To set the stage for examining the evidence in the upcoming section, let's do a little preliminary thinking to understand just why it is so important that Jesus actually did resurrect from death.

As we said earlier in this book, we live in a world filled with pain, tragedy, conflict, illness and death. We wonder why it's that way. How do we cope with it? We have an unquenchable longing to find meaning in all the mess we experience. Each one of us has a strong desire to know the answers to the deepest questions of life. This is why there has been such a proliferation of spiritual leaders, messiahs, gurus and prophets in human history claiming to answer our deepest questions—Muhammad, Plato, Buddha, Gandhi, Krishna, Joseph Smith, the Reverend Sun Myung Moon and Shirley MacLaine. At first appearance, Jesus seems to be in the same category as these people, another founder of a particular religion groping for answers to life's baffling questions.

On closer analysis, however, it becomes evident that Jesus is the only religious figure in history who transcends this group. What he offers is really quite different from simply a way to live in a troubled world or a philosophic grid for coping with life. While Jesus does indeed offer this, he offers something qualitatively different from all the rest. He offers not merely a way to cope; he offers the real answers to our deepest longings. *We long for real love.* No other religion will tell you of a God who is so passionate about you that he left heaven to come to this messed-up earth and die for us so he could be with us forever. *We long for unconditional acceptance.* No other religion offers a God who loves us so much he accepts us as we are, sin and all, yet died to make us pure enough to live with him forever (see Rom. 5:8). *We also long for intimate understanding.* No other religion offers a God who came to earth and became one of us so he could actually experience what we go through and understand us intimately (see Heb. 2:18). And in this world where all relationships are damaged and eventually ruptured by conflict, partings or death, *we long for permanent, continuous, loving relationships.* No other religion offers a God who gives us a way to relate to him personally and forever in a state of unending joy and love.

There are many claims that various gods exist, but only one God cared enough to become a man and die on our behalf. Of the 99 names for Allah in Islam, not one of them is either Father or Love. Buddha did not come and personally indwell his disciples. No other religion besides Christianity will tell you of a God who loves his people so much that he will endure the hellish pain of the cross in order for us to know him personally.

The God of Christianity offers not merely a way of coping with the evil in the world, then escaping from it by fading into oblivion. Christianity offers a real solution to our problem of death and our longing for a life of love forever. Clearly, Christianity stands immeasurably above all religions. It's the only religion that offers us fulfillment of the deepest desires of our heart. In fact, it is the only true religion in existence. All others are either poor attempts at a solution to our problem, corruptions of Christianity or incomplete religions offering no real hope.

Now, let's get to the crux of the matter. The resurrection of Jesus is the key to all these promises of Christianity. None of the promises of eternal life with a loving God have any meaning unless the resurrection actually occurred. Christianity is just another pretty story of hope without substance unless Christ really died and rose again from the grave to defeat death and demonstrate that, through him, we can do the same thing. To put it bluntly, Christianity is worthless unless the resurrection is objectively true—a real event that actually happened at a given time and in an identifiable place in world history.

Christianity: The One True Religion

No other religion backs up its claims with such remarkable evidence as we find for the historical accuracy of Christianity. And this is absolutely crucial to our belief because it provides a basis for reason to lead us to the truth. If the resurrection actually took place in historical space-time, then all other religions and philosophies for coping with life fall short. This doesn't mean other religions are entirely false in everything they teach. Many religions offer profound insights about life. But it does mean that on core issues—the nature of God, salvation and the after-life—Christianity is uniquely true.

We fully realize how politically incorrect it is for us to say that Christianity is the only true religion and Jesus Christ is the only way to God. The truth is, Jesus is the one who made this claim in the first place! In today's culture of tolerance, that claim is denounced as arrogant and exclusive, for it implies that all other religions are wrong. Yet we repeat Christ's claim with confidence because we believe with conviction he is who he said he was. It is this truth—Christ being God—that can turn around our culture, and especially our kids, who are rapidly falling into the postmodern tolerance trap.

Nearly 1 in 2 conservative Protestant teens (48 percent) and 6 out of 10 young people in general (60 percent) believe that many religions may be true.[12] It would be nice if everybody could be right, but as simple reason and basic commonsense tell us, all religions cannot be true in their core beliefs. By its very nature, truth is exclusive. While all religions could possibly be wrong, it is not logically possible for all of them to be right when their claims differ from each other so radically. Either they are all wrong or only one is right. Consider the following chart:

	Beliefs About God	Beliefs About Salvation	Attitude Toward Other Religions
Buddhism	No God	Enlightenment	False
Hinduism	Many Gods	Reincarnation	All True
Islam	Allah	The Five Pillars	False
Judaism	Yahweh	The Law	False
Christianity	Trinity	Grace	False

What this chart shows graphically is that all religions are not the same, nor do they all point to God. In fact, different religions don't even claim to be the same. Every religion has its own specific idea of who God is (or is not) and how salvation may be attained.

Christians are often slammed today for claiming that only Christianity is true and only Christ is the way to God. Yet Christians are not the only group that claims to have the truth. Notice in the chart above the attitudes of each religion toward the others. Four of the five religions are exclusive. They believe that all other religions are false. It is simply wrong to pick out Christianity as the only intolerant religion. Every religious group (including atheists and agnostics) believes it is right.

In fact, Christianity is not exclusive at all. It is the most inclusive of religions. Everyone who will believe is invited into Christ. Unlike Mithraism, which apparently excluded women, or Mormonism, which formerly excluded blacks from the priesthood, the message of Jesus has always been for *everyone*.

Colossians 3:11 says, "In this new life, it doesn't matter if you are a Jew or a Gentile, circumcised or uncircumcised, barbaric, uncivilized, slave, or free. Christ is all that matters, and he lives in all of us." Christ makes no human distinctions—he died and rose again so that all people could have a personal relationship with the living God.

Christianity excludes no one who will believe, yet Christ himself offers the only way to be reconciled with God. As philosopher Stephen Davis explains, "The resurrection of Jesus, then, is God's decisive proof that Jesus is not just a great religious teacher among all the great religious teachers in history. It is God's sign that Jesus is not a religious charlatan among all the religious charlatans in the world. The resurrection is God's way of pointing to Jesus and saying that *he* is the one in whom you are to believe. *He* is your savior. *He* alone is Lord."[13] The resurrection was a practical way God could demonstrate to all the truth of what he had said about Jesus at his baptism: "This is My beloved Son, in whom I am well-pleased" (Matt. 3:17, *NASB*). If you are an honest enquirer into the truth of Christianity, the resurrection of Jesus is the place to begin.

So you can see why knowing whether the resurrection is an actual, historical fact is so critical. It is the key to the whole of Christianity and confirms for the whole world that Jesus is the Lord of all. The apostle Paul, who had seen the risen Jesus, wrote that Jesus was "declared the Son of God with power by the resurrection from the dead" (Rom. 1:4, *NASB*). This is why the gospel of Jesus is considered good news. If Jesus truly is God in human flesh, then God is like Jesus. It means that God is not remote, arbitrary or unreal. He is a God who loves us and who came to earth so we could know him in a personal way.

The resurrection of Jesus answers one of our most pressing questions: Is death the end? The resurrection answers that question with a resounding NO! Death is not the end. We will be together someday in a place of love and joy beyond our wildest imagination. This brings us back to the crucial question that begs for an answer: Is it really true? Did the resurrection actually occur? The writers of the New Testament encourage us to make up our minds regarding the answer to this question, and they urge us to accept the truth they knew to be real: the resurrection was a factual event.

It is important that you determine the answer to this question for yourself. This is not merely an intellectual exercise to go through and then continue with your life as before. Finding the true answer can transform your life. The question for you personally is not merely whether the claims of Jesus Christ are true. While this question is of the utmost importance, the greater question regards how you will respond to this truth. Will you trust the resurrected Jesus? Will you look to him for answers and guidance in this life? Will you fall on your knees as Thomas did when he saw the risen Jesus and cry out, "My Lord and my God" (John 20:28)?

To answer these questions, we urge you to carefully consider the evidence we present in the following chapters.

THE CONFIRMATION OF HISTORY

The aim of the first two sections of this book was to present the relational meaning of the resurrection. There can be no relational meaning, however, unless the resurrection of Christ occurred as an actual historical event.

Some claim that the actual historical event of the resurrection is not what is important for the Christian life. What is important, they think, is the example that Christ has set for us to follow and that we live as if the resurrection was true. According to this viewpoint, whether or not the tomb was empty on the third day is irrelevant. The important thing is that Christ has personally risen in our own lives—that we have our own "Easter faith."

We believe, however, that it is in fact through the historical death and literal resurrection of Jesus that God has seen fit to make possible the salvation of the human race. If the historical events were not true, two major consequences follow. First, human sinfulness has not been taken seriously. It is through Jesus' life, death and resurrection that God has conquered sin and death. If these events did not happen, then, as Paul says, "your faith is worthless; you are still in your sins" (1 Cor. 15:17).

Second, we no longer have the possibility of restoring humanity's lost relationship with God. The value of Christ's death and resurrection is that it removes the sin barrier between humankind and God and demonstrates a future in which death will be overcome and we will be reunited with him in a new pristine environment of peace and love. Part of the value of the history of the events is that we can see God's love and forgiveness in concrete form. God doesn't merely reveal the truths to us in written form; he reveals them personally through his son, Jesus. God didn't just reveal the path to heaven to us; he blazed the trail by his death and resurrection. His death and resurrection makes possible our future life with him.

The purpose of this section, therefore, is to set forth the evidence for the credible resurrection as an actual event in history. We hope the three sections of this book will enable you to "know Him and the power of His resurrection and the fellowship of His suffering, being conformed to His death" (Phil. 3:10, *NASB*).

As we stated in the previous section, the resurrection of Christ must be examined by the same criteria used in examining any other event in history. The faith of the early church was founded on the experiences of people observing verifiable events in the factual realm. For example, Luke says:

> Inasmuch as many have undertaken to compile an account of the things accomplished among us, just as they were handed down to us by those who from the beginning were eyewitnesses . . . it seemed fitting for me as well, having investigated everything carefully from the beginning, to write it out for you in consecutive order . . . so that you may know the exact truth about the things you have been taught (1:1-4, *NASB*).

Luke's careful intention was to relate actual historical facts.

Wolfhart Pannenberg, professor of systematic theology at the University of Munich, has been primarily concerned with the relationship between faith and history. This brilliant scholar says, "Whether the resurrection of Jesus took place or not is a historical question, and the historical question at this point is inescapable. And so the question has to be decided on the level of historical argument."[1]

Philosopher Stephen Davis observes, "It seems clear—indeed, axiomatic—that if the resurrection of Jesus actually occurred, then it is a fact about the past as it occurred. And if the word *history* is understood as *the events that occurred in the real past and that historians attempt to discover*, then it follows that the resurrection of Jesus was an event in history."[2] William Lane Craig explains:

The hypothesis of the resurrection is both verifiable and falsifiable: verifiable through proving the historicity of the empty tomb, the appearances, and the origin of the Christian Way; falsifiable by either disproving the above or providing naturalistic explanations of them. In fact, I should go so far as to say that there is not a single event in the resurrection narratives that is not *in principle* historically verifiable or falsifiable.[3]

In other words, the empty tomb, the linen cloth, the appearances of Jesus and the removal of the large stone are either merely ideas in the mind or events in history. Hence, historical research is necessary to determine what truly happened that first Easter.

Is Historical Knowledge Really Possible?

Before we examine the historical evidence for the resurrection, we need to address this one preliminary question: Is it even possible to determine just what happened in the past? In today's postmodern culture it is often said that knowledge of the past is impossible, since the people who wrote down the historical accounts were biased and had their own political or religious agendas. Since we cannot personally revisit the past to determine what happened, as many critics claim, we can have no certainty of what occurred. This theory of history, which pervades many of our public schools and universities, is called *historical relativism*. This theory, if true, would preclude an historical investigation into the resurrection of Jesus, since we would be unable to gain an accurate picture of the events.

It is important to keep in mind that the goal of historical investigation is probability, not mathematical certainty. While it is true that no historian can have absolute certainty, it does not follow that history is unknowable. Historian Richard Evans writes: "No historians really believe in the *absolute* truth of what they are writing, simply in its *probable* truth, which they have done their utmost to establish by following the usual rules of evidence."[4]

Let's briefly consider four charges often made by historical relativists and test their viability:

1. *We cannot know historical facts because they cannot be directly observed.* While it is true that historical facts cannot be "observed," they can still be known with a great deal of probability. In fact, there are many things scientists believe exist because they infer their existence, not because they directly observe them. Subatomic particles (protons, neutrons and electrons) are not directly observable, but are inferred from equations and laboratory results. Dinosaurs have not been directly observed, but their existence is inferred from bones and other evidence.

2. *We cannot know historical facts because there is bias or subjectivism on the part of the person who wrote the original account.* Merely because a historian was biased does not mean that his account is false; it still may be that he recorded the events correctly. In fact, many times biased writers have made the most accurate historical accounts of certain events. It has been pointed out that scientists are also susceptible to bias, but this has not led them to conclude that their own accounts of experimental results are untrustworthy. Ideally we would want writers to be unbiased, but they must also have sufficient interest in a topic to want to write on a subject. In the case of the disciples, even though they were biased, it is clear that they were concerned to report the truth. This is most evident by their willingness to follow the facts, even if it cast them in a negative light.[5] N. T. Wright observes, "It must be asserted most strongly that to discover that a particular writer has a 'bias' tells us nothing whatever about the value of the information he or she presents. It merely bids us be aware of the bias (and of our own, for that matter), and to assess the material according to as many sources as we can."[6]

3. *We cannot know historical facts because historians are naturally conditioned by the culture in which they live.* While it is true that a historian's perspective will be colored by the assumptions of his or her culture, the same is true for *any* field of knowledge.

If it is not possible to know something because it was reported by a "culturally conditioned" person, then all knowledge would be impossible because there are no people who are not culturally conditioned to report the facts objectively. Since we do have some knowledge, we must not be completely conditioned by our culture.

4. *We cannot know historical facts because historical accounts are based on fragmentary evidence and selective facts.* But again, all fields of knowledge have the same constraints: they are also based on partial evidence, and their theories are constructed by people who have been selective in the facts they consider. Michael Licona notes, "Since data mostly comes to us fragmented, an exhaustive or even complete narrative is unattainable. Thus, historians do not expect full accounts of the past but narratives that are partial and intelligible. Historians seek an adequate accounting of the data where they get it right, even if not in an exhaustive sense."[7]

While historical relativism is a popular philosophy, there is no sufficient reason to conclude that historical knowledge is impossible. Regarding the knowability of history, Dr. Norman Geisler concluded:

But we cannot reject all history without engaging in some history of our own. The statement that "The past is not objectively knowable" is itself an objective statement about the past. Hence, the position against the knowability of history slits its own throat.[8]

We conclude, then, that the facts of history are objectively knowable with sufficient evidence, and thus we proceed with our historical investigation of the resurrection.

Sufficient Evidence Needed

The evidence for Jesus' death and resurrection must be approached with an honest, fair and open mind. Although we too have our own preconceived notions and conclusions about the matter, we must not let the investigation be prejudiced by them. Let the evidence speak for itself. Historian Ronald Sider writes, "We have a right to demand good evidence for an alleged event which we have not experienced, but we dare not judge reality by our limited experience. And I would suggest that we have good evidence for the resurrection of Jesus of Nazareth."[9]

Historian Ethelbert Stauffer gives further suggestions on historical research:

What do we (as historians) do when we experience surprises which run counter to all our expectations, perhaps our convictions and even our period's whole understanding of truth? We say as one great historian used to say in such instances: "It is surely possible." And why not? For the critical historian nothing is impossible.[10]

Historian Philip Schaff adds: "The purpose of the historian is not to construct a history from preconceived notions and to adjust it to his own liking, but to reproduce it from the best evidences and to let it speak for itself."[11]

If one is to judge the historicity of Jesus, then it ought to be judged as impartially as that of any other figure in history. The late Dr. F. F. Bruce, professor at the University of Manchester in England, testified that, "The historicity of Christ is as axiomatic for an unbiased historian as the historicity of Julius Caesar. It is not historians who propagate the 'Christ-myth' theories."[12]

What we are establishing here is the historical reliability of the Scriptures, not their inspiration. While the reader may come to the conclusion that the Scriptures are inspired, such a conclusion is not necessary to examine the life, death and resurrection of Jesus as an historical event. We repeat: The historical reliability of the Scriptures should be tested by the same criteria by which all historical documents are tested, and while that search is being conducted, any bias against supernatural occurrences or inspiration should not cloud the investigator's objectivity.

DO ACCOUNTS OF MIRACLES UNDERMINE CREDIBILITY?

We have noted that many scholars dismiss the historical accuracy of the New Testament on the basis that the biblical writings report miracles. According to the worldview of these critics, miracles cannot occur, therefore the biblical accounts of Jesus, his deeds, his virgin birth and his resurrection cannot be historically accurate. We have also pointed out that a true historian will set aside his or her biases and worldviews and allow the evidence alone to indicate whether an account is historical. And we have outlined the accepted principles for determining the validity of evidence. Yet we find that when evidence comes up against worldviews containing an anti-supernatural bias, the bias often overrides the obvious conclusion demanded by the evidence. Critics who doggedly hold to a purely naturalistic worldview that excludes all possibility of miracles will sometimes construct elaborate theories or manipulate dates in order to make historical evidence square with their bias.

Lest we be accused of allowing our own bias to color our view of history, let's pause in this chapter and consider the question of miracles. Is it possible that the critics have a strong point? Are miracles too far-fetched to believe? If a historical account seems to support a miraculous event, should we suspend our affirmation of it and look for an alternative explanation? Or is it possible that the bias against miracles has no basis?

We must first consider the possibility of miracles before we can openly examine the evidence for the resurrection. If miracles are impossible per se, then the resurrection could not have occurred, and we must look for some naturalistic explanation of the events that seem to affirm it. But if we conclude that miracles are at least *possible,* then we can be open to following the evidence without bias.

As we make this study, we will do well to keep in mind two important considerations pointed out by New Testament scholar Dr. Craig Blomberg:

There is an intuitive sense with which even the most devout believer must share the tension that the skeptic feels when it comes to the credibility of miracle stories. Moreover, even the person open to the possibility of miracles does not believe every strange tale of the supernatural.[1]

In other words, whenever we hear of an event that seems contrary to the common workings of the laws of nature, we naturally raise our guard. We don't want to be duped and we rightly apply rigid standards of judgment before we believe a report of anything outside the way nature works—according to set and predictable patterns.

Defining Miracles

Our first task is to define exactly what a miracle is. Dr. Richard Purtill, professor of philosophy at Western Washington University defines a miracle as "an event in which God temporarily makes an exception to the natural order of things, to show that God is acting."[2] Note that by his definition a true miracle must have five qualifications:

First, the exception to the natural order is *temporary*. The raising of Jesus from the dead is an exceptional, one-time event that in no way affects our certainty about the general uniformity of nature.

Second, the event is an *exception* to the ordinary course of events. The resurrection of Jesus is a supernatural event that does not happen in the ordinary course of nature.

Third, in order to have a miraculous event, it is necessary to maintain a belief in *the natural order of things*. You cannot recognize an event that is not according to the laws of nature unless you know and believe in the constant laws of nature. You can recognize the resurrection as a miracle only if you agree that in the ordinary course of events, dead people stay dead. If nature were chaotic and unpredictable, then miracles could not be contrasted with what we ordinarily expect.

Fourth, a miracle must be the result of the *power of God*.

Fifth, miracles are signs of God's action, momentarily overriding the normal workings of nature.

To sum it up, we might say that a miracle is an event caused by a direct act of God in which the laws of nature are temporarily suspended in order to accomplish a purpose for which the set laws of nature would be inadequate.

Challenging the Possibility of Miracles

Even when an event fits all five elements of Dr. Purtill's criteria, it is often dismissed from being historical because of a pervasive, modern attitude we call the "Hume hangover." The Hume hangover is rooted in the argument of the eighteenth-century Scottish philosopher David Hume that belief can be justified by probability and that probability is based upon the uniformity or consistency of nature. Nature always behaves in a certain way, Hume says, therefore it is probable that it always will behave in that way. Based on this probability he concludes that exceptions to nature's laws are so infinitely improbable as to be effectively impossible. The unchangeable laws of nature outweigh any evidence that could ever be offered for a miracle. In other words, anything that is unique to normal human experience—such as a miracle—should be, according to the Hume hangover, rejected outright.

For example, which is more probable: that the witnesses of Christ's resurrection were mistaken, or that Jesus was raised from the dead? According to Hume's rigidly naturalistic approach, the answer is obvious, even without considering the evidence because he believes the laws of probability tell us that miracles simply cannot happen.

Though they reach their conclusion by a different philosophy, naturalistic scientists also reject any possibility of miracles. Many of them reject miracles outright because of the scientific principle known as *methodological naturalism*. According to methodological naturalism, science must restrict itself solely to blind natural causes and unbroken laws of nature. Simply put, science must be confined to exclusively naturalistic explanations. Consequently, miracle claims are excluded from the start. Methodological naturalists do not necessarily assume that nature is all that exists, but for the sake of scientific investigation, one must only appeal to natural causes. They believe that the universe is a closed system in which no supernatural element can intervene. According to a naturalist, every event—past, present and future—must always have a natural explanation. This viewpoint completely rules out the intervention of the supernatural, and means that any evidence that points to a supernatural occurrence must either be false, misinterpreted or have another explanation besides the apparent one. No matter what the event or how strong the evidence for it, this attitude dictates that the miraculous must always be rejected, even in spite of the evidence.

To illustrate how naturalistic people think and react, I (Josh) was invited to be a guest lecturer in a philosophy class. The professor was the head of the entire philosophy department for the university. After I presented literary and historical evidence for the deity of Christ, the professor began to badger me with hostile questions and accusations concerning the resurrection. He did not believe the event happened, and he tried to make me look backward and stupid for believing it. After about 10 minutes, a student interrupted and asked the professor a very perceptive question.

"Sir, what do you think happened that first Easter?"

"I don't know what happened," the professor replied, "but it wasn't a resurrection!"

"Is your answer the result of examining the evidence?" the student responded.

"No!" the professor replied. "It is because of my philosophical outlook."

The man was heavily biased, but at least he was honest! Many who deny the resurrection hide behind the artificial cover of pseudo-science in an attempt to legitimize their naturalistic philosophy. The conclusion of this professor was not the result of careful examination of the facts; it was a conclusion made in spite of the facts. This is the attitude that many people adopt regarding miracles, and specifically the resurrection. They are unwilling to consider the evidence because they—like Hume—believe simply that miracles do not occur.

The Limitations of Hume

Even though David Hume has had a profound impact on the history of religion and philosophy, scholars today generally agree that he overstated his case. Philosopher Anthony Flew, even while he was still a preeminent atheist, believed Hume's argument to be defective.[3] We simply cannot discount the possibility of miracles before examining the evidence. If we do, we reveal nothing more than simple bias.

New Testament scholar and philosopher Dr. Norman Geisler has pointed out two of the fatal flaws in Hume's argument:

Hume speaks of "uniform" experience against miracles, but this seems to beg the question or else be special pleading. It begs the question if Hume presumes to know the whole field of experience to be uniform in advance of looking at the evidence for uniformity. For how can one know that all possible experience will confirm naturalism, unless one has access to all possible experiences, including those in the future? If, on the other hand, Hume simply means by *uniform experience* the select experiences of *some* persons, then this is special pleading. For there are others who claim to have experienced miracles. Why should their testimony be inferior to that of others who report uniformity?[4]

Another major problem with Hume's argument is that it is simply unscientific to determine the outcome of an investigation before examining the facts. To demonstrate the problem, consider the following true story. Near the end of the eighteenth century the Western world first encountered the duck-billed platypus. The platypus, which was indigenous to Australia, had fur over its entire body, was the size of a rabbit and had webbed feet. Yet since it laid eggs, it reproduced like a reptile! When the skin of a platypus was first brought to Europe, it was greeted with complete amazement. Was it a mammal or a reptile? The platypus seemed so bizarre that—despite the physical evidence of the skin and the testimony of the witnesses—many Londoners dismissed it as a sham.

Not until a pregnant platypus was shot and brought to London for observers to see with their own eyes did people begin to believe. Until this happened, some of the greatest thinkers refused to accept the existence of the platypus, and others doubted the unique claims about its physiology. The problem, according to apologist Ross Clifford, was that "It did not fit some people's view of how the world operated, so they rejected it and they reached their verdict *even though the weight of the evidence said otherwise.*"[5]

The reaction of people to the story of the platypus is similar to the way many react to the resurrection. Many are unwilling to consider the evidence for the resurrection because such an event does not fit their view of the world. Of course, such a reaction reveals a failure of objectivity, allowing biases to overrule reason in considering evidence. Even atheist Michael Goulder, a staunch critic of supernatural elements in the resurrection story, says, "We ought not to rule out 'miracles' as explanations of striking events."[6] In other words, we ought to consider the evidence before determining the verdict.

Another significant problem with Hume's critique of miracles is that it says we should always follow the odds and never believe the improbable. Even a novice can recognize the error in this thinking. While most outcomes do tend to favor the odds, are we in a position to say that we should *never* believe otherwise? Following this train of thought we should never believe that a person has been dealt a royal flush, since the odds against it are 0.15 x 10 (to the -5 power). Yet occasionally a royal flush shows up in a hand. The odds against winning a state lottery are usually millions to one, yet someone wins. According to Hume, even if you were dealt a royal flush or held a winning lottery ticket, you would not be justified in believing it was true. But surely it is perfectly reasonable to believe that an improbable event can at least occasionally occur. Wise people consider the weight of the odds but ultimately base their belief on the facts.

Rather than concluding before sufficient investigation that miracles are impossible—or even that miracles are certain to occur—we ought to assume a neutral ground that admits miracles may or may not occur. Then we can examine the evidence objectively and see where it leads us.

Do We Live in a Closed Universe?

As we explained above, many people discount miracles because they believe the entire universe is a closed system, operating solely by natural law where there can be no supernatural influences. With the passing of the Newtonian epoch, however, we need to leave room for the unpredictable, the unexpected and the incalculable. Quantum physics reveals elemental structures in the universe that, at this point, defy all explanation. This has led several people to open their minds to broader possibilities. As Professor C. Stephen Evans noted, "In our post-modern situation, we have no good grounds for assuming that the natural world is a closed mechanistic system."[7]

Even during the Newtonian era, allowing for the miraculous was never considered to be inherently unscientific. Those who defend the possibility of miracles do not deny the validity of the regularity of nature. People who believe in miracles have always assumed that the world operates by predictable natural laws. In fact, this assumption that the world is as science describes it is necessary before a miracle can be identified as a miracle. An event can be a miracle only if it is an exception to the way we all know the world normally works. If we did not believe in a universe operating by scientific law, everything that happened would be equally random and unpredictable, and the term *miracle* would be meaningless. Indeed, many modern scientists do believe in the possibility of miracles. In his immense work *A Marginal Jew*, John Meier lists a significant number of these men and women.[8]

Dr. Craig Blomberg explains the position of those who defend the validity of both scientific law and the existence of miracles:

> Despite all the marvelous advances of physics, no one has yet proved, if God as traditionally conceived by Jews and Christians exists, why he might not occasionally suspend or transcend the otherwise fixed regularities of nature . . . physical science today seems to be much more open to the possibility of God than it has been for generations.[9]

Norman Geisler explains it in this way:

Belief in miracles does not destroy the *integrity* of scientific methodology, only its *sovereignty*. It says in effect that science does not have sovereign claim to explain all events as natural, but only those that are regular, repeatable and/or predictable.[10]

Philosopher William Lane Craig has observed:

Science can neither bar gnomically impossible events from history nor force us to assimilate anomalous events to natural law. Philosophy cannot preclude either the occurrence or identification of a miracle. Therefore, so long as the existence of God is possible, it seems that such events' being caused by God cannot be ruled out. The historian ought first, as a methodological principle, to seek natural causes; but when no natural cause can be found that plausibly accounts for the data and a supernatural hypothesis presents itself as part of the historical context in which the event occurred, then it would not seem to be illicit to choose the supernatural explanation.[11]

Miracles are impossible only if it is assumed that God does not exist. Short of an absolute proof of atheism, one has to be open to the possibility that God has intervened directly in the world and thus also to evidence that he has done so.

Limitations of the Scientific Method

In the modern scientific age it is not uncommon for people to believe that nothing can be confirmed as true unless it can be proven scientifically. Students constantly ask, "Can you prove the resurrection scientifically?"

Scientific proof, based on observation through repetition, shows that something is a fact by repeating the event in the presence of the person questioning the fact. A controlled environment is set up, the experiment is conducted, observations are made, data is drawn and hypotheses are empirically verified or falsified.

Since the effectiveness of science depends on its being able to collect data from continuous observation of the testing of a hypothesis, the modern scientific method, while highly effective in a given sphere, is severely limited. It is applicable only to repeatable events or facts. It is unfortunate that the modern awe of science has led people to mistakenly assume that the scientific method can be used to determine all truth. It cannot, and it never could. It does not even apply to all scientific fields, such as geology or evolutionary biology. Historical events, by their very nature, occur only once in time and are not repeatable. We cannot prove scientifically that Hannibal crossed the Alps because we cannot rouse him from the grave, set up his army, train his elephants again and repeat the event. But this gives us no reason to look at the historical discipline as a "weak" science. Most reasonable people have confidence in the facts of history because we have other valid methods of determining their truth.

As a unique event in history, the resurrection of Jesus Christ is outside the realm of the scientific method. The inability to repeat the event in a controlled environment does not dismiss its reality. It can be determined by the unique and effective tools of historical investigation and validation. The scientific method is invalid as a tool for every kind of proof.

How Do We Know Anything at All?

People will often say, "The only things we can know *for sure* are what science tells us is true." This sentence is what philosophers call a *self-defeating* statement because the sentence contradicts itself. Other examples of self-defeating statements are, "There are no English sentences with more than three words," or "There are no truths." The former sentence contradicts itself because it is an example of an English sentence that has more than three words. The latter statement is self-defeating because, if correct, it would be an example of a truth.

Similarly, the sentence "The only things we can know for sure are what science tells us is true," is self-defeating because this statement itself cannot be proven by science. This statement is an example of something thought to be true but that is known outside the realm of science.

There are many avenues through which we can acquire knowledge. We can know things through the testimony of others. In fact, most things we know (or believe we know) are based on the testimony of other people. We can also know things through memory and introspection, as well as through the different disciplines required to know such subjects as philosophy, history, mathematics and law. While science is a crucial discipline for determining truth, it is simply false to assume that it is the only way we do or can gain access to truth.

Fact, Not Fable

Since the writings of the New Testament scholar Rudolph Bultmann, many people have believed that Jesus' contemporaries were naïve, primitive and prone to believe easily in myths and natural impossibilities. They assume that in that ancient, pre-scientific age, people couldn't tell the difference between fact and fable, reality and fantasy. Research, however, reveals a tremendous exaggeration regarding the naiveté of first-century men and women. Indeed, a simple reading of the New Testament could have dispelled the error. New Testament writers often put a high premium on believing on the basis of hard facts.

The apostle Peter proclaimed, "For we did not follow cleverly devised tales (mythos) when we made known to you the power and coming of our Lord Jesus Christ, but we were eyewitnesses of His majesty" (2 Pet. 1:16, *NASB*). The apostle Paul warned people not to "pay attention to myths and endless genealogies" (1 Tim. 1:4, *NASB*). Then there is Joseph, the fiancé of Mary. When he found that she was with child, he decided to call off the wedding in spite of her claim to be impregnated by God's Holy Spirit. Why? Because he knew how nature worked. He knew where babies came from, and to him, her claim was a wild fantasy. No gullibility in this man. But then when God himself told Joseph the truth, he knew that a miracle had occurred and dedicated himself to Mary and her son.

Even though in the first century men did not have the knowledge of the laws of nature that we have today, they knew that blind men usually stay blind. That's why they were astonished when Jesus healed the blind man. "Since the beginning of time," they said, "it has never been heard that anyone opened the eyes of a person born blind" (John 9:32, *NASB*).

They also knew that *dead men tend to stay dead*. Paul's brilliant address on Mars Hill in Greece (see Acts 17:16-34) shows that the resurrection was just as difficult for people to believe in the ancient world as it is today.

There was also Thomas, known by many today as "doubting Thomas." When the disciples reported to him that they had seen Jesus alive, his response was, in effect, "Look, it's not every day that somebody gets resurrected from the dead. I need a little evidence." His demand was quite emphatic: "Unless I see in His hands the imprint of the nails, and put my finger into the place of the nails, and put my hand into His side, I will not believe" (John 20:25, *NASB*). No ignorant, primitive gullibility here.

When Jesus showed himself to Thomas, he said, "Reach here with your finger, and see My hands; and reach here your hand and put it into My side; and do not be unbelieving, but believing." After feeling Jesus' wounds, Thomas replied, "My Lord and my God!" (vv. 27-28, *NASB*).

Dr. Gregory Boyd, professor of theology at Bethel College, concludes, "Many scholars have argued that the notion that ancient writers were largely gullible and uninterested in historical accuracy—being unable to adequately distinguish fact from fiction, reality from myth—is simply not tenable in the face of the evidence."[12]

Historical Research Needed

Dr. Wolfhart Pannenberg, professor of systematic theology at the University of Munich, observes, "The decision on the issue of the resurrection of Jesus as an event in the history of humankind is . . . a matter of purely historical examination of the early Christian tradition and of specifically historical judgment not of a prior determination."[13] In other words, we must do our historical research and let the determination rest solely on the evidence, not on any preconception or bias against supernatural occurrences.

Dr. John Warwick Montgomery, writing about those who still adhere to the concept of nature as a closed system (where all events must have a natural explanation), says:

> Since Einstein, no modern has had the right to rule out the possibility of events because of prior knowledge of "natural law." The only way we can know whether an event *can* occur is to see whether in fact it *has* occurred. The problem of miracles, then, must be solved in the realm of historical investigation, not in the realm of philosophical speculation.[14]

Dr. William Lane Craig observes:

Hume confuses the realms of science and history. In the realm of science the general experience of mankind has enabled us to formulate certain laws that describe the physical universe. That dead men do not rise is a generally observed pattern in our experience. But at most it only shows that a resurrection is naturally impossible. That's a matter of science. But it doesn't show that such a naturally impossible event has not in fact occurred. That is a matter of history . . . If the historical evidence makes it reasonable to believe that Jesus rose from the dead, then it is illegitimate to suppress this evidence because all other men have always remained in their graves.[15]

The testimony of history does seem to be one of consistency—dead men stay dead. When the billions of skeletons in history are contrasted with the resurrection and no other evidence is considered, the consistency of natural science does seem to weigh against the resurrection. Michael Licona has observed, however, that "what science has shown is that a person is not going to rise from the dead by *natural causes*. But this does not apply to Jesus' resurrection, since we are not claiming that Jesus came back to life naturally. The writers of the New Testament asserted that it was God who raised Jesus from the dead."[16]

In his article "History and Miracles," Dr. Frank Beckwith notes three factors that show that history is a viable tool for examining miracle claims.[17] First, history can examine the facts surrounding an alleged miracle without addressing its supernatural agency. Although historians may not have an interest in the theological implications of the resurrection of Jesus, it does not automatically follow that historical investigation is incapable of addressing any aspect of the alleged miraculous event. Historical investigation can still probe the occurrence of the actual events, regardless of the agency causing the events or the meaning behind them. Second, believers may very well be in a position to detect the supernatural agency behind an alleged miracle. When history determines the facts and those facts don't seem to be in accord with nature, experts other than historians may profitably use the facts to determine the meaning.

Third, and probably the most significant indication that historical investigation is a viable means of examining miracle claims, is that opponents of miracles implicitly assume the applicability of historical research to miracles whenever they try to disprove their occurrence. We saw this recently in the Discovery Channel movie *The Lost Tomb of Jesus*. The implication of the alleged finding of the bones of Jesus is that the resurrection was a farce. In taking such an approach, critics are implying that miracles can be investigated through the tools of history. This further advances our argument that historical investigation is vital to determining whether the miraculous occurrences in the New Testament are valid.

Background Information for Historical Investigation

Richard Swinburne, emeritus professor of philosophy at Oxford University, has pointed out the importance of background information when investigating an alleged miracle. He says:

> Any evidence that there is a God, and, in particular, evidence that there is a God of a kind who might be expected to intervene occasionally in the natural order will be evidence leading us to expect occasional violations of laws of nature. And any evidence that God might be expected to intervene in a certain way will be evidence supporting historical evidence that he has done so.[18]

If God truly exists, it is reasonable to expect that at some point he would intervene in history. Thus when investigating a miracle such as the resurrection, it is important to consider background evidence in favor of God's existence. (While the independent evidence for God's existence will not be given in this book, interested readers may want to consider some of the resources listed in the endnotes.)[19]

William Lane Craig concludes, "As long as God's existence is possible, then it is equally possible that He has acted uniquely at a point in history, in which case the question simply becomes whether such an event did take place. But then it is a question of evidence, not of principle, as Hume maintained."[20] Let's consider the evidence and be open to the possibility that a miracle actually occurred in the resurrection of Jesus.

EVIDENCES FOR DOCUMENT RELIABILITY

The New Testament provides the primary historical source for information on the resurrection. Because the New Testament makes claims about divine intervention in human affairs, many critics during the nineteenth, twentieth and twenty-first centuries have abandoned objectivity and attacked the reliability of the documents supporting the authenticity of the New Testament. Do these critics have a basis for their attack other than their doubt that the miraculous can occur? Let's look very briefly at two commonly accepted criteria for evaluating historical documents.

The first criterion is how chronologically close to the events they describe the documents were written. Naturally, the closer to the event the more authentic the document is likely to be. There is less time for memory to become unreliable and more chance of corroboration from others who witnessed the same events.

The second criterion for authenticating ancient documents is how reliable the copies of the original documents are. Obviously the New Testament as we have it is not based on original manuscripts written directly in the hands of the authors. The original manuscripts that Matthew, Mark, Luke, John, Paul and Peter actually wrote have long since decayed or been lost. The New Testament is based on copies of these original manuscripts—not only copies, but copies of copies through a period of almost 2,000 years. Logically, the earlier the copy was made and the more copies available, the better the original can be authenticated.

Reliability of copies can be largely confirmed by a large number of copies. The more copies we have of an ancient manuscript, the more it is possible to compare them and determine the exact form of the original document.

To evaluate the New Testament by the first criterion—how chronologically close to the events they describe the documents were written—some historians have evaluated them by the standards set in place by the U.S. judicial system. The "ancient document" principle contained in the Federal Rules of Evidence (the guidelines regulating evidence used in courts of law in the United States) permits the authentication of a document to be made by showing that the document: (1) is in such condition as to create no suspicion concerning its authenticity, (2) was in a place where, if authentic, it would likely be, and (3) has been in existence 20 years or more at the time it is offered.[1] How do the ancient documents supporting the New Testament measure up to these standards?

Dr. John Warwick Montgomery, retired professor of law and humanities at the University of Luton, England, comments about the application of the "ancient documents" rule to the New Testament documents: "Applied to the gospel records, and reinforced by responsible lower (textual) criticism, this rule would establish competency in any court of law."[2] Similarly Pamela Binnings Ewen, a partner in the prestigious international law firm of Baker and Botts, concludes that "the Gospels are documents of the requisite age, coming from the proper custody, and free of suspicious appearances. They meet all of the requirements for authentication under the rules of evidence."[3]

F. C. Bauer, along with other critics, assumed that the New Testament Scriptures were not written until late in the second century A.D. He believed that these writings came basically from myths or legends that had developed during the lengthy interval between the lifetime of Jesus and the time these accounts were set down in writing. By the end of the nineteenth century, however, archaeological discoveries had confirmed the accuracy of the New Testament manuscripts. Discoveries of early *papyri* manuscripts bridged the gap between the time of Christ and existing manuscripts from a later date.[4]

As a result of this incontrovertible evidence, William Albright, once the world's foremost biblical archaeologist, said, "We can already say emphatically that there is no longer any solid basis for dating any book of the New Testament after A.D. 80, two full generations before the date between 130 and 150 given by the more radical New Testament critics of today."[5] These findings greatly increased the confidence of scholars in the reliability of the Bible.

Coinciding with the *papyri* discoveries, an abundance of other manuscripts came to light in other archaeological discoveries. Dr. John A. T. Robinson, best known for playing a key role in the "Death of God movement," was one of England's most distinguished critics of supernaturalism in the Bible. Robinson accepted the consensus typified by German criticism that the New Testament was written years after the time of Christ, at the end of the first century. But as "little more than a theological joke," he decided to investigate the arguments on the late dating of all the New Testament books, a field largely dormant since the turn of the century.

The results stunned Dr. Robinson. He said that owing to scholarly "sloth," the "tyranny of unexamined assumptions" and "almost willful blindness" by previous authors, much of the past reasoning upon which Bible criticism was based was untenable. He concluded that the New Testament is the work of the apostles themselves, or of contemporaries who worked with them, and that all the New Testament books, including John, had to have been written before A.D. 64.

Robinson places Matthew between A.D. 40 and 64, Mark between A.D. 45 to 60, Luke before A.D. 57 to 64, and John between A.D. 40 and 64. If correct, this would mean that one or two of the Gospels could have been written as early as seven years after Christ's death. At the latest, the Gospels were all composed among eyewitnesses and contemporaries of the events. Robinson challenged his colleagues to try to prove him wrong. If scholars reopened the question, he claimed, the results would force "the rewriting of many introductions to—and ultimately, theologies of—the New Testament."[6]

The noted Roman historian Colin Hemer has more recently offered powerful support in favor of Robinson's conclusions. He has argued persuasively that Acts was written between A.D. 60 and 62. Here are some of the reasons that led him to this conclusion:

1. Acts abruptly concludes with Paul's house arrest in Rome. The most plausible explanation is that Luke was still writing at the time of the events he was describing. If so, we must date Acts no later than A.D. 62.

2. Acts records the martyrdom of Stephen (7:54-60) and the apostle James (12:1-2), yet it says nothing regarding the deaths of Paul and Peter (mid A.D. 60s), and James, Jesus' brother (about A.D. 62).

3. Accounts of the Jewish war with the Romans (beginning in A.D. 66) and the destruction of Jerusalem (A.D. 70) are oddly absent from Acts.

4. There is no hint of the deterioration of relations between the Christians and Romans during the Neronian persecution of the late A.D. 60s.

5. Acts speaks as if the Sadducees have a prominent authority in Rome. Yet after A.D. 70, their political influence collapses.

6. There are specialized details that would have been known only to a contemporary researcher such as Luke who traveled widely. These details include exact titles of officials, identification of army units and information about major routes. [7]

As these observations show, the book of Acts records no historical event occurring after A.D. 62, a strong indication that it was written at about that time. Today it is widely accepted that the same author wrote both Luke and Acts (see Luke 1:1-4; Acts 1:1). If Acts was composed on or before A.D. 62 and Luke was written before Acts, then Luke was written within 30 years of the death of Jesus. John Wenham has persuasively argued that Luke was even likely written between A.D. 50 and 55. [8] Even if this earlier date is not accepted, Luke was still a contemporary to the life, death and resurrection of Jesus.

The internal evidence of the literary relationship between Matthew, Mark and Luke has lead many scholars to conclude that Mark was written before the other two Synoptic Gospels. Craig Blomberg says, "All of this adds up to a strong case that all three [Synoptic] Gospels were composed within about thirty years of Christ's death (probably A.D. 30) and well within the period of time when people could check up on the accuracy of the facts they contain."[9] While the Gospel of John is typically placed in the A.D. 90s, this is still far closer to the events than the manuscripts of many ancient biographies that historians accept without question. For example, the two earliest biographers of Alexander the Great, Plutarch and Arian, wrote more than 400 years after Alexander's death in 323 B.C., yet their writings are generally accepted as trustworthy by historians.[10]

Ancient Manuscript Authority

Now we will consider the second class of evidence concerning the New Testament documents: the proximity of copies to the original manuscript and the number of manuscript copies available. The closer the copies to the original manuscript, the more likely it is to be accurate. As we all know, when copies are made, errors are likely to creep in. An unscrupulous copier could even choose to insert his own thinking into the document. One of the primary criteria for the reliability of manuscript copies is how close they are chronologically to the original. The more copies available, the more they can be compared, and the closer we can come to determining the authentic content of the original.

Regarding the date between original composition and existing copies, most ancient works have a gap of more than 700 years, with some works, such as Plato and Aristotle, being twice that. In contrast, there are fragments of the Gospel of John dating within 40 to 50 years of composition (*John Rylands Papyri*) and a nearly complete copy of the New Testament within 100 to 150 years of original composition (*Chester Beatty Papyri*). Historically speaking, existing copies of the New Testament books (or parts of books) are astonishingly close to the originals.

When I (Josh) finished my research into biblical reliability and released the first *Evidence That Demands a Verdict* in 1973, I was able to document 14,000 manuscripts of the New Testament alone. Now, after the release of *The New Evidence That Demands a Verdict*, I am able to document nearly 25,000 manuscripts. This number of copies makes the New Testament far and away the best-documented writing in ancient history. Its nearest competitor is Homer's *Iliad* with 643 manuscript copies extant. Some recent critics, such as Bart Ehrman (*Misquoting Jesus*), have claimed that there are too many variants across these manuscripts to reconstruct the original with confidence. But this conclusion is far too hasty. For one thing, 80 percent of the variations are simply spelling errors that are easily accounted for. While there are a handful of minor texts upon which New Testament scholars disagree, *there is no textual variation that threatens a central Christian doctrine.*

The significance of the number of manuscripts and their closeness to the original documents authenticating the New Testament motivated Sir Frederick Kenyon, regarded as one of the greatest archaeologists ever, to write:

The interval, then, between the dates of original composition and the earliest extant evidence becomes so small as to be in fact negligible, and the last foundation for any doubt that the Scriptures have come down to us substantially as they were written now has been removed. Both the authenticity and the general integrity of the books of the New Testament may be regarded as finally established.[11]

John A. T. Robinson concluded, "The wealth of manuscripts, and above all the narrow interval of time between the writing and the earliest extant copies, make it by far the best attested text of any ancient writing in the world."[12] Even the renowned scholar Anthony Flew, who recently announced his newly found belief that God exists, agrees with this statement.[13]

F. F. Bruce makes the following observation:

The evidence for our New Testament writings is ever so much greater than the evidence for many writings of classical authors, the authenticity of which no one dreams of questioning. And if the New Testament were a collection of secular writings, their authenticity would generally be regarded as beyond all doubt.[14]

Eyewitness Accounts

Another reason for trusting the New Testament records of Christ is that they were written by eyewitnesses or from eyewitness accounts. Historian Dr. Louis Gottschalk, in writing about the examination of the accuracy of a source, says, "Ability to tell the truth rests in part upon the witness's nearness to the event. *Nearness* is here used in both a geographical and a chronological sense."[15]

- 2 Peter 1:16 says, "For we did not follow cleverly devised tales when we made known to you the power and coming of our Lord Jesus Christ, but we were *eyewitnesses* of His majesty" (*NASB,* emphasis added).

- 1 John 1:1: "We proclaim to you the one who existed from the beginning, whom we have heard and seen. We saw him with our own eyes and touched him with our own hands. He is the Word of life."

- The disciples said, "He also presented Himself alive after His suffering, by many convincing proofs, appearing to them over a period of forty days . . ." (Acts 1:3, *NASB*).

- Acts 2:32: "This Jesus God raised up again, to which we are all *witnesses*" (*NASB*, emphasis added).

- John says, "And he who has seen has testified, and his testimony is true; and he knows that he is telling the truth, so that you also may believe" (John 19:35, *NASB*).

- Luke, the physician, wrote, "Inasmuch as many have undertaken to compile an account of the things accomplished among us, just as they were handed down to us by those who from the beginning were *eyewitnesses* and servants of the word, it seemed fitting for me as well, having investigated everything carefully from the beginning, to write it out for you in consecutive order . . . so that you may know the exact truth about the things you have been taught" (Luke 1:1-4, *NASB*, emphasis added).

In recording the events of the resurrection, the disciples followed the Jewish law, which commanded them to be honest witnesses. John Ankerburg and John Weldon put it this way: "The fact that the apostles constantly appealed to such eyewitness testimony is all the more believable in light of their own unique Jewish heritage. No religion has ever stressed the importance of truth or truthful testimony more than the Jewish religion."[16] In the Jewish Scriptures, God's people were constantly warned to be truthful. In fact, the disciples knew that if they were giving false testimony, they would be considered false witnesses against God himself and could be punished by death (see Exod. 20:16; 23:1; Deut. 17:6; 19:15; Prov. 19:5,9).

In further support of their testimony, the apostles refused to renounce their beliefs regarding the resurrected Christ even though they faced harsh persecution and martyrdom for believing. As scientist and philosopher Blaise Pascal once said:

The hypothesis that the Apostles were knaves is quite absurd. Follow it out to the end and imagine these twelve men meeting after Jesus' death and conspiring to say that he had risen from the dead. This means attacking all the powers that be. The human heart is singularly susceptible to fickleness, to change, to promises, to bribery. One of them had only to deny his story under these inducements, or still more because of possible imprisonment, tortures and death, and they would all have been lost. Follow that out.[17]

The disciples went to the grave with the conviction that they had seen the risen Jesus. It is more than fair to conclude that we can trust their testimony.

The Presence of Hostile Eyewitnesses

Another reason there was no room for myths, legends or inaccuracies in the accounts of the life and teachings of Christ is that these accounts were circulated in the presence of knowledgeable people who were extremely hostile to the new Christian movement.

Concerning the value of hostile eyewitnesses, law professor Dr. John Montgomery observes, "This rule underscores the reliability of testimony to Christ's resurrection which was presented contemporaneously in the synagogues—in the very teeth of opposition, among hostile cross-examiners who would certainly have destroyed the case for Christianity had the facts been otherwise."[18]

The apostle Paul affirmed the widespread knowledge of the reports of Christ's resurrection when he was brought before King Agrippa and the Roman official Festus to defend his teachings. In Acts 26:25-26 Paul said, "What I am saying is the sober truth. And King Agrippa knows about these things. I speak boldly, for I am sure these events are all familiar to him, for they were not done in a corner!" If the events were widely known and even those hostile to the new faith could not refute the facts, it gives the reports enormous credibility.

F. F. Bruce says concerning the value of the New Testament records being scrutinized by vocal opponents, "Had there been any tendency to depart from the facts in any material respect, the possible presence of hostile eyewitnesses in the audience would have served as a further corrective."[19]

The enemies of the Christian movement were prepared to challenge any over-zealous disciple who might have desired to exaggerate the story to make it sound more appealing. These hostile witnesses were ready to correct any distortion of the things Jesus did and taught. Theologian Stan Gundry notes, "Is it possible that they would have allowed false statements to pass as facts concerning His life which they also knew so well? Christianity would have opened itself to ridicule if it had created such stories to perpetuate itself."[20]

Archaeological Confirmation

Further corroboration for the New Testament documents comes from the discipline of archaeology. Where the data of the Gospels can be tested, archaeological discoveries have constantly proven the documents to be remarkably accurate. Louis Gottschalk explains the significance of archaeology to the New Testament documents: "Conformity or agreement with other known historical [geographic] or scientific facts is often the decisive test of evidence, whether of one or of more witnesses."[21]

Sir William Ramsey, one of the greatest geographers of all time, was a student of the German historical school of the mid-nineteenth century. He became firmly convinced that the book of Acts was a product of the mid-second century A.D. In his research to make a topographical study of Asia Minor, he was compelled to consider the writings of Luke as a guide to his quest. As a result of the book's incredible accuracy, he completely reversed his beliefs and dated the book as being near contemporary to the events it described due to the overwhelming evidence uncovered in his research. He found that in references to 32 countries, 54 cities and 9 different islands Luke did not make a single mistake.[22]

Here are just a few examples of how archaeology has confirmed the biblical record:

- For centuries there had been no record of the court where Pilate tried Jesus. William Albright shows that this court was the court of the Tower of Antonia, the Roman military headquarters in Jerusalem.[23]

- The pool of Bethesda, as mentioned in John 5:2, can now be identified, "with a fair measure of certainty in the northeast quarter of the old city (the areas called Bezetha, or 'New Lawn') in the first century A.D., where traces of its earlier existence were discovered in the course of excavations near the Church of St. Anne in 1888."[24]

- In 1990, the burial ground of Caiphas, the Jewish high priest who sent Jesus to Pilate, and his family was found in Jerusalem.[25]

Yale archaeologist Millar Burrows concludes, "On the whole such evidence as archaeology has afforded thus far . . . strengthens our confidence in the accuracy with which the text has been transmitted through the centuries."[26]

Extra-Biblical Evidence

Sources outside the Bible provide significant support for the story of Jesus as recorded in the New Testament documents. While these sources do not provide the detail of the Gospels, they do provide powerful corroborative evidence for the portrait of Jesus as portrayed in the Gospels.

Historical Jesus expert Gary Habermas has argued that "ancient extra-biblical sources do present a surprisingly large amount of detail concerning both the life of Jesus and the nature of early Christianity."[27] He notes that, "Overall, at least seventeen non-Christian writings record more than fifty details concerning the life, teachings, death, and resurrection of Jesus, plus details concerning the earliest church."[28]

Edwin Yamauchi, professor of history at Miami University, lists what can be known regarding Jesus through non-Christian writers alone:

> (1) Jesus was a Jewish teacher; (2) many people believed that he performed healings and exorcisms; (3) he was rejected by the Jewish leaders; (4) he was crucified under Pontius Pilate in the reign of Tiberius; (5) despite this shameful death, his followers, who believed that he was still alive, spread beyond Palestine so that there were multitudes of them in Rome by A.D. 64; (6) all kinds of people from the cities and countryside—men and women, slave and free—worshiped him as God by the beginning of the second century.[29]

Evidence from the New Testament Letters

While the majority of the details concerning the life of Christ in the New Testament are recorded in the Gospels, Paul's writings contain significant information that affirm and corroborate the events in the life of Christ. These letters are deemed to be authentic, as they were written so near the time of Christ—while many eyewitnesses to his life, death and resurrection were still alive. The three Pauline letters, Romans, 1 Corinthians and 1 Thessalonians, were likely written before any of the Gospels appeared.[30]

Professor Gary Habermas explains the significance of Paul's letters for the study of the historical Jesus:

Paul provides the most details concerning the last week of Jesus' life, speaking frequently of these events due to their centrality to the gospel. He gives particulars concerning the Lord's Supper, even citing the words Jesus spoke on this occasion (1 Corinthians 11:23-25). Paul speaks often of Jesus' death (Romans 4:25; 5:8), specifying crucifixion (Romans 6:6; Galatians 2:20) and mentioning the Jewish instigation of it (1 Thessalonians 2:14-15). He tells how Jesus was buried, rose again three days later, and appeared to numerous people, both individually and in groups (1 Corinthians 15:3-8).[31]

We conclude with the words of historian Paul Johnson:

What is clear beyond doubt is that whereas, in the 19th century, the tendency of history was to cast doubt of the veracity of the Judeo-Christian records, and to undermine popular faith in God and his Son, as presented in the Bible, in the 20th century it has moved in quite the opposite direction, and there is no sign of the process coming to an end. It is not now the men of faith, it is the skeptics who have reason to fear the course of discovery.[32]

Conclusion: The Gospel Writers Recorded Accurate History

Some New Testament critics assert that accounts of the life of Jesus were written down so long after the events that they were undoubtedly corrupted, just as words are garbled when passed orally in the child's game of Telephone. Thus, it is alleged, we do not have a trustworthy account of the actual words and life of Christ.

As we have shown in this chapter, this criticism is utterly invalid and based on old assumptions proven wrong by subsequent manuscript discoveries. We now have convincing reasons to conclude that the New Testament accounts are exceptionally accurate because of the extreme closeness of the original manuscripts to the actual events. William Albright observed that the period between Jesus' life and the written records is "too slight to permit any appreciable corruption of the essential character and even of the specific wording of the sayings of Jesus."[33]

Even with this short interval, we have good reason to believe the accounts to be accurate and that the information found in the Gospels was circulated accurately by word of mouth up to the time of their writing, even though that time was quite short by the standards of ancient document history. One reason for believing this is that the ancient Jewish world placed immense value on memorization skills. Elementary education was mandatory for youth ages 5 to 12. It was based entirely on rote memorization and focused on one topic: the Scriptures. Many Rabbis memorized the entire Old Testament as well as a considerable body of oral laws.

Another significant point is that as long as the key events of a narrative and their meaning were not changed, transmission of important ideas (not written down in Scripture) could involve a significant amount of flexibility in retelling the stories. This explains why the Synoptic Gospels have such similarities and differences: the writers had committed a considerable amount of material to memory regarding Jesus' sayings and actions, using their own styles and vocabularies in the process. Dr. Craig Blomberg gives six reasons why the Gospel writers felt free to recount what Jesus did and said in various forms, while preserving the truth of the narrative.[34] We will note three of these reasons here:

1. It is likely that a written form of various portions of the Gospel predate the appearance of the final form of the three Synoptic Gospels. This hypothetical, so-called "Q" document, which is composed of sayings of Jesus, was probably composed by at least A.D. 50. This brings the Gospel writings even closer to the time of Christ.

2. Rabbis and their followers often used a kind of shorthand to record important information they desired to preserve. It is likely that Jesus' disciples adopted this practice while he was

still alive. Even if they did not adopt this strategy, 80 percent of Jesus' teachings were in poetic or story form, and thus much easier to remember and memorize.

3. The center of apostolic leadership in Jerusalem, which existed from at least A.D. 30-60, periodically "checked up" on the Gospel story as it was being spread (Acts 8:14; 11:1-3; 15:1-2; 21:17-25). Thus, the child's game of Telephone is not analogous to the early transmission of information regarding Jesus, because in that game each participant is left alone to decipher the meaning and transmit it to the next participant. In the early church, however, the center of leadership acted as "check and balance" on the transmission of the sayings and actions of Jesus.

No wonder so many scholars have concluded that the New Testament is the best documented of all the ancient writings. In terms of the number and variety of documents and the time period between the events and the writings, none other matches it in its integrity.[35]

DO DISCREPANCIES UNDERMINE HISTORICAL RELIABILITY?

In the previous chapter we asserted that the first task of one searching for truth in ancient documents is to lay aside all biases and consider evidence for the veracity of the documents themselves. Our next question, therefore, is to ask whether we have reason to believe that the biblical accounts of Christ's resurrection are accurate history. Do they relate actual facts? Do they tell us the truth? Are they trustworthy?

Probably the most common objection to the trustworthiness of the resurrection narratives as found in the Gospels is that they contradict and therefore are not reliable historical documents. For example, the four Gospels tell us that Mary was the first to see the risen Jesus, whereas 1 Corinthians 15:5 says that the apostle Peter was the first witness. Mark says the women who went to the tomb to anoint Jesus "saw a young man clothed in a white robe sitting on the right side" (16:4-5), Matthew says an angel was there with a garment "as white as snow" (28:3), and Luke says "two men suddenly appeared to them, clothed in dazzling robes" (24:4). Don't these accounts hopelessly contradict each other, thus destroying their credibility?

Dr. John Feinberg has made a crucial observation regarding the nature of contradictory statements:

> To level the charge of contradiction is not to claim simply that two ideas do not fit together. Nor does it mean that though they fit together, we do not yet see how, though we may later. It does not even mean that God knows how they fit together, though we do not. It means that *there is no possible way for anyone ever to explain how the ideas can all be true and yet not contradict one another.*[1]

In other words, statements may differ and not be contradictions. There may be explanations for the differences that do not undermine the truth of either. Therefore, the burden of proof is on the one who claims that a statement is irreconcilably contradictory.

New Testament scholar Raymond Brown explains the significance of this to the charge that the Gospels hopelessly contradict:

> Too often commentators detect contradictions in the Gospel narratives and assume that one writer could not have been responsible for the text as it now stands or that the writer combined diverse sources without recognizing that they were irreconcilable. Such a solution is not impossible, but probabilities lie in another direction: The account as it now stands made sense to someone in antiquity, and so what seems contradictory to modern interpreters may not be really contradictory.[2]

While there are difficulties in the four Gospels, scholars should not be so quick to assume that they are genuine contradictions. Most scholars now agree that the genre of the Gospels is ancient Greco-Roman biography. This genre allowed the authors the same kind of flexibility in reporting that people typically employ in their daily conversations. Luke, for example, uses a technique called "telescoping," in which time is compressed to simplify the reporting of various stories. Specifically, he compresses the time of the resurrection, appearances of the risen Christ and his ascension in a way that could leave the impression that all these events occurred on Easter Sunday. But John's Gospel shows that they occurred over a longer period of time. Is this a contradiction? No. Rather, Luke's compression was an accepted stylistic device in the genre of Greco-Roman biographies. To claim such differences as a contradiction reveals an ignorance of genre rather than calling into question the credibility of the Gospels.

Seeming Discrepancies Do Not Invalidate the Historical Core

Even if the charge of discrepancies in the resurrection accounts were to be proven, the core material in the Gospels would still be historically valid.

Consider an example from classical history: Livy and Polybius give two seemingly irreconcilable accounts of Hannibal's passage through the Alps to attack Rome during the Second Punic War. While the accounts contradict, no one questions that Hannibal did carry out such a campaign.[3]

Even if it were shown that the Gospels did in fact contradict—which has not been proven—the core of the Gospels would *still* be considered reliable history.

Harmonization

Although there are differences in the way the four evangelists record the life of Jesus, there is remarkable consistency regarding the core facts.

Rather than focusing on apparent inconsistencies, a historian's task in studying any group of parallel writings is to see how they can be harmonized. All too often historians studying the Gospels turn this rule on its head and seem intent on finding contradictions. Sir Norman Anderson, an internationally respected legal figure who was offered a professorship for life at Harvard, explains:

> Is it not a matter of plain commonsense to make a reasonable attempt to resolve apparent inconsistencies in any web of evidence before jumping to the premature conclusion that the witnesses—or, indeed, one and the same witnesses—have presented us with "glaring" and "irreconcilable" contradiction?[4]

A witness can report the truth without reporting all the details and without reporting events in the order of occurrence. Some writers might use chronology as their organizing principle, whereas others might organize their material topically. No doubt you use both methods when dealing with the same material on your computer. Do you sometimes search your email list by date, sometimes by subject and sometimes by sender? Do the facts contained in your emails become doubtful because they are presented on the screen in different ways? Why wouldn't we give the Gospel writers the same flexibility? While we may never know the exact moment-by-moment order of events of Jesus' life, we can have confidence in the core truth of these events by the consistency of their various accounts.

John Wenham, in his book *Easter Enigma*, offers a plausible harmonization of the resurrection events. After his careful investigation of the Gospel writings, he concludes:

> I had no real doubts that the gospel writers were honest and well informed people . . . but I was by no means committed to the view that the accounts were correct in every detail. Indeed I was impressed in my early studies of the resurrection stories by the seemingly intractable nature of the discrepancies. . . .
>
> Reading all I could and studying the Greek text carefully, I gradually found many of the pieces of the jigsaw coming together. It now seems to me that these resurrection stories exhibit in a remarkable way the well-known characteristics of accurate and independent reporting, for superficially they show great disharmony, but on close examination the details gradually fall into place.[5]

Despite the differences, a closer analysis of the resurrection accounts reveals a hidden harmony. As philosopher Stephen Davis notes:

> Despite differences in details, the four evangelists agree to an amazing degree on what we might call the basic facts. All unite in proclaiming that *early on the first day of the week certain women, among them Mary Magdalene, went to the tomb; they found it empty; they met an angel or angels; and they were either told or else discovered that Jesus was alive.* There is also striking agreement between John and at least one of the Synoptics on each of these points: *the women informed Peter and/or other disciples of their discovery, Peter went to the tomb and found it empty, the risen Jesus appeared to the women, and he gave them instructions for the disciples.*[6]

This is why historian and theologian Craig Blomberg has concluded that "most of the charges have been answered adequately many times over by those who have written in defense of the Gospels' trustworthiness. The vast majority of readers of the Synoptic Gospels [Matthew,

Mark, and Luke] have been struck not by the differences among them but by their remarkable similarity."[7]

Apparent Discrepancies as Positive Evidence

Lawyers, philosophers, historians, journalists and others have found that the apparent discrepancies, rather than diminishing the trustworthiness of the Gospels, actually support their reliability. British scholar N. T. Wright observes that the inexactness and breathless quality of the Gospel narratives actually add to their value. "This," he says, "is what eyewitness testimony looks and sounds like."[8]

Dr. Paul Maier concludes that "the variations in the resurrection narratives *tend to support, rather than undermine, their authenticity*. They demonstrate that there were several independent traditions stemming from some event that must indeed have happened to give rise to them."[9]

Journalist William Proctor demonstrates that a key principle of journalism is that reporters covering the same story should expect their renditions to be somewhat different, just as we find in the accounts of the four Gospel writers. He explains:

> This kind of divergence in stories written about the same events is a common phenomenon when aggressive, independent reporters are at work—for a couple of reasons.
>
> First, no one journalist, no matter how skilled, can tell everything that happens in a confusing, fast-moving situation. Each will automatically select facts based on his or her insights, interests, and biases; consequently, the final stories are bound to be dissimilar.
>
> Second, one good reporter may dig a little deeper in one direction than anyone else, and another good reporter may explore in a quite different direction. In this situation, the results will inevitably be somewhat different, even though each report still represents facets of the same story."[10]

Proctor concludes that the four Gospels—because of their full agreement on the key facts, in spite of their apparent discrepancies—represent the finest kind of journalistic writing.

The famous lawyer Simon Greenleaf wrote a careful examination of the Gospel witnesses from a legal perspective. He asserted that "copies which had been as universally received and acted upon as the four Gospels, would have been received in evidence in any courts of justice, without the slightest hesitation."[11]

The apparent discrepancies in the Gospel accounts of the resurrection do not invalidate the truth of the event; they actually affirm it. The minor discrepancies of the writers give the unbiased, objective investigator no cause to dismiss the truth of the resurrection accounts as reliable history.

CRUCIAL FACTS ABOUT CHRIST'S CRUCIFIXION

We will begin our historical investigation into the reports and claims of Christ's resurrection by looking at the events leading up to it. It is important to have a good understanding of these prior events because they set the stage and provide valuable data that is crucial to our evaluation of the reports. So in this chapter we will look at the events surrounding the death of Christ and special precautions taken by those who crucified him to ensure that his death was accomplished. As we will see, ascertaining the historical fact of his death is a prerequisite to our conviction about his resurrection.

The Trials of Jesus

After his betrayal and arrest, Jesus went through six distinct trial cross-examinations before facing crucifixion. One was before Annas, the elder high priest (John 18:13); another was before Caiaphas, the Roman appointed priest (Matt. 26:57); the third was before the Jewish council, the Sanhedrin (Luke 22:66); the fourth was before the Roman governor Pontius Pilate (Matt. 27:2); the fifth was before Herod (Luke 23:7); and the sixth was again before Pilate (Luke 23:11-25). In total, there were three Jewish trials and three Roman trials.

Why all this concern over one man? Both the Roman and Jewish authorities had various concerns about Christ's remaining at large. N. T Wright gives five compelling reasons why the Jewish authorities wanted him executed:

1. Many of the Jewish leaders considered Jesus to be a "false prophet" who was leading Israel astray.

2. Jesus claimed authority over the greatest Jewish symbol: the Temple. The Temple was the center of Jewish national life as well as being considered the place of God's presence. Jesus claimed to personally replace the role the Temple had played in the religious life of the Jews.

3. Jesus saw himself as the Messiah, which meant he could potentially become the focus of serious revolutionary activity.

4. They saw Jesus as a political risk, whose actions might provoke the wrath of Rome upon the nation.

5. And finally, at the climax of the hearing, Jesus pleaded guilty to the above charges, and then he also made blasphemous claims placing himself alongside the God of Israel.[1]

James Montgomery Boice narrows the charges down to one central reason why the Jewish authorities sought Jesus' death:

No less than six separate charges had been brought against him. First, he had been charged with threatening to destroy the Jewish temple (Matthew 26:61). Second, he was accused of being an evil-doer (John 18:30). Third, he was charged with perverting the nation (Luke 23:2). Fourth, it was said that he had forbidden Jews to pay taxes to Caesar (Luke 23:2). Fifth, he was said to have stirred up the people (Luke 23:5). Sixth, he was cited for having made himself a king (Luke 23:2). Here were six serious accusations. But these charges were not the real reason for the hatred of the Jewish leaders for Jesus or their prosecution of the case against him before Pilate. The real accusation is that he had claimed to be the unique Son of God, which they judged blasphemy.[2]

According to the reputable scholar Raymond Brown, under Jewish law the death penalty was an appropriate punishment for Jesus' blasphemous claims.[3]

While the Jews were concerned with the religious implications of Jesus' actions, the Romans were far more concerned with politics, economics and the authority of Rome. They crucified him as a rebel against Rome. When Jesus replied to the governor's question, "Are you the King of the Jews?" by saying, "It is as you say," he gave them grounds for execution (Matt. 27:11, *NASB*). To say that Jesus was king was to imply that Caesar was not. While Jesus said, "My kingdom is not of this world" (John 18:36, *NASB*), it's doubtful that Pilate understood what he meant. However, the phrase "my kingdom" probably caught Pilate's attention. While Jesus claimed that his kingdom was not of this world, Pilate could take no chances. If Jesus truly were the King of the Jews it would unmistakably brand him as an enemy of Caesar. Therefore, he had to die.

Justice Haim Cohn, while a member of the Supreme Court of Israel, wrote an article titled "Reflections on the Trial of Jesus." He said, "There can be no doubt that a confession such as this was sufficient in Roman law for conviction of the defendant."[4] The offense was punishable with death, and the governor was vested with the right to pass the death sentence.

Dr. Craig A. Evans, Distinguished Professor of New Testament at Acadia Divinity College of Acadia University, sums up the reasons for Jesus' crucifixion: "Jesus provided the grounds for a sentence of death from both the Jewish authorities (i.e., capital blasphemy) and the Roman authorities (i.e., treason and sedition)."[5] N. T. Wright affirms this conclusion: "The leaders of the Jewish people were thus able to present Jesus to Pilate as a seditious trouble-maker; to their Jewish contemporaries (and later generations of rabbinic Judaism) as a false prophet and a blasphemer, leading Israel astray; and to themselves as a dangerous political nuisance. On all counts, he had to die."[6]

Pontius Pilate

Jesus was accused of sedition by Jewish religious rulers and brought for trial before the Roman governor, Pontius Pilate. For years the only historical evidence for Pilate's existence was literary, and some historians doubted his existence.[7] But in 1961 two Italian archaeologists excavated the Mediterranean port city of Caesarea that served as the Roman capital of Palestine. They uncovered a two-by-three foot inscription in Latin that reads: "Pontius Pilate, Prefect of Judea." This archaeological discovery of a historical reference to Pilate confirmed his existence and his position.

All available evidence shows Pilate to have been an extremely cruel and merciless despot. He was stubborn, proud, corrupt, brutal and spiteful. Philo records that he was responsible "for countless atrocities and numerous executions without any previous trial."[8] N. T. Wright observes:

> The later Christian adoption of Pilate as a hero, or even a saint, is many a mile from his characterization in the gospels. . . . He was the governor; he was responsible for Jesus' death; washing his hands was an empty and contemptuous symbol, pretending that he could evade responsibility for something that lay completely within his power. What emerges from the records is not that Pilate wanted to rescue Jesus because he thought he was good, noble, holy or just, but that Pilate wanted to do the opposite of what the chief priests wanted him to do because he always wanted to do opposite of what the chief priests wanted him to do.[9]

Finally after three Jewish trials and three Roman trials, the Jewish authorities, in conjunction with the Roman authorities, delivered up Jesus to be crucified. At this point, various "security precautions" were taken to make sure that Jesus was truly dead.

Death by Crucifixion

The Jews were well aware that Jesus had predicted his own resurrection. Fearing that his followers might take extraordinary measures to make it appear that Jesus had died and rose again, they took equally extraordinary precautions to be sure he was dead and remained dead. The first of these precautions was death by crucifixion. The death would be public, brutal and certain.

The History of Crucifixion

All four Gospels tell of Jesus' death by crucifixion (see Matt. 27:35-50; Mark 15:27-37; Luke 23:33-46; John 19:23-30). While the evangelists do not describe the process in detail, much can be ascertained regarding the nature of crucifixion through historical, literary and archaeological evidence.

Crucifixion was a common method of execution during the time of Christ. In fact, archaeological evidence indicates that crucifixion was known in the port of Athens as early as 700 years before Christ. The Romans did not invent crucifixion; it is likely that they adopted it from the Phoenicians in Carthage.

"As for crucifixion by Jews," writes biblical scholar Raymond Brown, "one of the earliest references to the practice is the execution in the early first century B.C. of 800 prisoners by Alexander Janaeus. As Roman armies began to interfere in Judea, crucifixion of Jews became a matter of policy, e.g., the governor of Syria crucified 2,000 Jews in 4 B.C." Brown continues, "In the first century A.D. Jesus is the first Jew whom we *know* to have been crucified. Otherwise Josephus records no crucifixions of Jews during the first part of the Roman prefecture in Judea (A.D. 6-40), though there is ample attestation of crucifixion during the second part of that prefecture (A.D. 44-66)."[10] Clearly crucifixion was an established historical practice in Judea during the time of Christ.

The Brutality of Crucifixion

Cicero called death by crucifixion "the most cruel and hideous of tortures" and the "extreme and ultimate penalty for a slave."[11] The great historian Will Durant wrote that "even the Romans . . . pitied the victims."[12]

Flavius Josephus, the Jewish historian, who was an advisor to Titus during the siege of Jerusalem, had observed many crucifixions and called them "the most wretched deaths."[13] Josephus reports that when the Romans threatened to crucify one of the Jewish prisoners, the entire Machaerus garrison surrendered in order to obtain safe passage. Crucifixion was so gruesome and degrading that the Romans usually excluded Roman citizens and reserved it for slaves or rebels to discourage uprisings. It was used primarily in political cases.

"The pain was absolutely unbearable," observes Alexander Metherell, M.D., Ph.D. "In fact, it was literally beyond words to describe; they had to invent a new word: *excruciating*. Literally, *excruciating* means 'out of the cross.' Think of that: they needed to create a new word, because there was nothing in the language that could describe the intense anguish caused during crucifixion."[14]

The Custom of Whipping

After the verdict of crucifixion had been pronounced by the court, it was customary to tie the accused to a post at the tribunal. The criminal was stripped of his clothes and then severely flogged by the soldiers (lictors). The Gospels record that Jesus was whipped thusly before his crucifixion (see John 19:1; Matt. 27:26; Mark 15:15).

The whip that was typically used, known as a flagrum, had a sturdy handle to which were attached long leather thongs of varying lengths. Sharp, jagged pieces of bone and lead were woven into the thongs. An article in the *Journal of the American Medical Association* records:

> As the Roman soldiers repeatedly struck the victim's back with full force, the iron balls would cause deep contusions, and the leather thongs and sheep bones would cut into the skin and subcutaneous tissues. Then, as the flogging continued, the lacerations would tear into the underlying skeletal muscles and produce quivering ribbons of bleeding flesh.[15]

Without medical attention these lacerations to the skin and muscle could kill a person within hours or a few days.[16]

The Jews were limited by their law to 40 lashes. The Pharisees, with their obsessive legalism, would limit their lashes to 39 so that if they miscounted they would not break their law. The Romans, on the other hand, had no such limitations. Out of disgust or anger, they could ignore the Jewish limitation, and probably did so in the case of Jesus.

In the *Martyrdom of Polycarp* we read: "For even when they [the Christians] were so torn by whips that the internal structure of their flesh was visible as far as the inner veins and arteries, they endured so patiently that even the bystanders had pity and wept."[17] Will Durant says it left the body "a mass of swollen and bloody flesh." It was the custom after flagellation to mock the individual, and the Roman soldiers did this to

Christ. They placed a purple robe, facetiously signifying royalty, around his shoulders and a "crown of thorns" on his head.

The Crown of Thorns
Which type of thorn was used as a mock crown for Jesus is uncertain. One possibility is a plant now called the Syrian Christ-thorn, a shrub about 12 inches high with 2 large, sharp, curved thorns at the bottom of each leaf. This plant is common in Palestine, especially around the site of Golgotha where Christ was crucified.

Another plant, simply called the Christ-thorn, is a dwarf-sized shrub four to eight feet high. The branches can be bent easily to form a crown, and the thorns, in pairs of different lengths, are stiff like nails or spikes.

The thorns of either plant, when pressed into the scalp, would cause deep and painful wounds and abrasions, which would bleed profusely, as scalp wounds do.

After placing the crown of thorns on his head, the soldiers began to mock Jesus, saying, "Hail, the King of the Jews." They also spit on him and beat him with a rod before leading him away to be crucified.

The Crossbar Burden
A man condemned to be crucified had to carry his own crossbar—the horizontal beam of the cross called the *patibulum*—from prison to the place of his execution. The patibulum weighed from 75 to 100 pounds and was strapped to the victim's shoulders, which meant that the weight rested on the lower neck and upper spine—areas deeply wounded from the whipping. If the victim stumbled and fell, he could be seriously injured. He was unable to protect his face since his hands were tied.

Crucifixion with Nails
On reaching the execution site, the condemned person was nailed or bound by ropes to the cross. The nails were driven into the wrists, which were considered part of the hand in the language of Jesus' day, as the palms could not support the entire body weight. Dr. Smalhout describes the pain that resulted from this:

One of the principle nerves, the median, crosses the wrist joint. . . . The nail almost always came into contact with this nerve. Touching or damaging a nerve causes the maximal amount of pain possible.[18]

And for the feet to be pierced with nails, the legs would have to be twisted into an unnatural and painful position.

Many have questioned the historical accuracy of the nailing of the hands and feet because there has been almost zero historical evidence of the practice. Dr. J. W. Hewitt, in his *Harvard Theological Review* article entitled "The Use of Nails in the Crucifixion," said, "To sum up, there is astonishingly little evidence that the feet of a crucified person were ever pierced by nails."[19] He went on to say that the victim's hands and feet were tied to the cross by rope.

For years Dr. Hewitt's statement was quoted as the final word. The conclusion, therefore, was that the New Testament account of Christ being nailed to the cross was false and misleading. Crucifixion by use of nails was considered legendary. It was believed that nails would have ripped the flesh and could not have supported a body on the cross. Then a revolutionary archaeological discovery was made in June 1968. Archaeologist V. Taaferis, under the direction of the Israeli Department of Antiquities and Museums, discovered the remains of a victim, named Yohanan, who had been crucified. The tomb he was found in dates back to the first century A.D. A seven-inch spike had been driven through Yohanan's ankle bone with small pieces of the olive wood cross still attached.

This discovery from the time of Christ adds solid archaeological evidence that crucifixion by nailing was definitely practiced. No longer is the claim based solely upon literary evidence.

Breaking the Victim's Legs

The bones of Yohanan confirm another passage in the New Testament: "So the soldiers came and broke the legs of the two men crucified with Jesus. But when they came to Jesus, they saw that he was already dead, so they didn't break his legs" (John 19:32-33). Dr. N. Haas, of the department of anatomy of the Hebrew University and the Haddash Medical

School, examined Yohanan's skeletal remains. He concluded that his legs were broken by a *coup de grace*, and that "the percussion, passing the already crushed right calf bones, was a harsh and severing blow for the left one, attached as they were to the sharp-edged wooden cross."[20] Two other ancient sources also mention the breaking of legs during crucifixion, confirming the historical nature of the New Testament account.[21]

How Crucifixion Brings About Death

To understand why the legs of a crucified man were broken, it is necessary to understand crucifixion as a means of execution. While hanging from the cross, it was very difficult for the victim to breathe. To inhale and exhale properly, he had to pull himself up by his hands and feet, which caused searing pain. In time the victim became so exhausted from the effort and from loss of blood that he could no longer perform the breathing motions, and he suffocated.

If the Romans wanted to hasten the victim's death, the usual method of terminating a crucifixion was known as crucifracture. It consisted of the breaking of the leg bones with a club to prevent the victim from pushing upward in order to breathe. After the breaking of the victim's legs, death was imminent. The legs of the two thieves crucified with Christ were broken, but Christ's were not because the executioners observed that he already was dead.

The Spilling of Blood and Water

After Jesus was observed to be dead, one of the Roman executioners thrust a spear into his side, and "immediately blood and water flowed out" (John 19:34). This practice is mentioned in the late first century by Quintillian in *Declamationes maiores* 6:9: "As for those who die on the cross, the executioner does not forbid the burying of those who have been pierced." Many medical doctors have agreed that the release of blood and water from such a spear wound is a sure sign of death.[22] British author Michael Green explains the significance of this:

> We are told on eyewitness authority that "blood and water" came out of the pierced side of Jesus (John 19:34-35). The eyewitness

clearly attached great importance to this. Had Jesus been alive when the spear pierced His side, strong spouts of blood would have emerged with every heartbeat. Instead, the observer noticed semi-solid dark red clot seeping out, distinct and separate from the accompanying watery serum. This is evidence of massive clotting of the blood in the main arteries, and is exceptionally strong medical proof of death. It is all the more impressive because the evangelist could not possibly have realized its significance to a pathologist. The "blood and water" from the spear-thrust is proof positive that Jesus was already dead.[23]

Pilate required certification of Christ's death before the body could be turned over to Joseph of Arimathea.[24] He consented to the body's removal from the cross only after four executioners had certified Jesus' death.

Roman Executionary Efficiency

The efficiency of execution by crucifixion was quite well known in the time of Christ. John Ankerburg and John Weldon conclude:

Indeed, survival from crucifixions was unknown; just as today, men simply do not survive the firing squad, electric chair, lethal injection, or gas chamber. Because the law has decreed the prisoner's death, even if a first attempt fails, procedures are repeated until death occurs. Death by crucifixion was just as certain as by any modern method of execution; there was no escape.[25]

Dr. Paul L. Maier, professor of ancient history, writes:

True, there is a recorded instance of a victim being taken down from a cross and surviving. The Jewish historian Josephus, who had gone over to the Roman side in the rebellion of A.D. 66, discovered three of his friends being crucified. He asked the Roman general Titus to reprieve them, and they were immediately removed from their crosses.

Still, two of the three died anyway, even though they apparently had been crucified only a short time. In Jesus' case, however, there were the additional complications of scourging and exhaustion, to say nothing of the great spear thrust that pierced His rib cage and probably ruptured His pericardium. Romans were grimly efficient about crucifixions: Victims did *not* escape with their lives.[26]

We need have no doubt that these security precautions taken by the Romans to ensure the death of Jesus were efficient. They worked. Jesus was definitely dead. History does not doubt this fact at all. Dr. Gary Habermas points out that there is significant evidence for Jesus' death from non-Christian sources. These include Cornelius Tacitus (A.D. 55-120), who is considered by many to be the greatest ancient Roman historian; the Jewish scholar Josephus (A.D. 37-97); and the Jewish Talmud (A.D. 70-200). Habermas says of these non-Christian writings: "Most frequently reported is Jesus' death, mentioned by twelve sources. Dated approximately 20 to 150 years after Jesus' death, these secular sources are quite early by the standards of ancient historiography."[27]

This is why even contemporary liberal scholars such as John Dominic Crossan claim:

Jesus' death by execution under Pontius Pilate is as sure as anything historical can ever be. For if no follower of Jesus had written anything for one hundred years after his crucifixion, we would still know about him from two authors not among his supporters. Their names are Flavius Josephus and Cornelius Tacitus.[28]

By trying hard to prevent any kind of fraudulent later claims that the man they were to kill came back to life, Christ's enemies did investigators the great favor of providing powerful evidences of his certain death that we would not otherwise have. The fact that Jesus was actually killed is as certain as any event recorded in history.

CRUCIAL FACTS ABOUT CHRIST'S BURIAL

Many skeptics have focused on the events and environment surrounding the burial of Christ to find loopholes in the claim that he was resurrected from the dead. Therefore it is important that we look carefully at the historical facts and check out their accuracy and believability. In this chapter we will look at pertinent occurrences, customs and special precautions taken by those who buried Jesus to be sure that his body stayed in the tomb. As we will see, the officials took several security precautions to prevent any story from arising that Jesus had come back from the dead. First, we will examine the facts about the tomb itself.

A Solid Rock Tomb

All four Gospels record that Jesus' body was placed in a tomb cut into a rock, and a large stone was rolled against the entrance. Matthew, Luke and John state that it was a new and unused tomb (see Matt. 27:60; Luke 23:53; John 19:41). Matthew points out that the tomb belonged to Joseph of Arimathea. Concerning these two points, William Lane Craig observes, "Both these details are very likely, as a body a condemned criminal would defile the bodies of other family members resting in the tomb, and Joseph could not take liberties to deposit a criminal's body in any tomb he happened to find."[1]

Archaeologists have discovered three different types of rock tombs used during the time of Jesus. Craig describes them:

(1) *kokim* or tunnels perpendicular to the walls of the tomb, about six or seven feet deep, three in each of the three inner walls of the

tomb, into which the body was inserted headfirst; (2) *acrosalia* or semi-circular niches two-and-one-half feet above the floor and two to three feet deep containing either a flat shelf or a trough for the body; (3) bench tombs containing a bench that went around the three walls of the tomb on which the body could be laid. [2]

Craig continues:

Joseph's tomb is described as being a bench or *acrosalia* tomb; these types of tombs were scarce in Jesus' day and were reserved for persons of high rank. But such tombs were in fact used in Jerusalem during this period, as the tombs of the Sanhedrin attest. Near the Church of the Holy Sepluchre, the traditional site for Jesus' grave, *acrosalia* tombs from Jesus' time have been found.[3]

These tombs were closed by covering the opening with a disk-shaped stone weighing an average of two tons (more about the stone below). Each tomb had a groove, or trough, cut into the rock in front of it to act as a track for moving the stone. The trough was deepest immediately in front of the entrance, and angled upward. The disk-shaped stone was placed in the higher part of the groove, and a block was placed beneath it to keep it from rolling. When the block was removed, the stone would roll down and lodge itself in front of the opening.

Clearly when the body of Jesus was sealed into such a tomb, getting it out would take extraordinary effort.

Recently some scholars have questioned Jesus' burial by Joseph of Arimathea as recorded in the Gospels. John Dominic Crossan, for example, has postulated that, consistent with crucifixion customs, Jesus' body was either left on the cross after the crucifixion to be eaten by wild beasts or thrown in a shallow grave.[4]

After careful analysis, Craig had this to say about Crossan's argument:

I was well aware that the wide majority of New Testament critics affirm the historicity of the Gospel's assertion that Jesus' corpse was interred in the tomb of a member of the Jewish Sanhedrin, Joseph of Arimathea. Thus it puzzled me why a prominent scholar like Crossan would set his face against the consensus of scholarship on this question. . . . You can imagine my sense of disappointment when, consulting Crossan's works, I found that he had no particular evidence, much less compelling evidence, for his allegation; rather, it was just his hunch as to what happened to the body of Jesus.[5]

We have key reasons for confidence in the burial of Jesus as presented in the Gospels. First, Paul confirms the burial story in 1 Corinthians 15:3-5. There is conclusive evidence that Paul drew from material predating his writing that can be traced to within three to eight years of Christ's death.[6] Thus, the burial story can be traced back so close to the time of Christ's death that legendary development is impossible.

Second, the tradition of the burial is not surrounded by adornment or embellishment. It is told in a simple and straightforward manner.

Third, no conflicting tradition about the burial story exists. There are no early documents that refute the burial story as presented in the Gospels.

Fourth, how could the Jewish authorities—who had tried for so long to get rid of Jesus—not pay attention to his burial? Can we believe that they simply ignored where the body was taken?

Fifth, Christians inventing Joseph, a member of the court that condemned Jesus, is highly unlikely. Why would early Christians make a hero of a member of the very court that was responsible for Jesus' death?

Raymond Brown concludes: "That Jesus was buried is historically certain. . . . That the burial was done by Joseph of Arimathea is very probable."[7] Similarly, John A. T. Robinson, the late professor of Cambridge University, says that Jesus' burial in the tomb is "one of the earliest and best attested facts about Jesus."[8]

Jewish Burial Procedures

The New Testament makes it very clear that the burial of Christ followed the customs of the Jews. Jesus was taken down from the cross and covered with a sheet. The Jews were quite strict about not allowing the body to remain all night upon the cross.

Burial Before Sunset

Josephus says that it was the Jewish custom in Jerusalem prior to the fall in A.D. 70 to remove the crucified and bury them prior to sunset.[9]

The *Babylonian Talmud*, the Scripture commentaries of the Jews, records: "If he is left [hanging] overnight, a negative command is thereby transgressed. For it is written, his body shall not remain all night upon the tree, but thou shalt surely bury him the same day for he is hanged [because of] a curse against God."[10] The body was immediately transported to the place of burial—in Christ's case, to the private tomb of Joseph of Arimathea.

Body Preparation

The New Testament tells us that two men, Nicodemus and Joseph of Arimathea, prepared Christ's body for burial (see John 19:38-42). To understand the meaning and significance of this act, we offer the following historical information.

In preparing a body for burial, the Jews would place it on a stone table in the burial chamber. The body first would be washed with warm water. *The Babylonian Talmud* records that the washing of the body was so important to proper burial, the Jews permitted it even on the Sabbath.

A. P. Bender, in a *Jewish Quarterly Review* article, writes that according to the ancient customs of the Jews:

> The ceremonial of washing the corpse must not be performed by one person alone, not even in the case of a child. The dead must likewise not be moved from one position to another by fewer than two persons. The corpse is laid on a board, with its feet turned towards the door, and covered with a clean sheet. . . . The corpse is now washed from head to foot in lukewarm water, during which process the mouth is covered, so that no water should trickle down it.[11]

Bender explains that the washing was so thorough that the nails were cleaned and cut with a particular kind of pin and the hair was specially arranged.

The Use of Aromatic Spices

It was the custom, as verified in the New Testament, to prepare the corpse (after cleansing) with various types of aromatic spices. In the case of Christ's burial, 75 to 100 pounds of spices were used. One might regard this as substantial, but it was no great amount for a leader. For example, in the preparation of the body of Gamaliel, grandson of the distinguished Jewish scholar Hillel and a contemporary of Jesus, 86 pounds of spices were used. Josephus records that when Herod died, carrying the spices required 500 servants.[12]

The Use of Linen Cloth

After all the parts of the body were straightened, the corpse was clothed in grave vestments made of white linen. There could be not the slightest ornamentation or stain on the cloth.[13] The grave linens were sewn together by women. No knots were permitted. For some this indicated that the mind of the dead was "disentangled of the cares of this life."[14] To others, it indicated the continuity of the soul through eternity. No individual could be buried in fewer than three separate garments.

At this point, the aromatic spices, composed of fragments of an aromatic wood pounded into a dust known as aloes, were mixed with a gummy substance called myrrh. Starting at the feet, the body would be wrapped with linen cloth, with the spices mixed with the gummy myrrh placed between the folds. The preparers would wrap the torso to the armpits, put the arms down outside the wrapping, and then wrap to the neck. A separate cloth was wrapped around the head. The final encasement could weigh between 117 and 120 pounds.

John Chrysostom, in the fourth century A.D., commented that the "myrrh used was a drug which adheres so closely to the body that the graveclothes could not easily be removed."[15]

Security Precaution: The Enormous Stone

We have already briefly referred to the stone that covered the entrance to Jewish tombs. Now we will give you more facts about the size of these stones, as this information will become significant later. Matthew records in his writings that a large stone was rolled against the front of the tomb. The Gospel of Peter, a second-century apocryphal gospel, agrees that the stone was large. Mark, in his Gospel, said the stone was "extremely large" (16:4). Just how large was the stone rolled in front of Jesus' tomb?

After a lecture of mine (Josh) at Georgia Tech, two engineering professors went on a tour of Israel with other faculty members. They remembered the comments I had made about the enormity of the stone. So, being engineers, they took the type of stone used in the time of Christ and calculated the size needed in order to cover the doorway of the tomb.

Later, they wrote me a letter spelling out all their careful calculations in precise technical terms. They said a stone of that size would have had a minimum weight of one-and-one-half to two tons. No wonder Matthew and Mark said the stone was extremely large.

One might ask, "If the stone was that big, how did Joseph move it into position?" The answer is that he simply let gravity do it for him. As we explained above, it had been held in place with a wedge as it sat in a groove that sloped downward to the entrance of the tomb. When the wedge was removed, the heavy circular rock just rolled into position. Although it would be easy to roll the stone into place, it would take considerable manpower to roll it back uphill from the tomb entrance. The large stone would have provided additional security against the Jewish suspicion that the disciples of Jesus would try to steal his body.

Security Precaution: The Roman Security Guard

The Jewish officials panicked because thousands were turning to Christ. To avoid a political problem, it was to the advantage of both the Romans and Jews to make sure Jesus was put away for good. So after the crucifixion, the chief priests and Pharisees said to Pilate:

"Sir, we remember what that deceiver once said while he was still alive: 'After three days I will rise from the dead.' So we request that you seal the tomb until the third day. This will prevent his disciples from coming and stealing his body and then telling everyone he was raised from the dead! If that happens, we'll be worse off than we were at first." Pilate replied, "Take guards and secure it the best you can." So they sealed the tomb and posted guards to protect it (Matt. 27:63-66).

Some people argue that Pilate was actually saying, "Look, you have your Temple police. You take them and go make the tomb secure."

If it was the Temple police that guarded Christ's tomb, that unit would not have been slouches at their job. Temple guards were responsible for protecting the courts and gates of the Temple. A unit consisted of 10 Levites who were placed on duty at strategic locations about the Temple. There were 27 such units, or a total of 270 men on duty.

The guardsmen were thoroughly trained, and the military discipline of the guard was excellent. In fact, at night, if the captain approached a guard member who was asleep, he was beaten and burned with his own clothes.[16] A member of the guard also was forbidden to sit down or to lean against anything while on duty.[17]

We are convinced, however, that it was the Roman guard who was ordered to secure the tomb of Christ. A. T. Robertson, noted Greek scholar, says that Pilate's response to the Jews' request is phrased in the present imperative and can refer only to a Roman guard, not the Temple police. According to him, Pilate literally said, "Have a guard."

Robertson adds that the Latin form *koustodia*, the term Pilate used in this passage to designate the guard he authorized, occurs as far back as the Oxyrhynchus papyrus (A.D. 22). This term is always used only in reference to the Roman guard.[18] Pilate wanted to prevent any tampering with Jesus' tomb, so he was very likely to want his own soldiers guarding the tomb.

The great New Testament scholar Raymond Brown offers five reasons why the guard was Roman:

1. The apocryphal Gospel of Peter clearly understands Pilate to offer Roman soldiers to protect the tomb.

2. If the Jewish leaders had wanted to use their own Temple police, why would they request Pilate's help at all?

3. Matthew's use of *koustodia* matches the picture of a Roman prefect assigning Roman troops.

4. Matthew refers to the guards as "soldiers," the plural of *stratiotes*. Twenty-two of twenty-six uses of *stratiotes* in the New Testament refer to Roman soldiers. In another three references (Acts 12:4,6,18), *stratiotes* refers to the soldiers of King Herod Agrippa I. Never in the New Testament does the term refer to the Temple police.

5. If the guards were Jewish, why would they be responsible to the governor of Rome for failing to fulfill their duties, as Matthew 28:14 implies?[19]

Also worth noting is that John reports the involvement of a Roman cohort in the arrest of Jesus (see 18:12). This clearly indicates that the Roman authorities were deeply concerned with the fate of Jesus. As John Wenham has observed, "It is a great mistake to underestimate the anxiety which the following of Jesus caused the authorities."[20] The arrest of Jesus by a Roman cohort also gives precedence for the reporting of Roman troops to Jewish authorities in specially assigned instances.

As Dr. Brown notes above, if the priests had wanted to post Temple police at the tomb, they would not have needed the orders of the governor to do it. Their request indicates that they were seeking assignment to them of a unit of Roman soldiers. That this was indeed the case is affirmed by the fact that the Roman soldiers later came to the chief priests for protection because they knew that they would have influence over Pilate: "If the governor hears about it, we'll stand up for you so you won't get in trouble" (Matt. 28:14).

At this point a critic might say, "See, the guards came to the high priest. That shows that they were the Temple guard." The context is clear, however, that they came to the high priest because he had influence with the Roman authority, and appealing to him was the only possible way to save their necks from Roman reprisal for their failure. What was their failure? They were ordered to protect the tomb of Jesus to keep his body from being stolen, and the body was missing. They reported to the high priest that they saw an angel as bright as lightning come down from heaven and move the stone before they fainted dead away in terror. The high priest could not allow such a story to get out, so he bribed the guards into reporting that the disciples of Jesus stole his body while they were sleeping (see Matt. 28:11-15). Such a bribe would have been nonsensical if these guards had been the Temple police. Since the high priest was their supervisor, a simple order would have sufficed. Instead, the priest gave the guards money and assured them that he would intervene to save their lives when the news reached Pilate.

Some have objected to the guard story on the basis that it is highly improbable that the guard would have accepted a bribe from the Jewish authorities. Given what is known about Roman soldiers, it is claimed, accepting a bribe seems highly unlikely. The fact that the Roman army had remarkable discipline, however, does not make the bribe implausible, or even unlikely. In fact, Tacitus tells of an instance where careless guards fell asleep on watch and almost allowed their general to be caught. To protect themselves, they used the general's objectionable behavior (he was away from his post sleeping with a woman) as a shield. Raymond Brown concludes: "In other words, bargains could be struck; and it is not implausible that Pilate might have been as willing as the Jews to have the guards' resurrection story hushed up."[21]

Others claim that the guards would never have accepted the bribe because that would be the same as accepting their own death sentence. This criticism is guilty of *begging the question* because, to have any force, it has to assume that the events reported in Matthew are false. If Jesus was not resurrected, then of course they would be foolish to accept a bribe because they would likely be executed for allowing his body to be stolen, which they were specifically charged to prevent. If Matthew's story is true, however, then going to the Jews and accepting the bribe may have been their best chance of survival, for they would be complicit with the Jews and the Romans in covering up facts none of them wanted known.

What Was a Roman Guard?

Don't let the Greek word *koustodia* as applied to Roman soldiers mislead you. In this case, *custodian* did not mean someone who cares for a building. The renowned Roman legions were custodians in the sense that they were the instrument by which Caesar retained custody of his vast empire. The vast Roman Empire owed its existence and continuance to these impeccably trained warriors, who were among the greatest fighting machines ever conceived.

The importance of the Roman army is underscored by Flavius Vegitius Renatus. A military historian, he lived several hundred years after the time of Christ when the Roman army had begun to deteriorate in its discipline. He wrote a manual for the Roman Emperor Valentinian, encouraging him to instill the methods of offensive and defensive warfare used by the Romans during the first century, when they were still highly disciplined. Called *The Military Institutes of the Romans,* it is still a classic today. Vegitius wrote:

> Victory in war does not depend entirely upon numbers or mere courage; only skill and discipline will insure it. We find that the Romans owed . . . the conquest of the world to no other cause than continual military training, exact observance of discipline in their camps and unwearied cultivation of the other arts of war.[22]

T. G. Tucker, in his book *Life in the Roman World of Nero and St. Paul,* points out that when a guard joined his unit, "he is made to take a solemn oath that he will loyally obey all orders of his commander-in-chief, the emperor, as represented by that emperor's subordinates, his immediate officers. That oath he will repeat on each first of January and on the anniversary of the emperor's accession."[23]

Supercilious pictures of the tomb of Christ show one or two guards standing around with wooden spears and miniskirts. That's really laughable and could not be further from the truth. Many excellent resources attesting to the discipline of the Roman army tell us that a Roman guard unit was a 4-to-16-man security force. Each man was trained to protect

6 feet of ground. The 16 men in a square of 4 on each side were supposed to protect 36 yards and hold it against an entire battalion.[24]

Normally a unit charged with guarding an area would work in this way: 4 men were placed immediately in front of what they were to protect. The other 12 would sleep in a semi-circle in front of them with their heads pointing in. To steal what these guards were protecting, thieves would first have to walk over the guards who were asleep. Every four hours, another unit of four guards was awakened, and those who had been awake took their turn at sleep. They would rotate this way around the clock.

To illustrate, historian Dr. Paul Maier wrote of the incident in Acts where Peter had been imprisoned. "Peter would be guarded by four squads of four men each when imprisoned by Herod Agrippa (Acts 12), so sixteen would be a minimum number expected *outside* a prison. Guards in ancient times always slept in shifts, so it would have been virtually impossible for a raiding party to have stepped over all their sleeping faces without waking them."[25]

Even Matthew indicated a multi-man force when he wrote that "*some* of the guards went into the city and told the leading priests what had happened" (28:11, emphasis added). Thus both the biblical account and independent history tell us that the military unit guarding Jesus' tomb was a significant number of men, all highly trained and disciplined.

Responses to Objections Concerning the Roman Guard

Since *The Resurrection Factor* was first written in 1981, there have been a few primary objections raised as to the historicity of the Roman guard. We will note these objections and address them.

Objection #1: Probably the most common objection is that Matthew's story is an apologetic legend. It is often pointed out that the sentence "their story spread widely among the Jews, and they still tell it today" (28:15) suggests that the author was writing years after the actual events, thus allowing time for legendary growth. However, as we have already seen, there is powerful evidence that Matthew was written during the lifetime of those who had witnessed the events, which means that there was not enough time for legendary development.

Yet Anglican biblical scholar John Wenham said the guard story "bristles with improbabilities at every point: the Sabbath visit to the governor, the great earthquake, the flashing angel rolling back the stone, the reporting to the chief priests, the bribe to the soldiers to tell the tale *that they were asleep on duty*—everything invites, not belief, but incredulity. And how stupid, having introduced the useful apologetic idea of a closely guarded tomb, to give a handle to the opposition by even hinting that the guards did not do their job! It is a worthless piece of Christian apologetic at whatever date it was written, *unless is happens to be undeniably true.*"[26]

Probably the strongest argument in favor of the guard story (and against its being an apologetic legend) centers around the early Christian-Jewish debate over the resurrection. William Lane Craig explains:

> Think about the claims and counterclaims about the Resurrection that went back and forth between the Jews and Christians in the first century. The initial Christian proclamation was, "Jesus is risen." The Jews responded, "The disciples stole his body." To this Christians said, "Ah, but the guards at the tomb would have prevented such a theft." The Jews responded, "Oh, but the guards at the tomb fell asleep." To that the Christians replied, "No, the Jews bribed the guards to say they fell asleep."
>
> Now if there not had been any guards, the exchange would have gone like this: In response to the claim Jesus is risen, the Jews would say, "No, the disciples stole his body." Christians would reply, "But the guards would have prevented the theft." Then the Jewish response would have been, "What guards? You're crazy! There were no guards!" Yet history tells us that's not what the Jews said.
>
> This suggests the guards really were historical and that the Jews knew it, which is why they had to invent the absurd story about the guards having been asleep while the disciples took the body.[27]

It is highly unlikely that the early Christians would create a story about a guard at the tomb that many people, including the Jewish authorities, would have known was false.

Objection #2: Some have discounted the guard story because it only appears in one of the four Gospels: Matthew. While it is true that Mark, Luke and John do not mention the story, the apocryphal Gospel of Peter, probably written around A.D 150, does mention it. It is likely that the Gospel of Peter records a tradition of the guard story that is independent of Matthew, since there are virtually no word similarities between the two accounts.[28] Because the guard story has been transmitted through at least two different traditions, it is highly unlikely that it was a legend.

Objection #3: Some have wondered why the Jews placed guards at the tomb in the first place. Their doing so would have indicated that they had a better understanding of Jesus' resurrection in three days than the disciples did, which seems difficult to believe. Guard duty, however, was not uncommon in the Roman army. When necessary, guards regularly protected the bodies of executed criminals in various Roman provinces.[29]

Another possibility is that the guards were placed at the tomb to prevent any sort of tomb robbery or other potential disturbances during the Passover. Passover was a time of incredible activity in Jerusalem—the Roman army would not want to allow any possible disturbances during the festival.

The greatest possibility, however, is what we find in Matthew 27:62-64 where the Jewish authorities tell Pilate that they want the guard because they have heard of Jesus' prediction of his own resurrection, and they fear that his disciples will steal the body to make it appear that it really happened.

John Wenham believes that this passage has earmarks of truth: "There is certainly no reason why the Jewish authorities should not have heard talk about a resurrection on the third day. . . . In their search for watertight evidence they must have weighed every word, and it is hardly likely that Jesus' sayings about his rising on the third day would not have come to their ears. So it is probable that they really did fear consequences of a successful plot to simulate a resurrection."[30]

The story of the Roman guard at the tomb of Jesus, as these evidences show, has the earmarks of genuine historicity.

Security Precaution: The Roman Seal

Matthew records that "along with the guard they set a seal on the stone" (Matt. 27:66, *NASB*). A. T. Robertson says the stone could be sealed only in the presence of the Roman guards who were left in charge. The purpose of this procedure was to prevent anyone from tampering with the grave's contents.

After the guard inspected the tomb and rolled the stone in place, a cord was stretched across the rock and fastened at either end with sealing clay. Finally, the clay packs were stamped with the official signet of the Roman governor.

A parallel to this is seen in the Old Testament book of Daniel: "A stone was brought and laid over the mouth of the den; and the king sealed it with his own signet ring and with the signet rings of the nobles, so that nothing would be changed in regard to Daniel" (6:17).

Henry Sumner Maine, former member of the Supreme Council of India, and former regius professor of civil law at the University of Cambridge, said of the Roman seal, "Seals in antiquity were actually considered as a mode of authentication."[31] To authenticate something simply means to prove that it is real or genuine. Because the seal was Roman, it also verified the fact that Christ's body was protected from vandals by nothing less than the power and authority of the Roman Empire. Anyone trying to move the stone would have broken the seal and thus incurred the wrath of Roman law and power.

In Nazareth, a marble slab was discovered with a warning to grave robbers. It was written in Greek and read, "Ordinance of Caesar. It is my pleasure that graves and tombs remain perpetually undisturbed for those who have made them for the cult of their ancestors or children or members of their house. . . . Let it be absolutely forbidden for anyone to disturb them. In case of violation I desire that the offender be sentenced to capital punishment on charge of violation of sepulcher."[32]

Maier observes, "All previous Roman edicts concerning grave violation set only a large fine, and one wonders what presumed serious infraction could have led the Roman government to stiffen the penalty precisely in Palestine and to erect a notice regarding it specifically in Nazareth or vicinity."[33] It well could be a response to the commotion caused by Christ's resurrection. Dr. Norman Geisler concludes:

> A likely explanation is that Claudius, having heard of the Christian doctrine of resurrection and Jesus' empty tomb while investigating the riots of A.D. 49, decided not to let any such report surface again. This would make sense in light of the Jewish argument that the body had been stolen (Matt. 28:11-15). This is early testimony to the strong and persistent belief that Jesus rose from the dead.[34]

In this chapter we have set forth reports of events surrounding the burial of Jesus Christ, noting various accounts of skepticism and giving you the evidence supporting the strong likelihood that the reports of these events were absolutely true. All the information in this chapter and the previous one are preliminary to the verification of the events surrounding the resurrection of Christ. In the following chapters we will show you how the events we've explored here are crucial to understanding and verifying the fact of the resurrection.

RESURRECTION FACTS TO BE RECKONED WITH

Whatever one believes about Christ and his resurrection, everyone has to admit that something significant happened on that morning—significant enough to alter the course of history, even to the point of changing the calendar from B.C. (before Christ) to A.D. (the Latin *anno domini*—the year of our Lord).

That "something" was so dramatic that it completely changed 11 men's lives, enabling them from that time on to endure abuse, suffering and even death. That something was an empty tomb! An empty tomb that a 15-minute walk from the center of Jerusalem would easily have confirmed or disproved. Reports of that empty tomb and the resurrection appearances of Jesus Christ have shaken the foundations of thought and shaped the course of history from that time forward. Obviously, something happened. Something big.

If you wish to rationalize away the events surrounding Christ and his resurrection, you must deal with certain imponderables. In fact, you might say that both the Jews and Romans outwitted themselves when they took so many precautions to make sure Jesus was dead and remained in the grave. The fact that something happened in spite of the security precautions we noted in the previous chapters—crucifixion, burial, entombment, sealing and guarding the tomb—makes it very difficult for critics to defend their position that Christ has not been raised from the dead.

Let's consider these security precautions again and look at subsequent facts concerning them.

Fact Number 1: The Roman Seal Is Broken

On Easter morning the seal that stood for the power and authority of the Roman Empire was broken. No one denies this fact. The consequences for breaking the seal were severe. The FBI and CIA of the Roman Empire were called into action to find the person or people responsible. When they were apprehended, they would receive severe punishment. Would Christ's disciples have broken that seal? Hardly! After his arrest they showed signs of craven cowardice and hid themselves. Peter even denied that he knew Christ.

Fact Number 2: The Tomb Is Empty

Another obvious fact that Sunday morning was the empty tomb. No one ever denied that the tomb was empty. It is significant that after the resurrection, the suddenly emboldened disciples of Christ did not go off to Athens or Rome to preach that he had been resurrected; they went right back to the city of Jerusalem where, if what they were claiming was false, their message would have been easily disproved. The resurrection claim could not have been maintained for a moment in Jerusalem if the tomb had not been empty. Dr. Paul Maier explains:

> Where did Christianity first begin? To this the answer must be: "Only one spot on earth—the city of Jerusalem." But this is the very *last* place it could have started if Jesus' tomb had remained occupied, since anyone producing a dead Jesus would have driven a wooden stake through the heart of an incipient Christianity inflamed by His supposed resurrection.
>
> What happened in Jerusalem seven weeks after the first Easter could have taken place only if Jesus' body were somehow missing from Joseph's tomb, for otherwise the Temple establishment, in its imbroglio with the Apostles, would simply have aborted the movement by making a brief trip over to the sepulcher of Joseph of Arimathea and unveiling Exhibit A. They did not do this, because they knew the tomb was empty. Their official explanation for it—that the disciples had stolen the body—was an admission that the sepulcher was indeed vacant.[1]

Philosopher Stephen Davis observes, "Early Christian proclamation of the resurrection of Jesus in Jerusalem would have been psychologically and apologetically impossible without safe evidence of an empty tomb . . . in other words, without safe and agreed-upon evidence of an empty tomb, the apostles' claims would have been subject to massive falsification by the simple presentation of the body."[2]

Both Jewish and Roman sources and traditions acknowledge an empty tomb. These sources range from the Jewish historian Josephus to a compilation of fifth-century Jewish writings called the *Toledoth Jeshu*. Maier calls this "positive evidence from a hostile source, which is the strongest kind of historical evidence. In essence, this means that if a source admits a fact decidedly *not* in its favor, then that fact is genuine."[3]

Gamaliel, a member of the Sanhedrin, put forth the suggestion that the Christian movement was of God (see Acts 5:34-42). He could not have done this if the tomb had been occupied or if the Sanhedrin had known the whereabouts of Christ's body.

Even Justin Martyr in his *Dialogue with Trypho* (written around A.D 130) relates that the Jerusalem authorities sent special representatives throughout the Mediterranean world to counteract the story of the empty tomb with the explanation that his followers stole the body. This was the first counterargument to the claim of an empty tomb (see Matt. 28:11-15). Why would the Jewish authorities bribe the Roman guard and propagate the "stolen body" explanation if the tomb was occupied?

Historian Ron Sider concluded: "If the Christians and their Jewish opponents both agreed that the tomb was empty, we have little choice but to accept the empty tomb as a historical fact."[4] Likewise, Dr. J. P. Moreland observes that "the only explanations for the resurrection of Jesus for which we have evidence assume an empty tomb, regardless of whether the explanation is offered by a friend or foe of Christianity. This is strong evidence that the tomb was in fact empty."[5]

Cultic veneration of heroes' graves was well attested in the ancient world of Greece and Rome.[6] At least 50 tombs of prophets or religious leaders were venerated as shrines in Palestine during the time of Jesus.[7] Even today it is common for the burial place of a significant religious leader to be venerated as a shrine. Muslims take yearly pilgrimages to

Mecca in honor of Mohammed. Hindus and Buddhists visit the graves of their spiritual guides, and Jews visit the grave of Abraham in Hebron.

While the tomb of James, Jesus' brother, was well known,[8] no one today knows the location of Jesus' tomb. Why? Lawyer Frank Morrison explains: "We cannot find in the contemporary records any trace of a tomb or shrine becoming the center of veneration or worship on the ground that it contained the relics of Jesus. This is inconceivable if it was ever seriously stated at the time that Jesus was really buried elsewhere than in the vacant tomb. Rumor would have asserted a hundred suppositious places where the remains really lay, and pilgrimages innumerable would have been made to them."[9]

Why was Jesus' tomb not venerated as a shrine? J. P. Moreland answers, "The most reasonable answer must be that Jesus' body was not in the tomb, and thus the tomb was not regarded as an appropriate site for such veneration."[10] It is common knowledge that when Christians go to see Christ's burial spot, they go to see an empty tomb. What other religious group does this?

Some have objected to the empty tomb story claiming that it was the development of legend or an apologetic device rather than a historical fact. Stephen Davis responds: "The empty-tomb tradition just does not have the characteristics we would expect it to have if it were an invented apologetic device, designed to convince readers that Jesus really rose. For one thing, the empty tomb does not play an apologetic role in the New Testament. Far from being presented as an irrefutable argument for the resurrection, the empty tomb is rather depicted as an enigma, a puzzling fact that no one at first is able to account for."[11]

One of the most compelling evidences showing that the empty tomb story was neither an apologetic device nor a legend is the fact that it was first discovered to be empty by women. In first-century Palestine, women had a low status as citizens or legal witnesses. Except in rare circumstances, Jewish law precluded women from giving testimony in a court of law. Why would those who wanted to advance Christianity have contrived a legend that embarrassed the disciples—the essential proponents of the new faith—by having them flee during the crucifixion and yet have women courageously approaching the tomb and providing the first witness to its vacancy? Such a legend would not have served the purpose of advancing the cause. Common sense tells us that the only reason the women were reported as the first witnesses was because it was the truth. Even deist scholar Dale Allison observed, "The discovery of the empty tomb by Mary Magdalene and other women commends itself as likely nonfiction."[12]

Dr. Paul Maier accurately observes that "if the resurrection accounts had been manufactured . . . women would *never* have been included in the story, at least, not as first witnesses."[13]

One might reasonably ask, "Why would these women go to the tomb, since the Roman security unit was guarding the grave?" That's quite simple. The women were unaware that the guard unit had been posted, and they were coming to anoint Christ's body over the grave clothes with a mixture of spices and perfume. On Friday they had watched the body preparation in a private burial area. They lived in the Jerusalem suburb of Bethany and therefore were not aware of the Roman and Jewish action of putting extra security at the place of Christ's burial (remember there was no CNN!).

And finally, the empty tomb story, as told in the Gospels, does not fit typical legendary writings. W. L. Craig comments regarding the simplicity of the empty tomb story in Mark: "Fictional apocryphal accounts from the second century contain all kinds of flowery narratives, in which Jesus comes out of the tomb in glory and power, with everybody seeing him, including the priests, Jewish authorities, and Roman guards. Those are the way legends read, but these don't come until generations after the events, which is after eyewitnesses have died off. By contrast, Mark's account of the story of the empty tomb is stark in its simplicity and unadorned by theological reflection."[14] The simplicity of the Gospels' account of the empty tomb—compared to legendary accounts—is powerful evidence for its historicity.

In his book *The Son Rises,* Craig offers 10 lines of evidence for the empty tomb and shows how the resurrection of Jesus is the most likely explanation. After his historical analysis, Craig concludes, "We have seen that ten lines of historical evidence combine to place the weight of the evidence solidly in favor of the historical fact that Jesus' tomb was found empty on the Sunday after His crucifixion and burial."[15]

Even the highly respected and accomplished historian Michael Grant, himself not a follower of Christ, concludes: "But if we apply the same sort of criteria that we would apply to any other ancient literary sources, then the evidence is firm and plausible enough to necessitate the conclusion that the tomb was indeed found empty."[16]

Fact Number 3: The Large Stone Is Moved

The first thing that impressed the people who approached the tomb that Sunday morning was the unusual position that the one-and-a-half to two-ton stone had previously been lodged in front of the doorway. All the Gospel writers mention the removal of the enormous stone.

For example, Matthew 27:60 says that Joseph "rolled a great stone across the entrance and left." Here the Greek word for roll is *kulio*. Mark used the same root word in his Gospel, but in chapter 16 he added a preposition to explain the position of the stone after the resurrection. In Greek, as in English, to change the direction of a verb or to intensify it, you add a preposition. Mark added the preposition *ana*, which means "up or upward." So *anakulio* can mean "to roll something up a slope or an incline." Mark's use of that verb indicates that the new position of the stone was up a slope or an incline relative to its original position.

In fact, that stone was so far "up a slope" that Luke used the same root word *kulio*, but added a different preposition, *apo. Apo* can mean, according to the Greek lexicons, "a separation from" or "a distance from." *Apokulio*, then, means to roll one object from another so that it is "separated some distance from it." Luke is telling us that the women saw the stone moved away a distance from the tomb.

In fact, the stone was in such a position up a slope away from the entire massive sepulcher that John (in chapter 20 of his Gospel) had to use a different Greek verb, *airo*, which (according to the Arndt and Gingrich lexicon) means "to pick something up and carry it away."

Here is the question that arises from this: If the disciples had come and tiptoed around the sleeping guards, why would they have moved the one-and-a-half to two-ton stone up a slope away from the entire massive sepulcher to such a position that it looked like someone had picked it up and carried it away? The needless effort would have been noisy and taken valuable time and energy. Those soldiers would need to be deaf not to have heard the commotion.

Fact Number 4: The Roman Guard Goes AWOL

The Roman guard fled. They left their place of responsibility. This is a very odd fact that must be explained

Dr. George Currie, who carefully studied the military discipline of the Romans, reports that the death penalty was required for various duty failures such as desertion, losing or disposing of one's arms, betraying plans to an enemy, refusing to protect an officer and leaving the night watch. To the above, one can add "falling asleep." If it was not apparent which soldier had failed in duty, then lots were drawn to see who would be punished with death for the guard unit's failure.

One way a guard was put to death was by being stripped of his clothes, and then burned alive in a fire started with the garments. The history of Roman discipline and security testifies to the fact that if the tomb had not been empty the soldiers never would have left their position. Fear of the wrath of their superiors and the ensuing death penalty meant they paid close attention to the most minute details of their job.

Dr. Currie notes, "The punishment for quitting a post was death, according to the laws. The most famous discourse on the strictness of camp discipline is that of Polybius VI. 37, 38, which indicates that the fear of punishments produced faultless attention to duty, especially in the night watches."[17]

Dr. Bill White, who was formerly in charge of the Garden Tomb in Jerusalem, has extensively studied the resurrection and subsequent events following the first Easter. White makes several critical observations about the Jewish authorities bribing the Roman guard:

> If the stone were simply rolled to one side of the tomb, as would be necessary to enter it, then they might be justified in accusing the men of sleeping at their posts, and in punishing them severely. If the men protested that the earthquake broke

the seal and that the stone rolled back under vibration, they would still be liable to punishment for behavior which might be labeled cowardice.

But these possibilities do not meet the case. There was some undeniable evidence which made it impossible for the chief priests to bring any charge against the guard. The Jewish authorities must have visited the scene, examined the stone, and recognized its position as making it humanly impossible for their men to have permitted its removal. No twist of human ingenuity could provide an adequate answer or a scapegoat and so they were forced to bribe the guard and seek to hush things.[18]

Fact Number 5: The Graveclothes Tell a Tale

Even though there was no body in Christ's tomb on that Sunday morning, the tomb was not literally empty. It contained an amazing phenomenon. After visiting the tomb and seeing the stone rolled away, the women ran back and told the disciples. Then Peter and John took off running. John outran Peter and, upon arriving at the tomb, he did not enter. Instead, he leaned over and looked in and saw something so startling that he immediately believed that Christ had indeed risen from the dead.

He looked over to the place where the body of Jesus had lain. There were graveclothes, *in the form of the body, slightly caved in and empty*—like the empty chrysalis of a caterpillar's cocoon. Seeing that would make a believer out of anybody! He never did get over it.

The first thing that stuck in the minds of the disciples was not the empty tomb, but rather the empty graveclothes—undisturbed in their form and position. Michael Green has observed, "No wonder they were convinced and awed. No graverobber would have been able to enact so remarkable a thing. Nor would it have entered his head. He would simply have taken the body, graveclothes and all."[19]

Fact Number 6: Christ's Confirmed Appearances

Few scholars today doubt that the disciples at least believed that they had seen the risen Jesus. Reginald Fuller has boldly claimed that "within a few weeks after the crucifixion Jesus' disciples came to believe this is one of the indisputable facts of history."[20] What caused the disciples to have this belief? From the inception of the church it was claimed that Jesus appeared personally to his followers. Several vital factors often are overlooked when investigating Christ's post-resurrection appearances to individuals, and this has led to some skepticism as to whether they are valid. Let's examine the evidence for Jesus' post-resurrection appearances.

The Large Number of Eyewitnesses

When studying an event in history, it is important to investigate whether enough people who were participants or eyewitnesses to the event were alive when the facts about the event were published. Greater numbers of witnesses help to validate the accuracy of the published report. For instance, if we all witness a murder, and in a week the police report turns out to be composed of fabricated lies, we as eyewitnesses can refute the report. When a book is written about an event, the accuracy of its content can be validated if enough eyewitnesses or participants in the event are alive when the book is published.

One of the earliest records of Christ's appearing after the resurrection is by Paul in 1 Corinthians 15:3-8:

> I passed on to you what was most important and what had also been passed on to me. Christ died for our sins, just as the Scriptures said. He was buried, and he was raised from the dead on the third day, just as the Scriptures said. He was seen by Peter and then by the Twelve. After that, he was seen by more than 500 of his followers at one time, most of whom are still alive, though some have died. Then he was seen by James and later by all the apostles. Last of all, as though I had been born at the wrong time, I also saw him.

Virtually all scholars agree that in these verses Paul records an ancient creed, or tradition, that dates before the writing of 1 Corinthians (mid-50s A.D.). In fact, most scholars who have investigated this creed date it to within three to eight years after Christ's crucifixion.[21]

It is believed that Paul received this creed when he visited Peter and James in Jerusalem three years after his conversion, which was one to four years after the crucifixion of Jesus (see Gal. 1:18-19). This is why historian Hans von Campenhausen claims that this text "meets all the demands of historical reliability that could possibly be made of such a text."[22]

While some have argued that the original creed did not include the appearance to the 500, Craig notes that "it does not mean that these appearances are any less reliable, for Paul still received the information about them from the earliest witnesses, probably during his Jerusalem visit."[23]

In these verses, Paul appeals to his audience's knowledge of the fact that Christ had been seen by more than 500 people at one time. Paul reminds them that the majority of these people were still alive and could be questioned. This statement is as strong evidence as anyone could hope to find for something that happened 2,000 years ago.

Likewise, C. H. Dodd has observed, "There can hardly be any purpose in mentioning the fact that most of the five hundred are still alive, unless Paul is saying, in effect, 'the witnesses are there to be questioned.'"[24]

This is why Dr. Norman Geisler has concluded that the appearance to the 500 "has the ring of truth about it,"[25] and William Lane Craig claims that "it is nearly indisputable that this appearance took place."[26] Paul never could have claimed that Jesus appeared to 500 witnesses so soon after the event if the event had not actually occurred.

If each of these 500 people were to testify in a courtroom for only six minutes each, including cross-examination, you would have an amazing 50 hours of firsthand eyewitness testimony. Add to this the testimony of the many other eyewitnesses and you could well have the largest and most lopsided trial in history.

The Variety of Witnesses and Locations

The second factor often overlooked in assessing the validity of the witnesses is the variety of people who saw the risen Jesus and the variety of locations in which they saw him. Professor Merrill C. Tenney writes:

It is noteworthy that these appearances are not stereotyped. No two of them are exactly alike. The appearance to Mary Magdalene occurred in early morning; that to the travelers to Emmaus in the afternoon; and to the apostles in the evening, probably after dark. He appeared to Mary in the open air. Mary was alone when she saw Him; the disciples were together in a group; and Paul records that on one occasion He appeared to more than 500 at one time.

The reactions also were varied. Mary was overwhelmed with emotion; the disciples were frightened; Thomas was obstinately incredulous when told of the Lord's resurrection, but worshipped Him when He manifested Himself. Each occasion had its own peculiar atmosphere and characteristics, and revealed some different quality of the risen Lord.[27]

In no way can one say his appearances were stereotyped.

The Inclusion of Hostile Witnesses

A third factor crucial to interpreting Christ's appearances is that he also appeared to those who were hostile to or unconvinced of his resurrection. In an attempt to dilute the overwhelming impact of the eyewitness accounts, skeptics often claim that his post-resurrection appearances were all to friends and followers. Despite the popularity of this claim, it is patently false.

No informed individual would regard Saul of Tarsus to have been a follower of Christ. He despised Christ and persecuted Christians, aiming to eradicate the entire Christian movement. Yet Saul, whose name was later changed to Paul, became one of the greatest propagators of the Christian movement in history. What could account for this radical transformation? Nothing short of a personal appearance by the risen Jesus could have sufficed (see 1 Cor. 9:1; Acts 22:4-21).

Consider James, the brother of Jesus. The Gospel record indicates that none of Jesus' brothers believed in him during his lifetime (see John 7:5; Mark 3:21-35). In fact, they tried to fool Jesus into a death trap at a public feast in Jerusalem. Yet James later became a follower of his brother and joined the band of persecuted Christians, becoming a key leader in the church and one of its early martyrs, as attested by Josephus, Hegesippus, and Clement of Alexandria.[28] What caused such a change in his attitude? The best historical explanation is that the risen Jesus appeared also to James.

It is equally possible that all to whom he appeared became followers. This perhaps explains the conversion of many of the Jerusalem priests as well as Jesus' other brothers (see Acts 6:7; 1 Cor. 9:5).

Our purpose in this chapter has been to show you that in spite of the elaborate lengths to which the Jews and Romans went to ensure Christ's death, and in spite of the elaborate precautions they took to protect his body in the tomb, several facts attest to the conclusion that he returned to life and left the tomb.

In conclusion, we turn to Tom Anderson, former president of the California Trial Lawyers Association and co-author of the Basic Advocacy Manual of the Association of Trial Lawyers of America. "Let's assume that Christ did not rise from the dead. Let's assume that the written accounts of His appearances to hundreds of people are false. I want to pose a question. With an event so well publicized, don't you think that it's reasonable that one historian, one eyewitness, one antagonist would record for all time that he had seen Christ's body: 'Listen, I saw that tomb—it was not empty! Look, I was there, Christ did not rise from the dead. As a matter of fact, I saw Christ's body.' The silence of history is deafening when it comes to testimony against the resurrection."[29]

ATTEMPTS TO "EXPLAIN AWAY" THE RESURRECTION

Many theories have been advanced attempting to show that the resurrection of Jesus Christ was a fraud. Since most of the facts surrounding the resurrection are undeniable, most of these attempts have involved putting a different interpretation on these facts, seeking either a legendary or mythical one or a naturalistic explanation. Few skeptics deny the essential events—the trial, the crucifixion, the burial, the guards, the seal or the empty tomb—because the historical evidence supporting these events is too strong. They simply deny that these events mean that a dead man came to life again. Their attitude can be summed up as, "Yes, but there's got to be some other explanation."

It takes more faith to believe some of these theories than to accept the explanation that is offered in the New Testament. We agree with John Ankerburg and John Weldon, who say, "Virtually every theory ever proposed to explain the empty tomb, other than the resurrection of Christ, is considerably more difficult to believe than the resurrection itself."[1] Indeed, as we shall see, skeptical historians actually must resort to becoming anti-historical in order to advance some of their ideas.

Two Principles to Remember

When evaluating the options regarding what happened that first Easter, one needs to apply two principles. First, the theories or alternate explanations must take into account *all* the facts surrounding the resurrection. J. N. D Anderson, head of the Institute for Advanced Legal Studies in London, emphasizes that "the evidence must be considered as a whole.

It is comparatively easy to find an alternative explanation for one or another of the different strands that make up this testimony. But such explanations are valueless unless they fit the other strands in the testimony as well. A number of different theories, each of which might conceivably be applicable to part of the evidence but which do not themselves cohere into an intelligible pattern, can provide no alternative to the one interpretation which fits the whole."[2]

The second principle to follow in the examination of historical events is not to force the evidence into a preconceived conclusion, but rather to let it speak for itself. Historian Philip Schaff warns that "the purpose of the historian is not to construct a history from preconceived notions and to adjust it to his own liking, but to reproduce it from the best evidence and to let the evidence speak for itself."[3]

With these two principles in mind, let's examine the various alternative theories offered as explanations for the events surrounding Christ's resurrection.

Natural Explanation: The Myth Theory

Many debate whether the resurrection of Jesus was an actual historical event or merely a myth patterned after the various "dying and rising" fertility gods of ancient pagan religions (e.g., Osiris, Adonis, Isis). In fact, many college professors, liberal authors and Internet skeptics have claimed that the New Testament rendition of Christ's death and resurrection was derived from pagan "mystery" religions.[4] Those who support the theory that Jesus' resurrection was borrowed from pagan myths often fail to realize the theory's quite fragile foundation. There are five basic arguments showing the weaknesses of this theory:

1. The many supposed "parallels" between the Christian doctrine of the resurrection and the dying and rising pagan gods are greatly exaggerated. Scholars often describe pagan rituals in language they borrowed from Christianity. Words like "baptism" and "resurrection" are often uncritically assigned to the acts of pagan deities, even when they have little in common with Christian beliefs.

2. The chronology does not support an early Christian dependence on the mystery religions. Most scholars believe that the available sources for the pagan deities (with anything resembling a resurrection story) date from the second, third and fourth centuries A.D., years after the completion of the New Testament canon.

3. It is highly unlikely that Paul—with his strict monotheism and Jewish roots—would have borrowed from the pagan religions. He commonly warned the early Christian churches against this very thing.

4. The death and resurrection of Jesus Christ took place within history, at a historically specified time and place. The mystery religions, on the other hand, were essentially nonhistorical. They are timeless depictions of annual events in nature, not specifically dated events that actually took place.

5. The genuine parallels that remain after the exaggerations have been accounted for may reflect a Christian influence on the pagan religions, rather than vice versa.[5]

Historian Michael Grant concluded, "To sum up, modern critical methods fail to support the Christ-myth theory. It has again and again been answered and annihilated by first-rank scholars."[6]

Natural Explanation: The Unknown Tomb Theory

One of the earliest theories presented to explain away the resurrection is that the actual tomb of Jesus was unknown. This theory is even held by some today.[7] Basically, proponents of this view claim that Jesus' body was thrown into a common pit for the executed rather than laid in a new tomb.

One possible support for this theory was the belief that those who were crucified were customarily tossed into a common pit. The discovery in 1968 of the remains of Yohanan Ben Ha'galgal in a family tomb outside of Jerusalem struck at the very heart of this theory. Yohanan had been crucified, yet he was entombed at his burial. As mentioned before, Josephus also recorded the common practice of the Romans' allowing the Jews to bury their own dead.

This theory also disregards totally the straightforward historical narrative detailing the events surrounding Christ's burial and the post-resurrection scene. The Gospel record indicates that Joseph of Arimathea, as we have seen, took the body to his own private tomb. Philosopher Stephen T. Davis concludes, "Moreover, the story of Joseph of Arimathea's involvement in the burial of Jesus seems so strongly supported and inherently trustworthy that it renders the argument for an unknown tomb quite implausible."[8]

Furthermore, the body of Christ was prepared according to the burial customs of the Jews as the women sat opposite the tomb and watched. If, for some unfathomable reason, the disciples and the women did not know the location of the tomb, certainly Joseph of Arimathea did. Also, the Romans obviously knew where the tomb was, as they had stationed a guard there.

The unknown-tomb fabrication fails to apply either of the two principles of historical research discussed above. It does not fit or explain all the facts, and it forces upon the facts a preconceived conclusion based on bias against the possibility of the supernatural.

The Wrong-Tomb Theory

This theory is similar to the previous one. It presumes that when the women returned on Sunday morning to honor Christ, they went to the wrong tomb.

Professor Kirsopp Lake, one of the initiators of this theory, surmises that the women did not know where Jesus was buried and mistakenly went to the wrong tomb. As a result of arriving at an empty tomb, they were convinced that Jesus had resurrected.[9]

Professor Lake's theory does not meet the requirements of our two research principles. First, it ignores just about all the evidence. Second, it constructs the theory entirely according to a preconceived notion.

In fact, Lake actually distorts the evidence to suit his theory. For example, he has the young man at the tomb saying to the women, "He is not here, but see the place where they laid him." The complete biblical text actually reads: "He isn't here! He is risen from the dead, just as he said would happen. Come, see where his body was lying" (Matt. 28:6). Without any literary or historical justification whatsoever, Lake omits the phrase of the angel, "He isn't here! He is risen from the dead."

The literary evidence for the inclusion of this phrase in Scripture is as strong as for any phrase in the New Testament. Although the wrong-tomb theory sounds ingenious, it hinges on arbitrarily omitting the phrase "He is risen." These women had carefully noted where the body of Jesus was interred less than 72 hours before (see Matt. 27:61; Mark 15:47; Luke 23:55). This wasn't a public cemetery, but a private burial ground. How could any rational person forget so quickly where a dearly beloved one was laid to rest?

To believe the wrong-tomb theory, one would have to say that not only did the women go to the wrong tomb, but also that Peter and John did as well, and that the Jews then went to the wrong tomb, followed by the Jewish Sanhedrin and the Romans. You would then have to say that the guard returned to the wrong tomb. And finally, you would have to say that the angel appeared at the wrong tomb. It would take a lot of faith (and blind faith at that) to believe something so absurd.

Craig points out that "if the resurrection was a colossal mistake based on the women's error, then the enemies of Christianity would have been more than happy to point that out, indicating where the correct tomb was or maybe even exhuming the body. The idea that the resurrection stemmed from the women's going to the wrong tomb is too shallow."[10] Remember, any alternate theory must account for *all* of the facts. The wrong-tomb theory does not account for the conversions of Paul or James.

The Legend Theory

Some argue that the resurrection accounts are legends, cropping up years after the time of Christ.

In reality, this would be impossible. Resurrection accounts were circulated and written down by the original eyewitnesses. Paul related that in the mid-50s A.D. there were almost 500 firsthand eyewitnesses still alive. And, as we have seen, this was already well known within three to eight years of the time of Christ.

Peter Kreeft and Ronald Tacelli observe that "there was not enough time for myth [legend] to develop. . . . several generations have to pass before the added mythological elements can be mistakenly believed to be facts. Eyewitnesses would be around before that to discredit the new, mythic versions. We know of other cases where myths and legends of miracles developed around a religious founder—for example, Buddha, Lao-tzu and Muhammad. In each case, many generations passed before the myth surfaced."[11]

Dr. J. N. D Anderson concludes that it is "almost meaningless to talk about legends when you're dealing with the eyewitnesses themselves."[12]

The Spiritual Resurrection Theory

A fourth theory claims that Christ's body decayed in the grave and his real resurrection was spiritual. Jehovah's Witnesses espouse a form of this theory. Rather than believing that Jesus' body decayed in the grave, however, they believe that God destroyed the body in the tomb and that Jesus rose in an immaterial body. Both of these "spiritual resurrection" theories have insurmountable problems.

First, to have any meaning, a resurrection must entail the physical. In the view of Palestinian Judaism, a spiritual resurrection without the physical body would not be a resurrection at all. Dan Cohn Sherbock, a Jewish rabbi and visiting professor at Cambridge, observed:

> Either Jesus was physically resurrected or he wasn't. It's as simple as that. The Gospel account of the empty tomb and the disciples' recognition of the risen Christ point to such a historical conception of the resurrection event. To them it would make no sense that in some spiritual—as opposed to physical sense—Jesus' body was revivified.[13]

British scholar N. T. Wright has demonstrated that although there were various conceptions of the afterlife in first-century Judaism, "resurrection" had a particular meaning. Wright explains:

However wide that spectrum may have been and however many positions different Jews may have taken upon it, "resurrection" always denotes *one position within* that spectrum. "Resurrection" was not a term for "life after death" in general. It always meant reembodiment.[14]

Wright also demonstrates that "there is no evidence for Jews . . . using the word *resurrection* to denote something essentially nonconcrete."[15] If Jesus had been raised in an immaterial body, the disciples would not have described it as a *resurrection*.

Jesus himself completely demolished the spiritual-resurrection theory. When his startled disciples thought they were seeing a spirit, Jesus admonished them: "See My hands and My feet, that it is I Myself, touch Me and see; for a spirit does not have flesh and bones as you see that I have" (Luke 24:39, *NASB*). Later, Christ ate fish with his followers, further demonstrating his flesh and bone. Matthew records that when they met Jesus they took hold of his feet and worshiped him (see Matt. 28:9). You don't grab the legs of a spirit! Some have argued that Jesus temporarily manifested himself in a physical body so the disciples would recognize him. While this is a creative response, it is arbitrary, and what is worse, it would involve deception on Jesus' part, which is clearly inconsistent with his character and nature.

Paul also demolishes the spiritual-resurrection theory in his discussion of the resurrection body in 1 Corinthians 15:29-58. As a former Pharisee, Paul firmly believed in a physical resurrection. Basing his theology on the resurrection of Christ, Paul argues that we too will be physically raised someday. While resurrected bodies are physically different from our current bodies, the difference involves enhancement; they are nonetheless thoroughly physical.

Some have disagreed with this interpretation, basing their argument on Paul's claim in 1 Corinthians 15:44 that "it is sown a *natural* body, it is raised a *spiritual* body." "See," they claim, "Paul believed in an immaterial resurrection!" What this objection fails to consider is that the word *spiritual*, in this context, does not connote *immaterial*. We often refer to the Bible as a "spiritual" book, yet we clearly don't mean that it is immaterial!

Michael Licona did a nearly exhaustive historical investigation of the Greek terms translated "natural" and "spiritual" in 1 Corinthians 15:44 in ancient texts from the eighth century B.C. through the third century A.D. He concluded, "Although I did not look at all of the 846 occurrences, I viewed most. I failed to find a single reference where *psuchikon* [the word translated *natural* in 15:44] possessed a meaning of 'physical' or 'material.' "[16] It is simply false to say that Paul was contrasting a physical body with a nonphysical body. Stephen Davis warns:

> We should not be misled by Paul's use of the term "spiritual body." He is not using this term to signify a body "formed out of spirit" or made of "spiritual matter," whatever that might mean, but rather a body that has been glorified or transformed by God and is now fully dominated by the power of the Holy Spirit.[17]

A good example of this is when Paul speaks of "those who are spiritual" in 1 Corinthians 2:15. He clearly did not mean invisible, immaterial people with no physical body; he meant those who are guided by the power of the Holy Spirit.

Others object to a physical resurrection because in 1 Corinthians 15:50 Paul says that "flesh and blood cannot inherit the kingdom of God." "See," they say, "Jesus' body had to be immaterial so he could be in heaven!" Geisler responds to this assertion: "The phrase, 'flesh and blood,' in this context apparently means *mortal* flesh and blood, that is, a mere human being."[18] His interpretation is supported throughout Scripture. For example, in Matthew 16:17 Jesus says, "Blessed are you, Simon Barjona, because *flesh and blood* did not reveal this to you, but My Father who is in heaven" (*NASB*, emphasis added).

The spiritual-resurrection theory completely ignores our two principles of research. The facts of the case don't even begin to fit the theory, and they are forced into a preconceived conclusion about what happened.

The Hallucination Theory

One of the most prevalent theories for explaining away the resurrection of Christ is that the witnesses only thought they had seen the risen Jesus. In reality, they were hallucinating. By this theory, all the post-resurrection appearances of Christ can be dismissed.

The hallucination theory was the most popular naturalistic explanation for the resurrection of Christ until it fell out of scholarly favor about 100 years ago. Today, however, the hallucination theory has made a semi-comeback. Yet it probably suffers from more believability problems than any naturalistic theory.[19]

The word "hallucination" is an anglicized form of the Latin term *alucination*, which means "a wandering of the mind, idle talk, prating."[20] The American Psychiatric Association's official glossary defines a hallucination as "a false sensory perception in the absence of an actual external stimulus."[21] Medical and psychological observations agree that a hallucination is an apparent act of vision for which there is no corresponding external object. Hallucinations result from purely inner psychological causes—not from the presence of an actual external object. Hallucinations are also sometimes known as "subjective visions." In other words, hallucinating people see something that is really not there.

Why is the hallucination theory so weak? First, it contradicts various conditions that most psychiatrists and psychologists agree must be present to have a hallucination. Unless the appearances of Christ correspond to these essential conditions, referring to them as hallucinations is meaningless.

The first principle is that, generally, only particular kinds of people have hallucinations—usually paranoid or schizophrenic individuals, with schizophrenics being the most susceptible, patients nearing death or people under the influence of drugs. In the New Testament, however, we have all different kinds of people from different backgrounds, different ages, different occupations, in different moods and from different studies claiming to have seen the risen Jesus. Dr. Gary Habermas observes, "That these different individuals in each of these various circumstances would all be candidates for hallucinations really stretches the limits of credibility."[22]

Second, hallucinations are linked to an individual's subconscious and to his particular past experiences, making it very unlikely that two or more persons could have the same hallucination at the same time.

Christ appeared to many people, and descriptions of the appearances involve great detail, which psychologists regard as an indication that those individuals were in contact with reality.

Michael Licona has observed, "Hallucinations are like dreams. They are private occurrences. . . . You could not share an hallucination you were having with someone else any more than you could wake up your spouse in the middle of the night and ask them to join you in a dream you were having."[23]

If two people cannot initiate or sustain the same vision without any external object or reference, how could more than 500 do so at one time? It is not only contrary to this principle of hallucinations but also strongly militates against it.

Christ also ate with those to whom he appeared. And he not only exhibited his wounds, but he also encouraged a closer, tactile inspection of them. A hallucination does not sit down and have dinner with you and it cannot be scrutinized by various individuals at will. The many claimed hallucinations would constitute a far greater miracle than the miracle of the resurrection.

Clinical psychologist Gary Collins explains, "Hallucinations are individual occurrences. By their very nature only one person can see a given hallucination at a time. They certainly are not something which can be seen by a group of people . . . Since a hallucination exists only in the subjective, personal sense, it is obvious that others cannot witness it."[24]

Collins concludes that the evidence against the hallucination hypothesis is so convincing that skeptics "would have to go against much of the current psychiatric and psychological data about the nature of hallucinations."[25]

A third principle of hallucinations is that they usually are restricted as to when and where they can happen. In the New Testament situations, favorable circumstances are missing. And the appearances recorded are much more than simple glimpses. Time was involved. We have a record of 15 different appearances—and one of these was to more than 500 people.

Consider the variety of times and places in which these hallucinations would have occurred: One was an early morning appearance to the women at the tomb. Another was on the road to Emmaus, followed by a couple of private interviews in broad daylight. Another was by the lake early one morning. Indeed, the variety of times and places of Christ's appearances defies the hypothesis that they were mere hallucinations. Dr. Habermas concludes: "The accounts of men and women, hard-headed and soft-headed alike, all believing that they saw Jesus, both indoors and outdoors, provide an insurmountable barrier for hallucinations."[26]

A fourth principle is that hallucinations usually come to people with an anticipating spirit or hopeful expectancy that causes their wishes to become the stimulus of the hallucinatory illusion. The last thing these disillusioned and disappointed disciples expected was a resurrection. They thought Christ had been crucified, buried and that was the end of it.

The late theologian Paul Little made an acute observation about the anticipatory attitude of the alleged hallucinators:

> Mary came to the tomb on the first Easter Sunday morning with spices in her hands. Why? To anoint the dead body of the Lord she loved. She was obviously not expecting to find Him risen from the dead. In fact, when the Lord finally appeared to the disciples, they were frightened and thought they were seeing a ghost.[27]

Not only did the disciples not expect Jesus to be resurrected, they didn't believe it at first. Neither the women nor Peter nor Thomas nor the 11 believed that Jesus had been resurrected when they first heard. Far from being anticipatory, they were terrified. They thought he was a ghost, and he had to show his wounds or eat something to prove to them that he was not.

A fifth principle is that hallucinations are inner phenomena. Peter Kreeft and Ronald Tacelli note that "hallucinations come from within, from what we already know, at least unconsciously."[28] If that is true, then the disciples never would have hallucinated Jesus' resurrection. N. T. Wright points out that the resurrection of Jesus involved two radically new concepts for Judaism: (1) It was a resurrection of an individual alone, not of the whole group; and (2) it was during the course of history, not at the end times.[29] William Lane Craig eloquently states that even if the disciples did hallucinate:

[T]hey would never have concluded that He had been raised from the dead, an idea that ran contrary to Jewish concepts of the resurrection; rather they would have concluded that God had translated Him into heaven, from where He appeared to them, and therefore the tomb was empty. The fact that the disciples proclaimed not the translation of Jesus, as with Enoch and Elijah, but—contrary to all Jewish concepts—the resurrection of Jesus, proves that the origin of the disciples' belief in Jesus' resurrection cannot be explained as their conclusion from the empty tomb and visions.[30]

In chapter six of his excellent book *Cross Examined*, Michael Licona studies the effects of hallucinations on Navy Seals, the Special Forces of the U.S. Navy. Navy Seal training is extremely difficult. At the beginning of their training they have "Hell Week," where the trainees are forced to run night and day for basically an entire week. They are under constant physical and emotional stress. They get only three to five hours of sleep the entire week.

During Hell Week many of the trainees have brief hallucinations. One guy "saw" a train coming at him, another thought he was paddling into a clay wall and another believed that an octopus came up out of the water and waved at him! While many of them hallucinated, they all had their own individual experiences. And a few moments after the experience, they all realized that they had hallucinated. None of their experiences caused them to have new beliefs. Hallucinations simply do not cause new beliefs in sane, rational people.

Finally, hallucinations have no spectrum of reality. They have no objective reality whatsoever. The hallucination theory in no way accounts for the empty tomb, the broken seal, the guard units and, especially, the subsequent actions of the high priests. To account for these facts, another naturalistic theory must be posited alongside the hallucination.[31]

Considering all the facts about hallucinations, it is difficult to believe that this phenomenon was the impetus for the disciples' belief in the resurrected Jesus. Licona concludes, "It appears to me that it wasn't [the disciples'] faith which led to the appearances. It was the appearances which led to their faith. . . . Neither hallucinations nor delusions explain the empty tomb, which is an historical fact."[32]

The Muslim Substitution Theory

The Qur'an claims that Jesus was not crucified on the cross. Rather than allowing Jesus, who was one of Allah's servants, to be crucified, Allah is said to have respected his prophet and saved him by crucifying a bystander who was made to appear to be Jesus. This is known as the "substitution theory" (Surah 4:157). Typically, Judas Iscariot or Simon of Cyrene is understood to be the substitute for Jesus. Instead of being crucified, Jesus ascended to heaven, where he remains alive until his return to earth before the end of time.

Historical Problems with the Substitution Theory

The Muslim substitution theory has serious historical problems. First, the Old Testament predicted the Messiah's death (see Isa. 53:5-10; Ps. 22:16; Dan. 9:26; Zech. 12:10), and in dying Jesus fulfilled these prophecies (see Matt. 4:14; 5:17-18; 8:17; John 4:25-26; 5:39). There are no predictions in the Old Testament that someone would be substituted for the Messiah; *all* references indicate that he would die personally.

Second, Jesus predicted his own death many times throughout his ministry (see John 2:19-21; Matt. 12:40; Mark 8:31). He never predicted that someone else would be substituted in his place. All of the predictions for Jesus' resurrection in both the Old and New Testaments are based on the fact that he would personally die (see Ps. 16:10; Isa. 26:19; Dan. 12:2; Matt. 12:40). Obviously Jesus could not have been resurrected if someone else had died in his place. There are virtually no scholars today—that are not already committed to Islamic theology—who accept the substitution theory.[33]

Moral Problems with the Substitution Theory

The Muslim claim that someone was substituted for Jesus is vulnerable to three moral critiques. First, why would God have allowed an innocent bystander to be tortured and victimized? If God intended to preserve Jesus' life by raising him to heaven, then why should anyone have been crucified at all? Second, would God not have considered Jesus' family and friends? Jesus' mother Mary, his disciple John, and many of his other friends were present at the crucifixion (see John 19:25). If the substitute was made to look like Jesus, then surely they would have all believed it was actually Jesus on the cross. Why would God put them through the anguish of watching him be tortured and killed if he was to be spared such suffering? Why would God not have allowed Jesus' mother Mary—who is revered in Islam—to be in on the illusion? Third, if the person who was crucified was made to look like Jesus, then can we blame the disciples for believing it truly was him? Did they found the entire Christian faith on a fraud? If the substitution theory were true, then God would be directly responsible for one of the greatest deceptions in history.

In light of these three critiques, Islam expert John Gilchrist has concluded:

> The event [the substitution of someone for Jesus] served no apparent purpose other than to victimize an innocent man, traumatize the followers of Jesus, and result in the formation of a religion based on a fallacy—all of Allah's own scheming and devising. Highly unlikely indeed![34]

In the book *Paul Meets Muhammad*, Michael Licona raises another dilemma for the Muslim substitution theory. In Mark 12:1-11 Jesus tells the parable of the landlord who leases his vineyard to farmers. There is near unanimous agreement among scholars—including skeptical scholars—that Jesus told this parable, in which he predicts his violent death. Licona explains:

> Since Jesus predicted his violent death and Muhammad regards him as a prophet, if Jesus did not die a violent death, that makes him a false prophet, a fact that would be anathema to both Christians and Muslims. The argument looks like this:
>
> 1. Jesus predicted his violent death.
> 2. If Jesus died a violent death, the Qur'an is wrong, since it claims he escaped death by crucifixion.

3. If Jesus did not die a violent death, the Qur'an is again wrong, since it regards Jesus as a prophet, and if he did not die as he predicted, he would be a false prophet.

Either way, the Qur'an is wrong.[35]

In this chapter we have explored the most prominent attempts at explaining the facts of the resurrection by either mythic or natural means. In the process we have pointed out the basic flaws of the alternate theories and shown how they do not undermine the credibility of the resurrection as the most consistent and reasonable interpretation of the facts. In the next chapter, we will explore additional theories and show how they too fail to fit the principles set down for determining historical truth.

EXPLODING THE EMPTY-TOMB THEORIES

Quite obviously, the tomb was empty on the Sunday morning after Christ's crucifixion, death and burial. The historical evidence is too strong to deny.

As we have said before, all that was needed to show that Jesus did not resurrect was for the authorities to produce his body. The council and high priests were skillful dialecticians and practical politicians. They were brilliant in their handling of Pilate. If Christ's disciples had stolen his body, it would have been easy for these expert manipulators with strings connected to the halls of power to have squeezed the information from them. If the body of Christ was still in the tomb when Christ's followers began preaching the resurrection, all the Jewish authorities had to do was exhume it and the disciples would have been silenced forever. Instead, these Jewish authorities forcibly brought the apostles before their council and threatened them with death if they did not stop proclaiming a risen Christ (see Acts 5:17-42).

Dr. Bill White was formerly in charge of the Garden Tomb in Jerusalem, which many believe to be Jesus' burial place. White observed:

The Jewish hierarchy was furious at the apostles' preaching of the resurrection. They did all in their power to keep it from spreading, but their efforts were unavailing. If the body of Jesus still lay in the tomb where Joseph of Arimathea had placed it, what more simple and damaging refutation of the Apostles' claim than to show the populace the grave of Jesus, open it, and exhume the crucified body of this self-styled Messiah.[1]

It is significant that the thousands of early converts to Christianity—made so through the preaching of the resurrection—were all Jewish, either who lived in Jerusalem or visited there. In becoming a follower of Christ, they were accepting a revolutionary teaching that could have been easily disproved by a simple five-minute walk to a garden just beyond the city walls. Rather than disbelieving the resurrection, they eagerly spread the message far and wide. Each convert was a proof of the empty tomb, as opponents could have stopped Christianity dead in its tracks by simply displaying the body of Jesus.

Dr. Paul Maier observes from an historical perspective:

> If all the evidence is weighed carefully and fairly, it is indeed justifiable, according to the canons of historical research, to conclude that the tomb of Joseph of Arimathea, in which Jesus was buried, was actually empty on the morning of the first Easter. And no shred of evidence has yet been discovered in literary sources, epigraphy, or archaeology that would disprove this statement.[2]

Those who are dead set against believing in the resurrection have found various ways of dealing with the hard fact of the empty tomb. In this chapter we will explore those theories and show why they do not work. As we begin our examination, let's remember the two cardinal principles of historical investigation: (1) Any explanation needs to take into account and fit all the facts, and (2) one must not force the evidence to fit a preconceived conclusion but rather let the facts speak for themselves.

The Conspiracy Theory: The Body Was Stolen by Disciples

The first and one of the most prominent empty-tomb theories is that the followers of Jesus stole his body and fabricated the resurrection story. This theory was even noted by Matthew (see 28:11-15). As we have seen, the guards at the tomb went to the Jewish high priest to report what happened at the tomb. The high priest bribed the Roman guards and told them to spread the lie that the disciples had stolen the body of Jesus. In return, the high priest protected the guards by smoothing things over with Pilate.

Justin Martyr, in his *Dialogue Against Trypho #108* (A.D. 130), speaks of the story still being told: "One Jesus, a Galilean deceiver, whom we crucified; but his disciples stole him by night from the tomb, where he was lain when unfastened from the cross, and now deceive men by asserting that he has risen from the dead and ascended to heaven."[3]

This conspiracy theory was first refuted by the great historian Eusebius in his *Demonstratio Evangelica* (A.D. 314-318). Eusebius argues that it is inconceivable that such a well-planned and thought-out conspiracy could ever succeed. Eusebius gives a satirical speech that he imagines to have been delivered by the disciples in efforts to motivate each other:

> Let us band together to invent all the miracles and resurrection appearances which we never saw and let us carry the sham even to death! Why not die for nothing? Why dislike torture and whipping inflicted for no good reason? Let us go out to all nations and overthrow their institutions and denounce their gods! And even if we don't convince anybody, at least we'll have the satisfaction of drawing down on ourselves the punishment for our own deceit.[4]

Eusebius's conclusion is that if we distrust the disciples, then we must distrust all writers of history!

The news media continually show us that conspiracies eventually unravel. Either the opponents uncover the truth or someone on the inside slips or gives in to pressure. Chuck Colson, Special Counsel to President Nixon during the Watergate scandal, knows full well how difficult it is to keep a conspiracy together. Colson explains, "I know how impossible it is for a group of people, even some of the most powerful in the world, to maintain a lie. The Watergate cover-up lasted only a few weeks before the first conspirator broke and turned state's evidence."[5] As soon as pressure mounted and the conspirators realized they could be punished, they broke. Yet not even one of the disciples, even though they all faced horrendous persecution and even death, renounced his belief in the resurrection of Jesus.

Dr. Simon Greenleaf, a famous Harvard legal authority, argues conclusively that the apostles would have broken under pressure if Jesus Christ had not been raised from the dead.[6]

Bible expositor Alexander Maclaren wrote:

> There is only one explanation . . . Jesus Christ had risen from the dead. That drew them [the disciples] together once more. You cannot build a church on a dead Christ; and of all the proofs of the Resurrection, I take it that there is none that is harder for an unbeliever to account for, in harmony with his hypothesis, than the simple fact that Christ's disciples held together after he was dead, and presented a united front to the world.[7]

Who Would Die for a Lie?

Each of the disciples, except John, died a martyr's death. They were persecuted because they tenaciously clung to their beliefs and statements. As Paul Little wrote, "Men will die for what they *believe* to be true, though it may actually be false. They do not, however, die for what they *know* is a lie."[8] If the disciples had stolen the body of Jesus, they would have known that their resurrection claim was false. Nevertheless, they never wavered in their commitment to the risen Jesus. Not only did they die for this "lie," but as a testimony to the strength of their convictions, they placed the resurrection of Jesus as the centerpiece of their preaching.

U.S. Supreme Court Justice Antonin Scalia points out how crazy it is to hold the theft/conspiracy theory. Speaking with a twinge of sarcastic humor, he said, "The wise do not believe in the resurrection of the dead. It is really quite absurd. So everything from the Easter morning to the Ascension had to be made up by the groveling enthusiasts as part of their plan to get themselves martyred."[9] If the resurrection was a lie, it seems inconceivable that no disciple would recant it in the face of such harsh suffering. Yet if it was true, as the disciples firmly believed, then they had all the motivation in the world to go to their graves proclaiming the resurrection of their Lord, Jesus Christ.

Dr. Moreland notes, "They faced hardship, ridicule, hostility, and martyrs' deaths. In light of all this, they could have never sustained such unwavering motivation if they knew what they were preaching was a lie."[10]

Too Honorable for Deception

Another significant problem with the theft/conspiracy theory is that this action would be contrary to the disciples' known ethics. They were men of high moral standing and honor. The historian Edward Gibbon, in his analysis of the decline and fall of the Roman Empire, points out the "purer but austere morality of the first Christians"[11] as one of the five reasons for the rapid success of Christianity.

Proponents of the conspiracy theory would have to allege that the followers of Christ foisted a lie upon the people, which would be utterly contrary to what their Master taught. The British legal authority J. N. D. Anderson comments that this theory "would run totally contrary to all we know of the disciples: their ethical teaching, the quality of their lives, their steadfastness in suffering and persecution. Nor would it begin to explain their dramatic transformation from dejected and dispirited escapists into witnesses whom no opposition could muzzle."[12]

Philosopher and theologian John Stott concludes that the conspiracy theory "simply does not ring true. It is so unlikely as to be virtually impossible. If anything is clear from the Gospels and Acts, it is that the apostles were sincere. They may have been deceived, if you like, but they were not deceivers. Hypocrites and martyrs are not made of the same stuff."[13]

The Guards Prevented Theft

Even if the disciples did want to steal the body, they would have been unable to carry out their scheme because of the Roman guard. The guard had been placed for the very purpose of preventing the theft of the corpse. The existence of the guard presents three key problems to the claim that the disciples stole the body of Jesus:

1. In light of the remarkable discipline of the Roman Army, which we have mentioned before, it is ludicrous to believe

that the guards actually fell asleep on duty. Therefore, they would have had no problem stopping the disciples.

2. If the Roman guard had fallen asleep on duty, how would they have known that it was the disciples who stole the body?

3. It is preposterous to believe that the disciples could sneak by the guards, break the seal, roll away the one-and-a-half to two-ton rock and sneak away with the body—all while the guards rested peacefully!

A further problem for the theft/conspiracy theory is that it cannot account for the appearances of Christ to others in addition to the disciples. How can the appearances to skeptics such as James, Thomas and Paul be accounted for? What about the 500? And finally, why would the disciples steal the body, yet leave the grave clothes behind? Why would they strip the body first?

The Authorities Stole the Body

Another stolen-body theory is that the Roman or Jewish authorities moved the body from the tomb of Joseph of Arimathea to another tomb for safekeeping. Thus, the disciples found the tomb empty and were convinced Jesus had risen.

Does Not Square with the Facts

This theory sounds possible until one stops to ask: Why would the authorities do the very thing that caused all their problems? If the Jewish or Roman authorities had moved the body, then why did they accuse the disciples of stealing it? Such a charge would make no sense. Why would the soldiers have reported the body missing? Why the bribe to cover up what the soldiers saw? If the authorities had custody of the body, they would have happily produced it to stop the resurrection movement.

When the disciples began to preach the resurrection, why wouldn't the authorities say, "That's nonsense! We gave the orders to move the body." Why wouldn't they just take the doubters to the new resting place and settle things once and for all?

The highly respected scholar Raymond Brown concludes:

> In all this the clear and unanimous Gospel presentation is that Jesus is given a distinguishable burial in a place that could be remembered. His was not the type of common burial in which corpses could be confused; nor was he buried and then reburied, so that the women went to the wrong tomb on Easter and that is why they found it empty.[14]

Brown says that the burial/reburial thesis finds "no support in the Gospel text or in primitive Christian tradition."[15]

Concerning the whereabouts of the body, one might conclude that *the silence of the Jews speaks louder than the voice of the Christians.* Dr. John Warwick Montgomery explains: "It passes credulity that the early Christians could have manufactured such a tale, then preached it among those who might easily have refuted it simply by producing the body."[16]

The Resuscitation Theory: Jesus Swooned and Revived

While the swoon theory has been adequately refuted by scholars, it continues to appear in popular literature, on the Internet and on college campuses. In fact, an influential Muslim sect known as the *Ahmadiyas* holds this view.

This theory was first proposed by H. E. G. Paulus in his *Das Leben Jesu* (1828), but it has appeared in such recent publications as Hugh Schonfield's *The Passover Plot* (1965), Donovan Joyce's *The Jesus Scroll* (1972) and more recently in Barbara Thiering's *Jesus and the Riddle of the Dead Sea Scrolls* (1992).

The swoon theory asserts that Jesus did not really die on the cross. According to the theory, he was nailed to the cross and suffered from shock, pain and loss of blood. But instead of dying, he merely fainted (swooned) from exhaustion. He was thought to be dead because medical knowledge was not at that time advanced enough to distinguish between a swoon and death. Thus Jesus was mistakenly buried alive. The cold sepulcher in which he was placed revived him. His disciples, who ignorantly believed he had truly died, couldn't believe mere resuscitation revived him, so they insisted it was a resurrection from the dead. Some proponents of this theory, such as Hugh Schonfield, have suggested that Jesus even planned this! In our view, such a resuscitation would be more miraculous than the resurrection itself.

Consider first all that Jesus had been through: (1) He went through six trials—three Roman and three Jewish; (2) was beaten to bloody shreds by the Roman flagrum; (3) was so weak he couldn't carry his own patibulum to the crucifixion site; (4) had a crown of thorns thrust into his scalp; (5) had spikes driven through his hands and feet and hung bleeding for six hours; (6) the Romans thrust a spear deep into his side; (7) he was encased in wrapped linen and 100-plus pounds of spices—and somehow breathed through it all; (8) a large stone was lodged against his tomb's entrance; (9) a Roman guard was stationed outside; and (10) a seal was placed across the entrance.

Then, according to the swoon theory, an incredible thing happened. The cool damp air inside the tomb somehow revived and energized him. He split out of his garments, single-handedly pushed the stone away, either fought off the guards or somehow broke the seal and moved the stone without their noticing it, walked naked and barefoot on badly wounded feet through a city stirring in the morning, and appeared to his disciples as the Lord of life.

Nineteenth-century theologian David Strauss was one of the most bitter of all opponents of the supernatural elements in the Gospels and a man whose works did much to destroy faith in Christ. This man, despite all of his vicious criticisms and firm denials of anything involving the miraculous, said this about the theory that Jesus revived from a swoon:

> It is impossible that a being who has been stolen half-dead out of the sepulcher, who crept about weak and ill, wanting medical treatment; who required bandaging, strengthening and indulgence, and who still at least yielded to his sufferings, could have given to the disciples the impression that he was a Conqueror over death and the grave, the Prince of Life, an impression which

lay at the bottom of their future ministry. Such a resuscitation could only have weakened the impression which He had made upon them in life and in death, at the most could only have given it an elegiac voice, but could by no possibility have changed their sorrow into enthusiasm, have elevated their reverence into worship.[17]

Theologian Albert Schweitzer said that Strauss's critique delivered a "death blow" to the swoon theory forever.[18]

The Certainty of Jesus' Death

Probably the most significant problem for this theory is that it greatly underestimates the severity of Jesus' wounds and the evidence for his death. Raymond Brown noted:

> Except for the romantic few who think that Jesus did not die on the cross but woke up in the tomb and ran off to India with Mary Magdalene, most scholars accept the uniform testimony of the Gospels that Jesus died during the Judean prefecture of Pontius Pilate, which is usually dated between A.D. 26 and 36.[19]

Here are some of the facts that have lead scholars to believe that Jesus died during his crucifixion: (1) The nature of his injuries—his whipping, beating, lack of sleep, crown of thorns and his collapse on the way to his crucifixion while carrying the cross—indicate that his ordeal must have killed him. (2) The nature of crucifixion virtually guarantees death. (3) The piercing of Jesus' side, from which came "blood and water" (John 19:34), is medical proof that Jesus had already died. (4) Jesus said he was in the act of dying while on the cross: "Father, into your hands I commit my spirit" (Luke 23:46). John renders that he "gave up his spirit" (John 19:30). (5) The Roman soldiers, who were trained killers, were charged to make sure that he died. Even though it was customary for soldiers to break the legs of the victims to speed death, they did not even have to break the legs of Jesus, for their examination determined that he was already dead (see John 19:33). (6) Pilate summoned the centurion to make sure Jesus had actually died before giving the body to Joseph for burial (see Mark 15:44-45). (7) Jesus' body was wrapped in about 100-plus pounds of cloth and spices and placed in a sealed tomb for three days (see John 19:39-40; Matt. 27:60). If Jesus had not died from his previous torture, he would have died in the tomb from lack of food, water and medical treatment. (8) Medical experts who have studied the circumstances surrounding the end of Jesus' life have concluded that he actually died on the cross. (9) Non-Christian historians from the first and second centuries, such as Tacitus and Josephus, recorded the death of Jesus of Nazareth. (10) The earliest Christian writers after the time of Christ, such as Polycarp and Ignatius, verify his death by crucifixion on the cross as well.

Not only does historical evidence find the swoon theory lacking in credibility, its support of Jesus' crucifixion and death is, as we have seen, overwhelming. Even the atheist German scholar Gerd Ludemann noted, "The fact of the death of Jesus as a consequence of crucifixion is indisputable, despite hypotheses of a pseudo-death or a deception which are sometimes put forward."[20] Liberal scholar Marcus Borg concluded, "The most certain fact about the historical Jesus is his execution as a political rebel."[21]

Was Jesus a Deceiver?

Another significant problem for the swoon theory is that it makes Jesus into a deceiver. William Lane Craig explains:

> The necessary implication of the theory is that Jesus was a charlatan who tricked the disciples into believing that He had been raised from the dead. Such a portrait of Jesus is a figment of the imagination. Jesus was one of the world's great moral teachers, a deeply religious man, if nothing else. It is impossible to cast Him in the role of a hoaxer.[22]

Even Hugh Schonfield, author of *The Passover Plot*, admits, "We are nowhere claiming . . . that [his rendition of the swoon theory] represents what actually happened."[23] Yet he offered the theory as a possibility. Dr.

Samuel Sandmen of the Hebrew Union College best summarized Schonfield's creation: "Schonfield's imaginative reconstruction is devoid of a scintilla of proof. . . . In my view, this book should be dismissed as the mere curiosity it is."[24] Dr. Gary Habermas says the swoon theory as presented in *The Jesus Scroll* "contains an even more incredible string of improbabilities than Schonfield's."[25] Emory University professor Luke Timothy Johnson calls Barbara Thierings's version of the swoon theory "the purest poppycock, the product of fevered imagination rather than careful analysis."[26]

In response to the various swoon theories put forward, professor David Stanley says, "In general, most of these stories belong to sensational journalism."[27] To claim that Jesus survived the rigors of crucifixion and then convinced his disciples that he was Lord of life—as the swoon theory suggests—would be a greater miracle than the resurrection itself.

What Theory Best Fits the Facts?

The most prominent empty-tomb theories have all been carefully examined in light of the elaborate precautions taken at the tomb by the Roman and Jewish authorities. The question remains: What theory best fits *all* the facts?

Dr. Gregory Boyd sums it up:

> The simplest explanation, and the only one that accounts for all the data, is to admit that Jesus' tomb was empty and that a number of his disciples believed that they saw him in a postmortem state shortly after his death. If this much is not conceded, observers have to necessarily get very speculative and complex in their explanations. For they can no longer build their theory *upon* the available data: they must rather build their theory *around* the available data. And that, we have seen, is illegitimate as a historical methodology and is, in any case, exceedingly difficult to do.[28]

British scholar N. T. Wright concludes:

We are left with the secure historical conclusion: the tomb was empty, and various "meetings" took place not only between Jesus and his followers (including at least one initial skeptic) but also, in at least one case (that of Paul; possibly, too, that of James), between Jesus and people who had not been among his followers. I regard this conclusion as coming in the same sort of category, of historical probability so high as to be virtually certain, as the death of Augustus in AD 14 or the fall of Jerusalem in AD 70.[29]

Only one conclusion takes into account all the facts and does not adjust them to preconceived notions. It is the conclusion that Christ is in fact risen—a supernatural act of God in history.

THE CIRCUMSTANTIAL EVIDENCE

There is even further evidence of Christ's bodily resurrection. It is called circumstantial evidence. "Direct evidence" deals with the fact in issue, such as, "Did Christ rise from the dead?" *The Random House Dictionary of the English Language* defines the meaning of "circumstantial evidence" as "proof of facts offered as evidence from which other facts are to be inferred."

Direct Evidence vs. Circumstantial Evidence

In a trial for robbery, the testimony of a witness who saw the man pull out a gun and shoot the clerk is direct evidence. It deals directly with the fact. But evidence that (1) the man was seen entering the store immediately before the shooting; (2) a sales slip showing he had purchased the gun; (3) his fingerprints on the gun and the cash register; and (4) a ballistics report showing the bullet came from his gun—are all circumstantial evidence. They do not deal directly with the firing of the gun that shot the clerk, but rather with facts that can be used to infer that the defendant shot the clerk.

The inability of any single piece of circumstantial evidence to prove an ultimate fact does not make that evidence less valuable. Several pieces of circumstantial evidence can add up to a compelling case. As C. T. McCormick points out in his *Handbook of the Law of Evidence*, a brick is not a wall but several bricks can make a wall. Small pieces of evidence do add up to a substantial proof.[1]

In a court of law, circumstantial evidence is just as valuable as direct evidence. And often, strong circumstantial evidence is more trustworthy than direct evidence because it cannot be as easily fabricated. In fact some defendants have been convicted of first-degree murder on circumstantial evidence alone.[2]

In this chapter we will briefly consider six areas of circumstantial evidence that point to the fact of the resurrection because nothing else can explain them.

Circumstantial Evidence Number 1: The Church

The early success and continued existence of the Christian church is an historical phenomenon that must be explained. Within a brief period of time after Jesus' death, the Christian faith spread rapidly throughout Palestine and then beyond until it finally permeated the entire Roman Empire. Its origin can be traced directly back to the city of Jerusalem in Palestine about A.D. 30. It took root and thrived in the very city where Jesus was crucified and buried.

Do you believe for a moment that the early church could have survived for a week in its hostile surroundings if Jesus Christ had not been raised from the dead? The resurrection of the one on whom the church was founded was preached within a few minutes' walk to Joseph's tomb. As a result of the first sermon, in which Peter asserted that Christ had risen, 3,000 people believed (see Acts 2:41). Shortly thereafter, 5,000 more believed. Could all these converts have been made if Jesus had not been raised from the dead?

Dr. J. N. D. Anderson concludes from the evidence that the church owed its origin to the resurrection of Jesus Christ from the dead. He asks, "Is there really any other theory that fits the facts?"[3]

Dr. Daniel Fuller observes that "to try to explain this [the church] without reference to the resurrection is as hopeless as trying to explain Roman history without reference to Julius Caesar."[4]

Circumstantial Evidence Number 2: Sunday Worship

Fact number two is the sociological phenomenon of the Christian Sunday. The decision to change "the day of worship" from the Jewish Sabbath (Saturday) to the first day of the week (Sunday) is probably one of the most significant decisions ever made by a group of people in history. This is especially true when one considers the consequences the Jews believed would result if they were wrong.

The early Christians were devout Jews who were fanatical in their observance of the Sabbath. The Jews feared breaking the Sabbath, believing they would incur the wrath of God if they violated the strict laws concerning its observance. Yet something happened that caused these Jewish men and women to turn their backs on all their years of religious training and tradition.

They changed their day of worship to Sunday in honor of the anniversary of the resurrection of Jesus Christ. Can you think of any other historical event that is celebrated 52 times a year? The most rational explanation for this phenomenon is that Jesus appeared personally to people after his resurrection, convincing them of the truth of it.

Circumstantial Evidence Number 3: Baptism

Believers' baptism dates back to the early church. It is a public testimony by a new believer of faith in Jesus Christ and symbolizes that at the moment of salvation, he or she dies with Christ in the crucifixion (going into the water as if buried) and is raised with him in newness of life (coming out of the water as Jesus came from the grave) through the resurrection.

This sacrament of baptism finds its meaning in the fact of the historical resurrection of Jesus Christ. Dr. J. P. Moreland observes, "The practice of baptism in the early church was probably an adaptation of proselyte baptism practiced in Judaism. The change in meaning of the act of baptism by the church points to the Resurrection as a necessary precondition for such a change."[5]

Circumstantial Evidence Number 4: Communion

Communion is another sacrament in which the cup and bread symbolize Christ's death on the cross and the shedding of his blood for the sins of mankind. When believers participate in communion, they acknowledge with great joy that Christ died for them personally. Dr. Moreland explains the significance of communion:

> What's odd is that these early followers of Jesus didn't get together to celebrate his teachings or how wonderful he was. They came together regularly to have a celebration meal for one

reason: to remember that Jesus had been publicly slaughtered in a grotesque and humiliating way.

Think about this in modern terms. If a group of people loved John F. Kennedy, they might meet regularly to remember his confrontation with Russia, his promotion of civil rights, and his charismatic personality. But they're not going to celebrate the fact that Lee Harvey Oswald murdered him![6]

How could great joy accompany the acknowledgment of the horrifying death of the founder of one's religion unless that death was followed by a subsequent resurrection that offers personal redemption? The celebration of communion only makes sense on the basis of conviction that Jesus truly arose from the dead on the third day after his death, as the Scriptures record.

Circumstantial Evidence Number 5: Changed Social Structure

The Jews have survived through the ages unlike any other people in history. In spite of national calamity, persecution and massive attempts at genocide, the Jews still exist and thrive as a distinct people group today. Most other groups who lived before the time of Jesus—such as the Babylonians, Assyrians, Jebusites and Moabites—have gone out of existence. Some were crushed militarily while others intermarried and lost their sense of national distinctiveness. Dr. Moreland explains:

Why didn't that happen to the Jews? Because the things that made the Jews, Jews—the social structures that gave them their national identity—were unbelievably important to them. The Jews would pass these structures down to their children, celebrate them in synagogue meetings every Sabbath, and reinforce them with their rituals, because they knew if they didn't, there soon would be no Jews left. They would be assimilated into the cultures that captured them.

And there's another reason why these social institutions were so important: they believed these institutions were entrusted to them by God. They believed that to abandon these institutions would be to risk their souls being damned to hell after death.

Now a rabbi named Jesus appears from a lower-class region. He teaches for three years, gathers a following of lower- and middle-class people, gets in trouble with the authorities, and gets crucified along with thirty thousand other Jewish men who are executed during this time period.

But five weeks after he's crucified, over ten thousand Jews are following him and claiming that he is the initiator of a new religion. And get this: they're willing to give up or alter . . . the social institutions that they have been taught since childhood [to] have such importance both sociologically and theologically.[7]

Dr. Barry Leventhal, academic dean and professor at Southern Evangelical Seminary, demonstrates four of the radical social changes that the early Jewish converts to Christianity gave up to follow Jesus.[8] First, the new believers in Christ never offered another animal sacrifice after the cross, as Christ's death was sufficient to atone for all sin (see John 19:30; Heb. 10:26-31). Second, the new believers felt free to disregard certain ceremonial aspects of the Mosaic Law, which was the key element that identified them as God's chosen people (see Acts 15:14-29; Eph. 2:11-22). Third, while the new believers remained monotheistic, they also became Trinitarian. Rather than merely believing in God as one person, they came to believe that there is one God simultaneously existing in three persons (see Matt. 28:19). Fourth, the Jewish community was expecting a political and military deliverer, not a suffering Messiah. Yet, after Christ's resurrection, the early converts understood that the Scriptures taught that the Messiah must come first and suffer for the sins of the people before entering into glory (see Luke 24:25-27,44-48).

In light of this circumstantial evidence, Dr. Levanthal concludes:

Does the supporting evidence cited above point to the unique space-time resurrection of Yeshua the Messiah? Whatever our response, it cannot be denied that the early messianic community thought so—and many of them gave their lives rather than deny any part of it. The fact of his resurrection was the hope of their own resurrection. Jesus' impact as the resurrected Messiah seems as certain as any fact can be.[9]

The fact that these strict, law-observing Jews were willing to change their social and religious structure strongly indicates a firm belief that Jesus truly was resurrected from the dead, giving them a rationale for overcoming their fear of displeasing God by abandoning long-observed laws and traditions in favor of the worship practices of the Christian religion.

Circumstantial Evidence Number 6: Changed Lives

The radically changed lives of those early Christian believers are among the most telling testimonies to the fact of the resurrection. One of the most dramatic changes was their willingness to go everywhere proclaiming the message of the risen Christ. We must ask, what could have motivated such a change?

Had there been visible benefits accruing to them from their efforts—such as prestige, wealth or increased social status—we might logically account for their actions. As a reward, however, for their wholehearted and total allegiance to this risen Christ, these early Christians were beaten, stoned to death, thrown to the lions, tortured, crucified and subjected to every conceivable method of stopping them from talking. Yet they were the most peaceful of men and women, who continually demonstrated love and never forced their beliefs on anyone. Rather they laid down their very lives as the ultimate proof of their complete confidence in the truth of their message.

One evidence of changed lives was in the disciples themselves. When the authorities captured Jesus in the Garden of Gethsemane, the Bible tells us that "all the disciples deserted him and fled" (Matt. 26:56; see Mark 14:50). During Christ's trial, Peter went out and three times denied that he even knew Jesus (see John 18:15-27; Mark 14:66-72). After Christ was crucified, the fearful disciples hid themselves in an upper room and locked the doors (see John 20:19). These disciples were also skeptical when they first heard about the empty tomb. One of them refused to believe until he personally touched Jesus' wounds. And two disciples on the road to Emmaus doubted while they personally talked to Jesus!

But within days something happened to utterly change this group of cowardly followers into a bold band of enthusiasts who were willing to face a life of suffering for the cause of Christ. What happened? As we've said earlier, the most logical explanation is that after Jesus' resurrection "He appeared to Cephas [Peter], then to the twelve. After that He appeared to more than five hundred brethren at one time, most of whom remain until now, but some have fallen asleep; then He appeared to James, then to all the apostles" (1 Cor. 15:5-7, *NASB*).

The Resurrection Explains All the Facts

Harvard law professor Simon Greenleaf, who lectured for years on how to break down testimony and determine whether a witness is lying, concludes:

> The annals of military warfare afford scarcely an example of the like heroic constancy, patience, and unblenching courage. They had every possible motive to review carefully the grounds of their faith, and the evidences of the great facts and truths which they asserted. . . . It was therefore impossible that they could have persisted in affirming the truths they have narrated, had not Jesus actually risen from the dead, and had they not known this fact as certainly as they knew any other fact.[10]

Dr. George Eldon Ladd, writing of the historical significance of the change in the apostles, says:

> The historian must also admit that historical criticism has not yet found an adequate historical explanation for these facts; that for the historian the transformation in the disciples is an unsolved problem. He must also admit that the view that Jesus actually arose from the dead would explain all the facts.[11]

Each point in this chapter provides you with another brick that eventually will build a wall of truth so solid that you will find the resurrection to be the most plausible explanation of all the facts recorded in the New Testament and confirmed by secular history. Believers in Jesus Christ today can have the complete confidence, as did those first Christians, that their faith is based, not on myth or legend, but on the solid historical fact of the empty tomb and the risen Christ.

ШHAT'S NEXT?

How do you evaluate the historical evidence for the resurrection of Jesus Christ presented in this book? What is your decision about the documented fact of Christ's empty tomb? *What do you think of Christ?*

When I (Josh) was confronted with the overwhelming evidence for Christ's resurrection, I had to ask the logical question, "What difference does it make in my life whether or not I believe Christ died on the cross for my sins and rose again?"

In order to answer this question, you must consider the words of Jesus spoken to his disciples: "I am the way, the truth, and the life. No one can come to the Father except through me" (John 14:6). The apostle Peter underscored his Master's bold statement when he said, "Jesus is the [Messiah]. . . . There is salvation in no one else! There is no other name in all of heaven for people to call on to save them" (Acts 4:11-12).

Jesus claims to be the only means to a relationship with God the Father. On the basis of the overwhelming evidence for Christ's resurrection, and considering that Jesus offers forgiveness of sin and an eternal relationship with God, who would be so foolhardy as to reject him?

Christ is alive! He is living today! The most logical response to this reality is to trust Jesus Christ with your life and experience the personal transformation that only he can affect.

The Power of Christ

No matter what the critics may say, the Christ of the New Testament can change lives. Millions of people from all backgrounds, all nationalities, all races and all professions spanning more than 20 centuries are witnesses to the sin-breaking power of God's forgiveness through Jesus Christ. E. Y. Mullins writes:

> A redeemed drunkard, with vivid memory of past hopeless struggles and new sense of power through Christ, was replying to the charge that his religion was a delusion. He said: "Thank God for the delusion; it has put clothes on my children and shoes on their feet and bread in their mouths. It has made a man of me and it has put joy and peace in my home, which had been hell. If this is a delusion, may God send it to the slaves of drink everywhere, for their slavery is an awful reality.[1]

I am also a walking testimony that the Bible is true and that Jesus Christ was raised from the dead and lives today. My life was changed by the power of Christ. As a result, I have come to one conclusion: A relationship with the living Christ changes people. Jesus Christ can transform you. If you ask him to take control of your life, start watching your attitudes and actions, because the Christ of the New Testament is in the business of forgiving sin, removing guilt, changing lives and building new relationships.

The Focal Point of Christian Experience: Jesus Christ

Many people have the impression that Christian conversion is a psychologically induced experience brought about by brainwashing the subject with persuasive words and emotional presentations of Christian "myths." An evangelist is thought of as a psychologist manipulating weak, helpless minds into conformity with his own views.

Some have even suggested that the Christian experience can be explained on the basis of conditioned reflexes. They claim that anyone, after repeated exposure to Christian thought, can be caught in a type of "spiritual hypnosis" in which he or she will mechanically react in certain ways under certain conditions.

In his book *Know Why You Believe*, Paul Little concludes that "to explain all Christian experience on a psychological basis does not fit the facts." He adds that "Christian experience can be described psychologically, but this does not explain why it happens or negate its reality."[2] The *why* of Christian experience is the person of Jesus Christ. This fact distinguishes Christianity from all other religions, for it is only Christianity that provides a totally new source of power for living.

Robert O. Ferm comments on the uniqueness of Christian conversion: "For the Christian this new center of energy is the person of Christ. The difference between the Christian and the non-Christian turns out to be, not difference in psychological symptoms, but rather in the object about which the new personality is integrated. The thing that makes Christian conversion different, then, is Christ."[3] As I have written in my book *Evidence that Demands a Verdict:*

> [This] object of . . . faith is not some philosophical invention of man's mind, but a physical, historical reality. The God of Christianity is not an imperceptible unknown God, but one who has specific attributes and characteristics, which are revealed in the Scriptures. Unlike some of the religions devoted to a mystical god, Christians put their faith in a God who may be identified and who made Himself known in *history* by sending His Son, Jesus Christ. Christians can believe that their sins have been forgiven because forgiveness was accomplished and recorded in *history* by the shedding of Christ's blood on the cross. You can know that Christ is now living within them because He was raised from the dead in *history*.[4]

How You Can Respond to What Jesus Has Done for You

You can respond personally to what Jesus Christ has done for you through his death and resurrection through prayer. Prayer is simply talking with God. God knows your heart and is not as concerned with your words as he is with the attitude of your heart. If you have never trusted Christ, you can do so right now in prayer. Here are four important principles to understand as you approach God in prayer.

First, *God loves you and offers a wonderful plan for your life.* God's love is evident in John 3:16: "For God so loved the world that he gave his only Son, that everyone who believes in him will not perish but have eternal life." John 10:10 shows us God's wonderful plan for our lives.

Jesus said, "My purpose is to give life in all its fullness."

Second, *man is sinful and separated from God, thus he cannot know and experience God's love and plan for his life.* Romans 3:23 says, "For all have sinned; all fall short of God's glorious standard." Humankind was created to have fellowship with God, but because of our stubborn self-will we chose to go our own independent way, and fellowship with God was broken. This self-will, characterized by an attitude of active rebellion or passive indifference, is an evidence of what the Bible calls sin. Romans 6:23 says, "For the wages of sin is death," and death means spiritual separation from God.

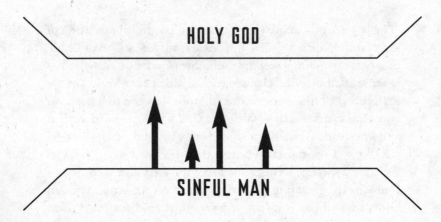

This diagram illustrates that God is holy and man is sinful. A great gulf separates the two. The arrows illustrate that man is continually trying to reach God and the abundant life through his own efforts, such as by trying to live a good life or through philosophy or religion.

Third, *Jesus Christ is God's only provision for man's sin.* Through him you can know and experience God's love and plan for your life. Jesus died in your place. According to Romans 5:8, "God showed His great love for us by sending Christ to die for us while we were still sinners." Jesus rose from the dead. First Corinthians 15:3-6 states, "Christ died for our sins. . . . He was buried, and he was raised from the dead on the third day, as the Scriptures said. He was seen by Peter and then by the twelve apostles. After that, he was seen by more than five hundred."

Jesus is the only way to God. He said, "I am the way, the truth, and the life; no one can come to the Father except through Me" (John 14:6).

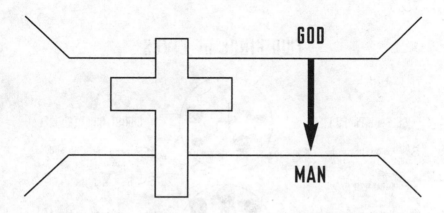

This diagram illustrates that God has bridged the gulf that separates us from him by sending his Son, Jesus Christ, to die on the cross in our place to pay the penalty for our sins.

It is not enough to know these first three principles or to give intellectual assent to them. The fourth principle defines how you can know and experience God's love and plan for your life: *by individually receiving Jesus Christ as Savior and Lord.* The Bible tells us we must receive Christ: "But to all who believed in him [Christ] and accepted him, he gave the right to become children of God" (John 1:12). We receive him by faith: "God saved you by his special favor when you believed. And you can't take credit for this; it is a gift from God. Salvation is not a reward for the good things we have done, so none of us can boast about it" (Eph. 2:8-9). When you receive Christ by faith, you experience a new birth (see John 3:1-8).

You receive Christ by faith through personal invitation. Jesus said, "Look! I stand here at the door and knock. If you hear me calling and open the door, I will come in " (Rev. 3:20). Receiving Christ involves turning to God from self (repentance) and trusting Christ to come into your life to forgive your sins and to make you the kind of person he wants you to be. Just to agree intellectually that Jesus Christ is the Son of God and that he died on the cross for your sins is not enough. Nor is it enough to have an emotional experience. You receive Jesus Christ by faith as an act of the will.

TWO KINDS OF LIVES

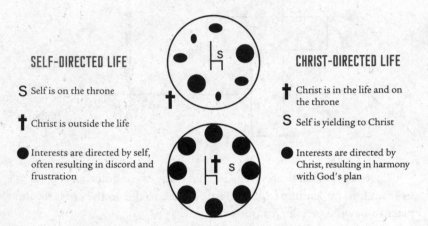

SELF-DIRECTED LIFE

S Self is on the throne

✝ Christ is outside the life

● Interests are directed by self, often resulting in discord and frustration

CHRIST-DIRECTED LIFE

✝ Christ is in the life and on the throne

S Self is yielding to Christ

● Interests are directed by Christ, resulting in harmony with God's plan

Which circle best represents your life?
Which circle would you like to represent your life?

Are you ready to trust Christ? If so, you can pray the following prayer:

Lord Jesus, I need you. Thank you for dying on the cross for my sins. I open the door of my life and receive you as my Savior and Lord. Thank you for forgiving my sins and giving me eternal life. Take control of the throne of my life. Make me the kind of person you want me to be.

Does this prayer express the desire of your heart? If it does, pray this prayer right now and Christ will come into your life, as he promised.

Did you pray to receive Christ into your life? Then, according to his promise in Revelation 3:20, where is Christ right now in relation to you? Christ said that he would come into your life. Would he mislead you?

No! You can be sure that God has answered your prayer because he and his Word are trustworthy.

The Bible promises that by receiving Christ you have eternal life: "And this is what God has testified: He has given us eternal life, and this life is in his Son. So whoever has God's Son has life; whoever does not have his Son does not have life. I write this to you who believe in the Son of God, so that you may know you have eternal life." (1 John 5:11-13).

Thank God right now that Christ is in your life and that he will never leave you (see Heb. 13:5). You can know on the basis of his promise that Christ lives in you and that you have eternal life, from the very moment you invite him in. He will not deceive you.

What's next? You were not meant to live the Christian life alone. God's Word urges you to meet with other Christians to grow and remain strong (see Heb. 10:25). Several logs burn brightly together; but put one aside on the cold hearth and the fire goes out. So it is with your relationship to other Christians. If you do not belong to a church, do not wait to be invited. Take the initiative. Call the pastor of a nearby church where Christ is honored and his Word is taught. Start this week, and make plans to attend regularly.

If you have established a relationship with God through Christ as you were reading these last pages, please write me and tell me about it. I would be delighted to send you some materials that will help you in your ongoing walk with God.

Josh McDowell Ministry
660 International Parkway
Richardson, TX 75081

ENDNOTES

Introduction: Christ's Resurrection—the World's Only Hope
1. "SuperNinjette," message posted at www.atheistnetwork.com, posted July 16, 2007.

Chapter 1: How Did Things Get So Messed Up?
1. Michael Green, *The Empty Cross of Jesus* (Downers Grove, IL: InterVarsity Press, 1984), p. 73.

Chapter 2: Are We Doomed?
1. David Kinnaman, *unChristian: What a New Generation Really Thinks About Christianity* (Grand Rapids, MI: Baker Books, 2007), p. 128.
2. Chap Clark, *Hurt: Inside the World of Today's Teenagers* (Grand Rapids, MI: Baker, 2004), pp. 50, 69.
3. Ibid., p. 51.
4. *Merriam-Webster's Collegiate Thesaurus*, tenth edition (Springfield, MA: Merriam-Webster, 1996), s.v. "happiness."
5. Dennis Prager, *Happiness Is a Serious Problem* (New York: Harper Collins, 1999), p. 44.
6. J. P. Moreland and Klaus Issler, *The Lost Virtue of Happiness* (Colorado Springs, CO: NavPress, 2006), p. 17.
7. Christian Smith, *Soul Searching* (New York: Oxford University Press, 2005), p. 149. Used by permission of Oxford University Press, www.oup.com.
8. Geoffrey Cowley, "The Science of Happiness," *Newsweek* (September 12, 2002), p. 48.
9. J. P. Moreland, *Love Your God with All Your Mind* (Colorado Springs, CO: NavPress, 1997), pp. 81-82.

Chapter 3: The Incredible Love of God
1. John R. W. Stott, *The Cross of Christ* (Downers Grove, IL: InterVarsity Press), p. 214.
2. Philip Yancey, *Disappointment with God* (Grand Rapids, MI: Zondervan, 1988), p. 122.
3. Michael Green, *The Empty Cross of Jesus* (Downer's Grove, IL: InterVarsity Press), p. 54.

Chapter 4: The Solution to Our Dilemma
1. John R. W. Stott, *The Cross of Christ* (Downers Grove, IL: InterVarsity Press), p. 220.
2. Josh McDowell and Thomas Williams, *The Incredible Rumor* (Dallas, TX: Josh McDowell Ministry, 2007), p. 96.
3. Stott, *The Cross of Christ*, p. 244.
4. N. T. Wright, *The Challenge of Jesus* (Downers Grove, IL: InterVarsity Press, 1999), p. 126.
5. Gerd Ludemann, *What Really Happened to Jesus: A Historical Approach to the Resurrection*, trans. by John Bowden (Louisville, KY: Westminster John Knox Press, 1995), p. 1.

Chapter 5: Freedom from the Fear of Death
1. These points were developed in Stephen T. Davis, *Risen Indeed* (Grand Rapids, MI: Eerdmans, 1993), pp. 203-204. Reprinted by permission of the publisher. All rights reserved.
2. Gary Habermas, *The Risen Jesus and Future Hope* (Lanham, MA: Rowman and Littlefield, 2003), pp. 173-183.
3. Randy Alcorn, *Heaven* (Carol Stream, IL: Tyndale, 2004), p. xx.
4. Ibid., p. 21.
5. Habermas, *The Risen Jesus and Future Hope*, p. 182.

Chapter 6: Our Hopes and Desires Will Be Fulfilled
1. N. T. Wright, as quoted in Randy Alcorn, *Heaven* (Carol Stream, IL: Tyndale, 2004), p. 409.
2. Mark Twain, *Letters from the Earth* (1962; repr., Greenwich, Connecticut: Fawcett Crest, 1966), p. 16.
3. Alcorn, *Heaven*, pp. 10-12.
4. Ibid, p. 241.
5. C. S. Lewis, *Miracles*, copyright © C. S. Lewis Pte. Ltd. 1960. Extract reprinted by permission.

Chapter 7: The Restoration of All Things

1. Dwight.L. Moody, "Shall We Meet Our Loved Ones Again?" Sermon found at http://www.je sus-is-savior.com/Books,%20Tracts%20&%20Preaching/Printed%20Sermons/DL_Moody/loved_ ones.htm.
2. Dan Kimball, *They Like Jesus but Not the Church* (Grand Rapids, MI: Zondervan, 2007), p. 69.
3. David Kinnaman, *unChristian: What a New Generation Really Thinks about Christianity* (Grand Rapids, MI: Baker Books, 2007), pp. 27, 185.
4. Kimball, *They Like Jesus but Not the Church*, p. 112.
5. Kinnaman, *UnChristian*, p. 219.

Chapter 8: Our New Life Begins Now

1. "Chris Farley: 1964-1997," *Rolling Stones*, edited by Erik Hedegaard (February 5, 1998), p. 42.
2. Francis S. Collins, *The Language of God* (New York: Free Press, 2006), pp. 19-20.
3. Henri Nouwen, *Here and Now: Living in the Spirit* (New York: The Crossroad Publishing Co., 1997), p. 35.
4. Erik Segalini, "Dying to Tell You," *Worldwide Challenge* (July/August, 1998), p. 25.
5. Liz Halloran, "Moving On," *US News & World Report* (March 26-April 2, 2007), p. 26.
6. N. T. Wright, *Evil and the Justice of God* (Downers Grove, IL: InterVarsity Press, 2006), p. 143.
7. Ibid., p. 160.
8. Jean M. Twenge, *Generation Me* (New York: Free Press, 2006), p. 110.
9. Marya Mannes, as quoted in "Wit and Wisdom," *The Week* (February 9, 2007), p. 17.
10. David Wilkerson, Surfing the Current, "Turning the Other Xbox," *The Journal of Student Ministries* (January/February, 2007), p. 16.
11. Wright, *Evil and the Justice of God*, p. 98, emphasis added.

Chapter 9: Is It True? Is It Believable?

1. George Barna, *Real Teens* (Ventura, CA: Regal Books, 2001), p. 92.
2. Christian Smith, *Soul Searching* (New York: Oxford University Press, 2005), p. 144.
3. Nancy Pearcey, *Total Truth* (Wheaton, IL: Crossway Books, 2004), p. 20.
4. As cited in "Youth Culture Update," *YouthWorker Journal* (July/August, 2006), p. 9.
5. Walt Mueller, *Youth Culture 101* (Grand Rapids, MI: Zondervan, 2007), p. 59.
6. Smith, *Soul Searching*, p. 138.
7. Ibid., p. 145.
8. N. T. Wright, *Evil and the Justice of God* (Downers Grove, IL: InterVarsity Press, 2006), pp. 30-31.
9. Dan Kimball, *The Emerging Church* (Grand Rapids, MI: Zondervan, 2003), p. 86.
10. Taken from James W. Sire, *Why Good Arguments Often Fail*, © 2006 by James W. Sire. Published with permission from InterVarsity Press, P.O. Box 1400, Downers Grove, IL 60515, www.iv press.com, pp. 150-152.
11. Ibid., p. 151.
12. Smith, *Soul Searching*, p. 74.
13. Stephen T. Davis, *Risen Indeed* (Grand Rapids, MI: Eerdmans, 1993), p. 197. Reprinted by permission of the publisher. All rights reserved.

Chapter 10: The Confirmation of History

1. Wolfhart Pannenberg, "A Dialogue on Christ's Resurrection," *Christianity Today*, vol. XII (April 12, 1968), p. 10.
2. Stephen T. Davis, *Risen Indeed* (Grand Rapids, MI: Eerdmans, 1993), pp. 24-25.
3. William Lane Craig, *Assessing the New Testament Evidence for the Historicity of the Resurrection of Jesus* (Lewiston, NY: Edwin Mellen, 1989), pp. 418-419.
4. Richard J. Evans, *In Defense of History* (New York: W. W. Norton and Company, 1999), p. 189.
5. See Luke 24:9-11, Luke 24:13-32, and John 20:24-31 for examples of the disciples reporting incidents that cast themselves in a negative light. The most likely incentive they would have for recording these incidents is that they are true. Why else would they make themselves look bad?

6. N. T. Wright, *The New Testament and the People of God* (Minneapolis, MN: Augsburg Fortress, 1992), p. 89.

7. Michael Licona, *The Historicity of the Resurrection of Jesus: Historiographical Considerations in the Light of Recent Debates*. A doctoral dissertation completed at the University of Pretoria (2008).

8. Norman L Geisler, *Baker Encyclopedia of Christian Apologetics* (Grand Rapids, MI: Baker Books, 1999), p. 531.

9. Ronald Sider, "A Case for Easter," *His* (April 1972), pp. 27-31.

10. Ethelbert Stauffer, *Jesus and His Story*, trans. by Dorothea M. Barton (New York: Knopf, 1960), p. 17.

11. Philip Schaff, *History of the Christian Church*, vol. 1 (New York: Charles Scribner's Sons, 1882), p. 175.

12. F. F. Bruce, *The New Testament Documents: Are They Reliable?* fifth edition (Downer's Grove, IL: Intervarsity Press, 1960), p. 119.

Chapter 11: Do Accounts of Miracles Undermine Credibility?

1. Craig Blomberg, *The Historical Reliability of the Gospels* (Downers Grove, IL: InterVarsity Press, 1987), p. 73.

2. Richard Purtill, "Defining Miracles," Taken from *In Defense of Miracles*, edited by R. Douglas Geivett and Gary R. Habermas. © 1977 by R. Douglas Geivett and Gary R. Habermas. Published by InterVarsity Press, P.O. Box 1400, Downers Grove, IL 60515, pp. 62-63.

3. Antony Flew, "Negative Statement," *Did Jesus Rise from the Dead?* edited by Terry L. Miethe (San Francisco: Harper & Row, 1987), p. 4.

4. Norman Geisler, "Miracles and the Modern World," *In Defense of Miracles*, edited by R. Douglas Geivett and Gary R. Habermas (Downers Grove, IL: InterVarsity Press, 1997), pp. 77-78.

5. Ross Clifford, *Leading Lawyers' Case for the Resurrection* (Edmonton, Alberta, Canada: Canadian Institute for Law, Theology & Public Policy, Inc., 1996), pp. 104-105, emphasis added.

6. Michael Goulder, "The Explanatory Power of Conversion-Visions," *Jesus' Resurrection: Fact or Figment?* edited by Paul Copan and Ronald K. Tacelli (Downers Grove, IL: InterVarsity Press, 2000), p. 102.

7. C. Stephen Evans, *The Historical Christ and the Jesus of Faith* (New York: Oxford University Press, Inc., 1996), p. 22.

8. John P. Meier, *A Marginal Jew: Rethinking the Historical Jesus,* vol. 2 (New York: Doubleday, 1991), pp. 509-534.

9. Blomberg, *The Historical Reliability of the Gospels*, pp. 75-76.

10. Norman L. Geisler, *Miracles and Modern Thought* (Grand Rapids, MI: Zondervan, 1982), p. 58.

11. William Lane Craig, *The Historical Argument for the Resurrection of Jesus During the Deist Controversy* (Lewiston, NY: Edwin Mellen Press, 1985), p. 516.

12. Gregory Boyd, *Cynic, Sage, or Son of God?* (Wheaton, IL: Bridgepoint, 1995), pp. 120-121.

13. Wolfhart Pannenberg, "History and the Reality of the Resurrection," *Resurrection Reconsidered*, edited by Gavin D'Costa (Rockport, MA: Oneworld Publications, 1996), p. 66.

14. John Warwick Montgomery, *Where Is History Going?* (Minneapolis, MN: Bethany Fellowship, 1967), p. 71.

15. William Lane Craig, *Reasonable Faith* (Wheaton, IL: Crossway Books, 1994), p. 151.

16. Gary Habermas and Michael Licona, *The Case for the Resurrection* (Grand Rapids, MI: Kregel Publishers, 2004), p. 136.

17. Francis J. Beckwith, "History and Miracles," *In Defense of Miracles*, edited by R. Douglas Geivett and Gary R. Habermas (Downers Grove, IL: InterVarsity Press, 1997), pp. 87-88.

18. Richard Swinburne, "Evidence for the Resurrection," *The Resurrection*, edited by Stephen Davis, Daniel Kendall and Gerald O'Collins (New York: Oxford, 1998), p. 198.

19. See J. P. Moreland, *Scaling the Secular City: A Defense of Christianity* (Grand Rapids, MI: Baker Academic, 1987); William Lane Craig, *Reasonable Faith: Christian Truth and Apologetics* (Wheaton, IL: Crossway Books, 2008); and Frank Turek and Norman Geisler, *I Don't Have Enough Faith to Be an Atheist* (Wheaton, IL: Crossway Books, 2004).

20. Craig, *The Historical Argument for the Resurrection of Jesus During the Deist Controversy*, p. 505.

Chapter 12: Evidences for Document Reliability

1. Federal Rules of Evidence 901(b)(8).

2. John Warwick Montgomery, "Legal Reasoning and Christian Apologetics," *The Law Above the Law* (Oak Park, IL: Christian Legal Society, 1975), pp. 88-89.

3. Pamela Binnings Ewen, *Faith on Trial* (Nashville, TN: B&H Publishers, 1999), p. 29.

4. See Josh McDowell, *The New Evidence That Demands a Verdict* (Nashville, TN: Thomas Nelson, 1999) for detailed information on these various manuscript discoveries.

5. William F. Albright, *Recent Discoveries in Biblical Lands* (New York: Funk and Wagnalls, 1955), p. 136.

6. John A. T. Robinson, *Time* (March 21, 1977), p. 95.

7. Colin J. Hemer, *The Book of Acts in the Setting of Hellenistic History*, edited by Conrad H. Gempf (Tubingen: Mohr, 1989), pp. 376-382.

8. John Wenham, *Redating Matthew, Mark and Luke* (Downers Grove, IL: InterVarsity Press, 1992), pp. 223-244.

9. Craig Blomberg, "Where Do We Start Studying Jesus?" *Jesus Under Fire* (Grand Rapids, MI: Zondervan, 1995), p. 29.

10. Ibid., pp. 29-30.

11. Frederick G. Kenyon, *The Bible and Archaeology* (New York: Harper and Row, 1940), p. 288.

12. John A. T. Robinson, *Can We Trust the New Testament?* (Grand Rapids: Eerdmans, 1977), p. 36. Reprinted by permission of the publisher. All rights reserved.

13. Gary R. Habermas and Antony Flew, *Did Jesus Rise from the Dead? The Resurrection Debate*, edited by Terry L. Miethe (San Francisco: Harper and Row, 1987), p. 66.

14. F. F. Bruce, *The New Testament Documents: Are They Reliable?* fifth edition (Downer's Grove, IL: Intervarsity Press, 1960), p. 15.

15. Louis Gottschalk, *Understanding History*, second edition (New York: Knopf, 1969), pp. 150, 161, 168.

16. John Ankerburg and John Weldon, *Knowing the Truth About the Resurrection* (Eugene, OR: Harvest House, 1996), p. 20.

17. Blaise Pascal, *Pensees* (New York: Penguin Books, 1995), first translated by A.J. Krailsheimer in 1966.

18. John Warwick Montgomery, "Legal Reasoning and Christian Apologetics," pp. 88-89.

19. Bruce, *The New Testament Documents: Are They Reliable?* p. 43.

20. Stan Gundry, *An Investigation of the Fundamental Assumption of Form Criticism*, thesis presented to the Department of New Testament Language and Literature, Talbot Theological Seminary, June 1963, p. 43.

21. Gottschalk, *Understanding History*, p. 168.

22. McDowell, *The New Evidence That Demands a Verdict*, pp. 62-64.

23. William F. Albright, *The Archaeology of Palestine*, revised edition (Baltimore, MA: Penguin Books, 1960), p. 141.

24. Bruce, "Archaeological Confirmation of the New Testament," in *Revelation and the Bible*, edited by Carl Henry (Grand Rapids, MI: Baker Book House, 1969), p. 329.

25. Markus Bockmuehl, *This Jesus: Martyr, Lord, Messiah* (Downers Grove, IL: InterVarsity Press, 1996), pp. 70-71.

26. Millar Burrows, *What Mean These Stones?* (New York: Meridian Books, 1957), p. 42.

27. Gary R. Habermas, *The Historical Jesus: Ancient Evidence for the Life of Christ* (Joplin, MO: College Press, 1996), p. 224.

28. Gary R. Habermas, "Why I Believe the New Testament Is Historically Reliable," in *Why I Am a Christian: Leading Thinkers Explain Why They Believe*, edited by Norman L. Geisler and Paul K. Hoffman (Grand Rapids, MI: Baker Books, 2001), p. 150.

29. Edwin Yamauchi, "Jesus Outside the New Testament: What Is the Evidence?" in *Jesus Under Fire*, pp. 221-222.

30. Craig Blomberg, "Where Do We Start Studying Jesus?" in *Jesus Under Fire*, p. 41.

31. Gary R. Habermas, "Why I Believe the New Testament Is Historically Reliable," in Geisler and Hoffman, *Why I Am a Christian*, pp. 157-158.

32. Paul Johnson, "An Historian Looks at Jesus," in *Crisis in Christology: Essays in Quest of Resolution*, edited by William R. Farmer (Livonia, MI: Dove Booksellers, 1995), p. 33.

33. William F. Albright, *From the Stone Age to Christianity*, second edition (Baltimore, MA: John Hopkins Press, 1946), pp. 297-298.

34. Blomberg, "Where Do We Start Studying Jesus?" in *Jesus Under Fire*, pp. 33-34.

35. Josh McDowell, *The New Evidence That Demands a Verdict* (Nashville, TN: Thomas Nelson, 1999).

Chapter 13: Do Discrepancies Undermine Historical Reliability?

1. John S. Feinberg, "The Incarnation of Jesus," taken from *In Defense of Miracles*, edited by R. Douglas Geivett and Gary R. Habermas. © 1977 by R. Douglas Geivett and Gary R. Habermas. Published by InterVarsity Press, P.O. Box 1400, Downers Grove, IL 60515, p. 229, emphasis added.

2. R. Raymond E. Brown, *The Death of the Messiah*, vol. 1 (New York: Doubleday, 1994), p. 8.

3. Murray J. Harris, *Raised Immortal* (Grand Rapids, MI: Eerdmans, 1983), p. 68. Reprinted by permission of the publisher. All rights reserved.

4. Norman Anderson, *A Lawyer Among Theologians* (London: Hodder and Stoughton, 1973), p. 111.

5. John Wenham, *Easter Enigma* (Oxford, UK: Paternoster Press, 1984), pp. 10-11. For another harmonization attempt, see *Jesus Christ: The Greatest Life Ever Lived*, compiled and translated by Johnston M. Cheney and Stanley Ellisen (Eugene, OR: Paradise Publishing, Inc, 1994), a revision of *The Life of Christ in Stereo* (Portland, OR: Western Baptist Seminary Press, 1969).

6. Stephen T. Davis, *Risen Indeed* (Grand Rapids, MI: Eerdmans, 1993), p. 69, emphasis added.

7. Craig Blomberg, *The Historical Reliability of the Gospels* (Downers Grove, IL: InterVarsity Press, 1987), p. 113.

8. N. T. Wright, "The Transformation of the Bodily Resurrection," in *The Meaning of Jesus: Two Visions*, Marcus Borg and N. T. Wright (New York: Harper San Francisco, 2000), pp. 121-122.

9. Paul Maier, *In the Fullness of Time: A Historian Looks at Christmas, Easter, and the Early Church* (Grand Rapids, MI: Kregel, 1998), p. 180, emphasis added.

10. William Proctor, *The Resurrection Report* (Nashville, TN: B&H Publishers, 2000), p. 41.

11. Simon Greenleaf, *An Examination of the Testimony of the Four Evangelists by the Rules of Evidence Administered in the Courts of Justice* (Grand Rapids, MI: Baker Book House, 1965), reprint of 1874 edition (New York: J. Cockroft & Co.), pp. 17-18.

Chapter 14: Crucial Facts About Christ's Crucifixion

1. N. T. Wright, *Jesus and the Victory of God* (Minneapolis, MN: Augsburg Fortress Press, 1997), pp. 551-552.

2. James Montgomery Boice, *The Gospel of John: Triumph Through Tragedy* (Grand Rapids, MI: Baker Book House, 1999), p. 1472.

3. Raymond E. Brown, *The Death of the Messiah*, vol. 1 (New York: Doubleday, 1994), pp. 531-532.

4. Haim Cohn, "Reflections on the Trial of Jesus," in *Judaism*, vol. 20, 1971, p. 11.

5. Craig A. Evans, "What Did Jesus Do?" in *Jesus Under Fire* (Grand Rapids, MI: Zondervan, 1995), p. 29.

6. Wright, *Jesus and the Victory of God*, p. 552.

7. In *The Antiquities*, Josephus refers to Jesus' trial and crucifixion under Pontius Pilate. Although the passage in which this information appears is hotly debated, most scholars agree that Josephus wrote a basic text (which includes the reference to Pilate) to which later Christians made additions.

8. Philo, *Logation and Gaium*.

9. Wright, *Jesus and the Victory of God*, pp. 545-546.

10. Brown, *The Death of the Messiah*, vol. 2, p. 946.

11. Cicero, *V in Verrem*.

12. Will Durant, *Caesar and Christ* (New York: Simon and Schuster, 1944), p. 572.

13. Flavius Josephus, *De Bello Judaico*, vol. 7.

14. Dr. Alexander Metherell was interviewed by Lee Strobel in *The Case for Christ* (Grand Rapids, MI: Zondervan, 1998), pp. 197-198.

15. William D. Edwards, Wesley J. Gabel and Floyd E. Hosmer, "On the Physical Death of Jesus Christ," *Journal of the American Medical Association*, vol. 255, no. 11 (March 21, 1986).

16. Professor Dr. B. Smalhout, *The Terrible Easter of A.D. 33*. First appeared in *De Telegraaf*, March 25, 1985. Also appears in *Bijbelse Tijdgenotentrans* (The Netherlands: Het Spectrum, 1997) translated by Brenda Vaughan, p. 10.

17. English translation by Michael W. Holmes in Michael W. Holmes, *The Apostolic Fathers: Greek Texts and English Translations*, second edition (Grand Rapids, MI: Baker, 1999), p. 227.

18. Smalhout, *The Terrible Easter of A.D. 33*, p. 4.

19. J. W. Hewitt, "The Use of Nails in the Crucifixion," *Harvard Theological Review*, vol. 25, 1932, pp. 29-45.

20. N. Haas, "Anthropological Observations on the Skeletal Remains from Giv' at ha-Mivtar," *Israel Exploration Journal* vol. 20, 1970, p. 57.

21. Cicero, *Orations*, Speech 13, 12:27; Gospel of Peter 4:14.

22. See William D. Edwards, Wesley J. Gabel and Floyd E. Hosmer, "On the Physical Death of Jesus Christ," pp. 1462-1463; C. Truman Davis, "The Crucifixion of Jesus," *Arizona Medicine*, March 1965, pp. 185-186; Stuart Bergsma, "Did Jesus Die of a Broken Heart?" *The Calvin Forum*, March 1948, p. 165; Alexander Metherell in Lee Strobel, *The Case for Christ*, p. 199.

23. Michael Green, *Man Alive* (Downers Grove, IL: InterVarsity Press, 1968), p. 33.

24. Ibid., p. 573.

25. John Ankerburg and John Weldon, *Knowing the Truth About the Resurrection* (Eugene, OR: Harvest House, 1996), p. 12.

26. Paul L. Maier, *First Easter* (New York: Harper and Row, 1973), p. 112.

27. Gary R. Habermas, "Why I Believe the New Testament Is Historically Reliable," in *Why I Am a Christian: Leading Thinkers Explain Why They Believe*, edited by Norman L. Geisler and Paul K. Hoffman (Grand Rapids, MI: Baker Books, 2001), p. 150.

28. John Dominic Crossan, *Who Killed Jesus?* (New York: Harper Collins, 1996), p. 5.

Chapter 15: Crucial Facts About Christ's Burial

1. William Lane Craig, *Assessing the New Testament Evidence for the Historicity of the Resurrection of Jesus* (Lewiston, NY: Edwin Mellen, 1989), pp. 185-186.

2. Ibid., p. 186.

3. Ibid., p. 187.

4. John Dominic Crossan, *Jesus: A Revolutionary Biography* (San Francisco: Harper and Row, 1994), chapter 6.

5. William Lane Craig, "Did Jesus Rise from the Dead?" *Jesus Under Fire* (Grand Rapids, MI: Zondervan, 1995), p. 142.

6. Gary R. Habermas, *The Historical Jesus: Ancient Evidence for the Life of Christ* (Joplin, MO: College Press, 1996), chapter 7.

7. R. Raymond E. Brown, *The Death of the Messiah*, vol. 2 (New York: Doubleday, 1994), p. 1240.

8. John A. T. Robinson, *The Human Face of God* (Philadelphia, PA: Westminster Press, 1973), p. 131.

9. Flavius Josephus, cited in *The Works of Josephus: Complete and Unabridged*, translated by William Whiston (Peabody, MA: Hendrickson, 1996, 1987), S. Wars 4.317.

10. Seder Nezikin, "Sanhedrin 46A," *The Babylonian Talmud* (London: The Sancino Press, 1935), p. 304.

11. A. P. Bender, "Beliefs, Rites, and Customs of the Jews, Connected with Death, Burial, and Mourning," *The Jewish Quarterly Review*, vol. 7, 1895, pp. 259-260.
12. Flavius Josephus, *Antiquities of the Jews*, vol. 3, chapter 8, section 3.
13. Bender, "Beliefs, Rites, and Customs of the Jews, Connected with Death, Burial, and Mourning," p. 261.
14. Ibid.
15. John Chrysostom, *Homilies of St. John* (Grand Rapids, MI: Eerdmans, reprint 1969), p. 321. Reprinted by permission of the publisher. All rights reserved.
16. The *Mishnah*, translated by Herbert Danby (London: Oxford University Press, 1933), Middoth 1.1-1.2.
17. Alfred Edersheim, *The Temple: Its Ministry and Services* (Grand Rapids, MI: Eerdmans, 1958), reprinted by Hendrickson Publishers, 1994.
18. A. T. Robertson, *Word Pictures in the New Testament* (Nashville, TN: Broadman & Holman, 1930), p. 239.
19. Brown, *The Death of the Messiah*, vol. 2, p. 1295.
20. John Wenham, *Easter Enigma* (Oxford, UK: Paternoster Press, 1984), p. 74.
21. Brown, *The Death of the Messiah*, vol. 2, p. 1311.
22. Flavius Vegitius Renatus, *The Military Institutes of the Romans*.
23. T. G. Tucker, *Life in the Roman World of Nero and St. Paul* (New York: Macmillan, 1910), p. 342.
24. Dr. George Currie, who did his doctoral dissertation on the Roman custodian (Graduate Council of Indiana University, 1928); Dr. William Smith, editor of the *Dictionary of Greek and Roman Antiquities*, revised edition (London: James Walton and John Murray, 1870); and more recently, Lawrence Keppie, *The Making of the Roman Army: From Republic to Empire* (Baltimore, MA: Johns Hopkins University Press, 1991).
25. Paul L. Maier, *First Easter* (New York: Harper and Row, 1973), p. 111.
26. Wenham, *Easter Enigma*, p. 79.
27. William Lane Craig, as quoted in an interview with Lee Strobel, *The Case for Christ* (Grand Rapids, MI: Zondervan, 1998), p. 212.
28. William Lane Craig, *Assessing the New Testament Evidence for the Historicity of the Resurrection of Jesus* (Lewiston, NY: Edwin Mellen Press, 1989), p. 207.
29. Lawrence Keppie, *The Making of the Roman Army* (London: B.T. Batsford Ltd., 1984), pp. 38, 57.
30. Wenham, *Easter Enigma*, pp. 72-73.
31. Henry Sumner Maine, *Ancient Law* (New York: Henry Holt and Company, 1888), p. 203.
32. Maier, *First Easter*, p. 119.
33. Ibid, pp. 118-119.
34. Norman L. Geisler, *Baker Encyclopedia of Christian Apologetics* (Grand Rapids, MI: Baker Books, 1999), p. 48.

Chapter 16: Resurrection Facts to Be Reckoned With
1. Paul L. Maier, "The Empty Tomb as History," *Christianity Today*, vol. 19, March 28, 1975, p. 5.
2. Stephen T. Davis, *Risen Indeed* (Grand Rapids, MI: Eerdmans, 1993), pp. 79-80.
3. Maier, "The Empty Tomb as History," p. 5.
4. Ronald Sider, "A Case for Easter," *HIS Magazine*, April 29, 1972, pp. 27-31.
5. J. P. Moreland, *Scaling the Secular City* (Grand Rapids, MI: Baker Book House, 1987), p. 163.
6. A. J. M. Wedderburn, *Beyond Resurrection* (Peabody, MA: Hendrickson Publishers, 1999), p. 63.
7. Edwin Yamauchi, "Easter—Myth, Hallucination, or History?" *Christianity Today*, vol. 4 (March 15, 1974), pp. 4-16.
8. Eusebius, *Hist. Eccl.* 2.23.18, as cited in Wedderburn, *Beyond Resurrection*, p. 63.
9. Frank Morrison, *Who Moved the Stone?* (Downers Grove, IL: InterVarsity Press, 1969), p. 94.
10. Moreland, *Scaling the Secular City*, p. 161.
11. Davis, *Risen Indeed*, pp. 72-73.

12. Dale C. Allison, *Resurrecting Jesus: The Earliest Christian Tradition and Its Interpreters* (New York: T. & T. Clark, 2005), p. 332.

13. Paul L. Maier, *First Easter* (New York: Harper and Row, 1973), p. 98.

14. William Lane Craig, as interviewed by Lee Strobel in *The Case for Christ* (Grand Rapids, MI: Zondervan, 1998), p. 220.

15. William Lane Craig, *The Son Rises* (Eugene, OR: Wipf and Stock Publishers, 2000), p. 88.

16. Michael Grant, *Jesus: An Historian's Review of the Gospels* (New York: Charles Scribner's Sons, 1977), p. 176.

17. George Currie, *The Military Discipline of the Romans from the Founding of the City to the Close of the Republic*, an abstract from his dissertation published under the auspices of the Graduate Council of Indiana University, 1928.

18. Bill White, *A Thing Incredible* (Israel: Yanetz Ltd., 1976).

19. Michael Green, *The Empty Cross of Jesus* (Downers Grove, IL: InterVarsity Press, 1984), pp. 22-23.

20. Reginald H. Fuller, *The Foundations of New Testament Christology* (New York: Scribner's, 1965), p. 142.

21. Gary R. Habermas, *The Historical Jesus: Ancient Evidence for the Life of Christ* (Joplin, MO: College Press, 1996), chapter 7.

22. Hans von Campenhausen, "The Events of Easter and the Empty Tomb," in *Tradition and Life in the Early Church* (Philadelphia, PA: Fortress, 1968), p. 44.

23. Craig, *The Son Rises*, p. 94.

24. C. H. Dodd, "The Appearances of the Risen Christ: A Study in the Form Criticism of the Gospels," in *More New Testament Studies* (Manchester, UK: University of Manchester Press, 1968), p. 128.

25. Norman L. Geisler, *Baker Encyclopedia of Christian Apologetics* (Grand Rapids, MI: Baker Books, 1999), p. 654.

26. Craig, *The Son Rises*, pp. 94-95.

27. Merril C. Tenney, "The Resurrection of Jesus Christ," in *Prophecy in the Making*, edited by Carl Henry (Carol Stream, IL: Creation House, 1971), p. 59.

28. Josephus, *Antiquities* 20:200; see Gary Habermas and Michael Licona, *The Case for the Resurrection* (Grand Rapids: Kregel Publishers, 2004), p. 68.

29. This comment was made in a conversation with Josh McDowell, January 1981.

Chapter 17: Attempts to "Explain Away" the Resurrection

1. John Ankerburg and John Weldon, *Knowing the Truth About the Resurrection* (Eugene, OR: Harvest House, 1996), p. 17.

2. J. N. D. Anderson, *Christianity: The Witness of History* (Carol Stream, IL: Tyndale, 1970), p. 105.

3. Philip Schaff, *History of the Christian Church*, vol. 1 (New York: Charles Scribner's Sons, 1882), p. 175.

4. Examples of people who have recently supported this theory are Evan Fales, "Successful Defense? A review of *In Defense of Miracles*," in *Philosophia Christi*, series 2, vol. 3, no. 1 (November 2001), pp. 26-35; Dan Barker, *Losing Faith in Faith: From Preacher to Atheist* (Madison, WI: Freedom from Religion Foundation, Inc, 1992), p. 373.

5. For a comprehensive refutation of the myth theory, see Gunter Wagner, *Pauline Baptism and the Pagan Mysteries* (London: Oliver and Boyd, 1967); Ronald H. Nash, *The Gospel and the Greeks* (Richardson, TX: Probe Books, 1992); J. Gresham Machen, *The Origin of Paul's Religion* (New York: Macmillan, 1925), rep. (Grand Rapids, MI: Eerdmans, 1970); William Lane Craig, "On the Empty Tomb of Jesus," and Gary Habermas, "On the Resurrection Appearances of Jesus," in *Philosophia Christi*, series 2, vol. 3. no. 1 (Nov. 2001), pp. 67-87. Reprinted by permission of the publisher. All rights reserved.

6. Michael Grant, *Jesus: An Historians Review of the Gospels* (New York: Macmillan, 1992), p. 200.

7. John Dominic Crossan, *Jesus: A Revolutionary Biography*; Charles Alford Guignebert, *Jesus* (New York: New York Univ. Books, Inc., 1956), p. 500.

8. Stephen T. Davis, *Risen Indeed* (Grand Rapids, MI: Eerdmans, 1993), p. 81.
9. Kirsopp Lake, *The Historical Evidence for the Resurrection of Jesus Christ* (New York: Putnam's Sons, 1907).
10. William Lane Craig, *The Son Rises* (Eugene, OR: Wipf and Stock Publishers, 2000), p. 42.
11. Peter Kreeft and Ronald K. Tacelli, *Handbook of Christian Apologetics* (Downers Grove, IL: Inter-Varsity Press, 1994), pp. 190-191.
12. J. N. D. Anderson, "The Resurrection of Jesus Christ," *Christianity Today* (March 29, 1968), p. 6.
13. Dan Cohn Sherbock, "The Resurrection of Jesus: A Jewish View," in *Resurrection Reconsidered*, p. 200.
14. N. T. Wright, "Christian Origins and the Resurrection of Jesus: The Resurrection as a Historical Problem," *Sewanee Theological Review*, vol. 41:2 (Easter 1998), p. 111, emphasis added.
15. N. T. Wright, "The Transforming Reality of the Bodily Resurrection," in *The Meaning of Jesus: Two Visions* by N. T. Wright and Marcus Borg (New York: HarperCollins Publishers, 1999), p. 115.
16. Michael Licona, "Paul on the Nature of the Resurrection Body" in *Buried Hope or Risen Savior? The Search for the Jesus Tomb,* edited by Charles L. Quarles (Nashville, TN: B&H Academic, 2008), pp. 177-198.
17. Davis, *Risen Indeed,* p. 56.
18. Norman L Geisler, *Baker Encyclopedia of Christian Apologetics* (Grand Rapids, MI: Baker Books, 1999), p. 662.
19. Gary Habermas and J. P. Moreland, *Beyond Death* (Wheaton, IL: Good News Publishers, 1998), p. 119.
20. Theodore R. Sarbin and Joseph B Juhaz, "The Social Contact of Hallucinations," *Hallucinations: Behavior, Experience and Theory*, edited by R. K. Siegel and L. J. West (New York: John Wiley & Sons, 1975), p. 242.
21. Ibid.
22. Habermas and Moreland, *Beyond Death,* p. 120.
23. Licona, *Cross Examined* (Virginia Beach, VA: TruthQuest Publishers, 1998), p. 90.
24. Gary Collins, PhD, in personal correspondence with Gary Habermas. Recorded in Gary R. Habermas, "The Recent Revival of Hallucination Theories," in *The Christian Research Journal*, vol. 23, no. 4 (August 13, 2001), p. 48.
25. Ibid.
26. Habermas, "The Recent Revival of Hallucination Theories," p. 47.
27. Paul Little, *Know Why You Believe* (Wheaton, IL: Scripture Press, 1967), pp. 68-69.
28. Kreeft and Tacelli, *Handbook of Christian Apologetics*, p. 187.
29. N. T. Wright, "The Transforming Reality of the Bodily Resurrection," *The Meaning of Jesus: Two Visions* by N. T. Wright and Marcus Borg (New York: HarperCollins Publishers, 1999), pp. 114-115.
30. Craig, *The Son Rises*, p. 133.
31. For an in-depth refutation of the hallucination theory, we recommend William Lane Craig and Gerd Ludemann, *Jesus' Resurrection: Fact or Figment?* edited by Paul Copan and Ronald K. Tacelli (Downers Grove, IL: Intervarsity Press, 2000).
32. Licona, *Cross Examined*, p. 94.
33. For a great response to the claims of Islam, see Norman L. Geisler and Abdul Saleeb, *Answering Islam: The Crescent in Light of the Cross* (Grand Rapids, MI: Baker, 1993) and answering-islam.org.
34. John Gilchrist, *Facing the Muslim Challenge* (South Africa: MERCSA, 1999), p. 122.
35. Michael Licona, *Paul Meets Muhammad: A Christian-Muslim Debate on the Resurrection* (Grand Rapids, MI: Baker Books, 2006), p. 55.

Chapter 18: Exploding the Empty-Tomb Theories

1. Bill White, *A Thing Incredible* (Jerusalem: Yanetz Ltd, revised edition, 1976), p. 9.
2. Paul L. Maier, *First Easter* (New York: Harper and Row, 1973), p. 120.
3. Justin Martyr, *Dialogue Against Trypho #108*.
4. Eusebius, *Demonstratio Evangelica*.

5. Charles Colson, *How Now Shall We Live?* (Wheaton, IL: Tyndale House Publishers, 1999), pp. 275-276.

6. Simon Greenleaf, *The Testimony of the Evangelists: The Gospels Examined by the Rules of Evidence* (Grand Rapids, MI: Kregel Classics, 1995), pp. 31-33.

7. Alexander Maclaren, *Expositions of Holy Scripture*, vol. 7, "Gospel of St. John" (Grand Rapids, MI: Eerdmans, 1959), p. 340. Reprinted by permission of the publisher. All rights reserved.

8. Paul Little, *Know Why You Believe* (Wheaton, IL: Scripture Press, 1967), p. 173.

9. Justice Antonin Scalia, as quoted in William Proctor, *The Resurrection Report* (Nashville, TN: B&H Publishers, 2000), p. 181. This article first appeared in the *Washington Post* and was quoted by the *Palm Beach Post*, April 10, 1996, p. 3A.

10. J. P. Moreland, *Scaling the Secular City: A Defense of Christianity* (Grand Rapids, MI: Baker Academic, 1987), p. 172.

11. Edward Gibbon, *The History of the Decline and Fall of the Roman Empire* (Chicago: William Benton, Publishers, reprinted 1952), p. 179.

12. J. N. D. Anderson, *Christianity: The Witness of History* (Carol Stream, IL: Tyndale, 1970), p. 92.

13. John Stott, *Basic Christianity*, second edition (Downers Grove, IL: InterVarsity Press, 1971), p. 50.

14. R. Raymond E. Brown, *The Death of the Messiah*, vol. 1 (New York: Doubleday, 1994), pp. 1206-1207.

15. Ibid.

16. Montgomery, *History and Christianity* (Downers Grove, IL: InterVarsity Press, 1964; reprinted 1971), p. 35.

17. David Friedrick Strauss, *The Life of Jesus for the People*, vol. 1, second edition (London: William & Norgate, 1879), p. 412.

18. Albert Schweitzer, *The Quest of the Historical Jesus: A Critical Study of Its Progress from Reimarus to Wrede*, translated by J. W. Montgomery from the 1906 German version (New York: Macmillan, 1968), pp. 56-67.

19. Brown, *The Death of the Messiah*, p. 1373.

20. Gerd Ludemann, *What Really Happened to Jesus* (Louisville, KY: Westminster John Knox Press, 1995) p. 17.

21. Marcus Borg, *Jesus: A New Vision: Spirit, Culture, and the Life of Discipleship* (San Francisco: Harper Collins, 1987), p. 179

22. William Lane Craig, *The Son Rises* (Eugene, OR: Wipf and Stock Publishers, 2000), p. 39.

23. Hugh Schonfield, *The Passover Plot* (New York: Bantam Books, 1965), p. 165.

24. *Saturday Review*, December 3, 1966, p. 43.

25. Gary Habermas, *The Verdict of History* (Nashville, TN: Thomas Nelson Publishers, 1988), p. 56.

26. Luke Timothy Johnson, *The Real Jesus* (San Francisco: HarperSanFrancisco, 1996), p. 30.

27. *Newsweek*, August 8, 1966, p. 51.

28. Gregory Boyd, *Cynic, Sage, or Son of God?* (Wheaton, IL: Bridgepoint, 1995), p. 293.

29. N. T. Wright, *The Resurrection of the Son of God* (Minneapolis, MN: Augsburg Fortress Press, 2003), p. 710.

Chapter 19: The Circumstantial Evidence

1. *McCormick's Handbook of the Law of Evidence* (St. Paul, MN: West Publishing Company, second edition, 1972), pp. 435-437.

2. Pamela Binnings Ewen, *Faith on Trial* (Nashville, TN: B&H Publishers, 1999), pp. 7-8.

3. J. N. D. Anderson, "The Resurrection of Jesus Christ," *Christianity Today* (March 29, 1968), p. 9.

4. Daniel Fuller, *Easter Faith and History* (Grand Rapids, MI: Eerdmans, 1965), p. 259. Reprinted by permission of the publisher. All rights reserved.

5. J. P. Moreland, *Scaling the Secular City: A Defense of Christianity* (Grand Rapids, MI: Baker Academic, 1987), p. 180.

6. J. P. Moreland, as quoted in Lee Strobel, *The Case for Christ* (Grand Rapids, MI: Zondervan, 1998), p. 253.

7. Ibid., p. 250.
8. Barry R. Levanthal, "Why I Believe Jesus Is the Promised Messiah," in *Why I Am a Christian: Leading Thinkers Explain Why They Believe*, edited by Norman L. Geisler and Paul K. Hoffman (Grand Rapids, MI: Baker Books, 2001), pp. 216-217.
9 Ibid., p. 218.
10. Simon Greenleaf, *The Testimony of the Evangelists: The Gospels Examined by the Rules of Evidence* (Grand Rapids, MI: Kregel Classics, 1995), p. 32.
11. George Eldon Ladd, *The New Testament and Criticism* (Grand Rapids, MI: Eerdmans, 1967), p. 188. Reprinted by permission of the publisher. All rights reserved.

ABOUT THE AUTHORS

Josh McDowell considered himself to be an agnostic as a young man and believed that Christianity was worthless. However, after being challenged to intellectually examine the claims of Christianity, Josh discovered compelling and overwhelming evidence for the reliability of the Christian faith. Josh came to believe in Jesus Christ, and his life was changed dramatically as he experienced the power of God's love.

After Josh's conversion, his plans for law school turned to plans for seminary and for telling a doubting world about the truth of Jesus Christ. He completed his college degree at Wheaton College and later earned a Master of Divinity degree from Talbot Theological Seminary. In 1964, Josh joined the staff of Campus Crusade for Christ International. Not long after, The Josh McDowell Ministry was formed to realize the vision of reaching young people worldwide with the truth and love of Jesus Christ.

Well known as an articulate speaker, Josh has spoken to more than 10 million young people through more than 23,000 talks in at least 113 countries. As he traveled to other countries, Josh quickly realized that where young people were sick, homeless and hungry, words alone were not enough. So in 1991 he founded Operation Carelift to meet physical and spiritual needs in orphanages, hospitals and prisons in the countries of the former Soviet Union. Since its inception, more than $46 million of humanitarian aid (food, clothing and medical supplies) has been delivered overseas.

During his 47 years of ministry, Josh has authored or co-authored 108 books, including *More Than a Carpenter* (Living Books, 1987), which has been translated into more than 85 languages, and *New Evidence That Demands a Verdict* (Thomas Nelson, 1999), which has been recognized by *World Magazine* as one of the century's most influential books. He has been nominated 36 times for the Gold Medallion Award and been chosen for that prestigious award on four occasions.

Josh and his wife, Dottie, have been married 37 years and have four children and two very precious grandchildren.

Sean McDowell is the head of the Bible department at Capistrano Valley Christian Schools, where he teaches the courses on Apologetics, Theology, and Old Testament. He graduated summa cum laude from Talbot Theological Seminary with a double Master's degree in Theology and Philosophy. Sean received the award for Educator of the Year for San Juan Capistrano in 2008, and his apologetics training was awarded Exemplary Status by the Association of Christian Schools International.

Sean is a popular speaker at camps, churches, schools and conferences nationwide. He has spoken for organizations including Focus on the Family, Campus Crusade for Christ, Youth Specialties, Wisdom Works and the Association of Christian Schools International. He is the national spokesman and a conference speaker for Wheatstone Academy (www.wheatstoneacademy.com), an organization committed to training young people with a biblical worldview. Sean has also appeared as a guest on radio shows such as *The Bible Answer Man, Family Life, Focus on the Family, Point of View, The Frank Pastore Show, The Michael Reagan Show, Converse with Scholars* and *Stand to Reason.*

Sean is the co-author of *Understanding Intelligent Design* (along with William A. Dembski). He is also the author of *Ethix: Being Bold in a Whatever World* (B&H Publishing Group, 2006) and *Apologetics for a New Generation* (Harvest House, 2008). He is the General Editor for *The Apologetics Study Bible for Students* (B&H Publishing Group, 2010). Sean has also contributed to *YouthWorker Journal, Decision Magazine* and the *Christian Research Journal,* and blogs regularly at www.conversantlife.com.

In April 2000, Sean married his high school sweetheart, Stephanie. They have two children, Scottie and Shauna, and live in San Juan Capistrano, California.

AUTHOR CONTACT INFORMATION

You can contact Josh McDowell
at the following:

Josh McDowell Ministry
P.O. Box 131000
Dallas, TX 75313
972-907-1000
josh@josh.org

Also visit:

www.josh.org
www.new.facebook.com/pages/Josh-McDowell/14589320545
Myspace.com/joshmcdowellministry
Joshmcdowell.blogspot.com
Youtube.com/joshmcdowell

For more information about Sean McDowell
and his ministry, or for speaking and booking
information, please visit:

www.seanmcdowell.org